THE
HOMELESS

OPPOSING VIEWPOINTS®

Other Books of Related Interest

Opposing Viewpoints Series

AIDS
American Values
America's Children
America's Cities
America's Prisons
Chemical Dependency
Child Abuse
Crime and Criminals
Drug Abuse
Education in America
The Elderly
The Family in America
Mental Illness
Poverty
Social Justice
Suicide
Violence
Work

Current Controversies Series

Alcoholism
Ethics
Hunger
Illegal Immigration
Youth Violence

At Issue Series

Immigration Policy
Legalizing Drugs

THE HOMELESS

OPPOSING VIEWPOINTS®

David Bender & Bruno Leone, *Series Editors*

Tamara L. Roleff, *Book Editor*

OPPOSING
VIEWPOINTS®
SERIES

Greenhaven Press, Inc., San Diego, CA

Cover photo: Dave Allen

Greenhaven Press, Inc.
PO Box 289009
San Diego, CA 92198-9009

Library of Congress Cataloging-in-Publication Data

The homeless : opposing viewpoints / Tamara L. Roleff, book editor.
    p.   cm. — (Opposing viewpoints series)
  Includes bibliographical references (p.   ) and index.
  ISBN 1-56510-361-0 (lib. ed. : alk. paper) —
ISBN 1-56510-360-2 (pbk. : alk. paper)
  1. Homelessness—United States. 2. Homeless persons—United States. 3. Housing policy—United States.
I. Roleff, Tamara, 1959– . II. Series: Opposing viewpoints series (Unnumbered)
HV4505.H65512   1996
362.5′8′0973—dc20   95-19809
                                     CIP

AUG 7 1996

"Congress shall make no law . . .
abridging the freedom of speech,
or of the press."

First Amendment to the U.S. Constitution

The basic foundation of our democracy is the First Amendment
guarantee of freedom of expression. The Opposing Viewpoints
Series is dedicated to the concept of this basic freedom and the
idea that it is more important to practice it than to enshrine it.

Contents

Why Consider Opposing Viewpoints?

"The only way in which a human being can make some approach to knowing the whole of a subject is by hearing what can be said about it by persons of every variety of opinion and studying all modes in which it can be looked at by every character of mind. No wise man ever acquired his wisdom in any mode but this."

John Stuart Mill

In our media-intensive culture it is not difficult to find differing opinions. Thousands of newspapers and magazines and dozens of radio and television talk shows resound with differing points of view. The difficulty lies in deciding which opinion to agree with and which "experts" seem the most credible. The more inundated we become with differing opinions and claims, the more essential it is to hone critical reading and thinking skills to evaluate these ideas. Opposing Viewpoints books address this problem directly by presenting stimulating debates that can be used to enhance and teach these skills. The varied opinions contained in each book examine many different aspects of a single issue. While examining these conveniently edited opposing views, readers can develop critical thinking skills such as the ability to compare and contrast authors' credibility, facts, argumentation styles, use of persuasive techniques, and other stylistic tools. In short, the Opposing Viewpoints Series is an ideal way to attain the higher-level thinking and reading skills so essential in a culture of diverse and contradictory opinions.

In addition to providing a tool for critical thinking, Opposing Viewpoints books challenge readers to question their own strongly held opinions and assumptions. Most people form their opinions on the basis of upbringing, peer pressure, and personal, cultural, or professional bias. By reading carefully balanced opposing views, readers must directly confront new ideas as well as the opinions of those with whom they disagree. This is not to simplistically argue that everyone who reads opposing views will—or should—change his or her opinion. Instead, the series enhances readers' depth of understanding of their own views by encouraging confrontation with opposing ideas. Careful examination of others' views can lead to the readers' understanding of the logical inconsistencies in their own opinions, perspective on why they hold an opinion, and the consideration of the possibility that their opinion requires further evaluation.

Evaluating Other Opinions

To ensure that this type of examination occurs, Opposing Viewpoints books present all types of opinions. Prominent spokespeople on different sides of each issue as well as well-known professionals from many disciplines challenge the reader. An additional goal of the series is to provide a forum for other, less known, or even unpopular viewpoints. The opinion of an ordinary person who has had to make the decision to cut off life support from a terminally ill relative, for example, may be just as valuable and provide just as much insight as a medical ethicist's professional opinion. The editors have two additional purposes in including these less known views. One, the editors encourage readers to respect others' opinions—even when not enhanced by professional credibility. It is only by reading or listening to and objectively evaluating others' ideas that one can determine whether they are worthy of consideration. Two, the inclusion of such viewpoints encourages the important critical thinking skill of objectively evaluating an author's credentials and bias. This evaluation will illuminate an author's reasons for taking a particular stance on an issue and will aid in readers' evaluation of the author's ideas.

As series editors of the Opposing Viewpoints Series, it is our hope that these books will give readers a deeper understanding of the issues debated and an appreciation of the complexity of even seemingly simple issues when good and honest people disagree. This awareness is particularly important in a democratic society such as ours in which people enter into public debate to determine the common good. Those with whom one disagrees should not be regarded as enemies but rather as people whose views deserve careful examination and may shed light on one's own.

Thomas Jefferson once said that "difference of opinion leads to inquiry, and inquiry to truth." Jefferson, a broadly educated man, argued that "if a nation expects to be ignorant and free . . . it expects what never was and never will be." As individuals and as a nation, it is imperative that we consider the opinions of others and examine them with skill and discernment. The Opposing Viewpoints Series is intended to help readers achieve this goal.

David L. Bender & Bruno Leone,
Series Editors

Introduction

"News stories about homelessness in America have increased a thousandfold from ten years ago: there are not a thousand times more homeless."

Richard W. White Jr., Rude Awakenings: What the Homeless
Crisis Tells Us, 1992

"A 1990 New York Times *poll reported that 68 percent of urban Americans see the homeless in the course of their daily routine . . . an 18 percent increase in just four years."*

Joel Blau, The Visible Poor, 1992

Homelessness is not a new phenomenon to the United States. Since colonial times, homeless people (who were called "vagrants," "tramps," "hoboes," and "bums" until the late 1970s) have been present in America. The number of homeless people fluctuated with America's economic booms and recessions, increasing during times of high unemployment and shrinking during periods of prosperity. During the Great Depression of the 1930s, the worst economic downturn in U.S. history, hundreds of thousands of people became homeless. The Great Depression also changed the faces of the homeless: A population that had formerly been almost exclusively male now included families with children who were forced into homelessness by bankruptcies and foreclosures.

During the economic boom that followed World War II and continued into the 1960s, homelessness declined sharply from the high numbers of the Depression. Those few Americans who remained homeless were mostly male alcoholics relegated to skid row areas in large cities. Many people expected homelessness to disappear entirely. In his book *Address Unknown: The Homeless in America*, James D. Wright notes that in the mid-1960s, due to the restoration of dilapidated urban areas and the aging of the skid row population, "the impending demise of skid row was widely and confidently predicted."

However, the skid rows never totally disappeared. In the late 1970s, some social activists began to notice the people who were living on the streets of American cities. Mitch Snyder and Mary

Ellen Hombs, two activists who became prominent advocates for the homeless, brought the issue of homelessness into public view. They insisted that homelessness was an extremely serious problem in the United States—a problem that would not go away without the government's help.

Many government officials and policymakers contended that Hombs and Snyder's characterization of homelessness was a gross exaggeration. Throughout the 1980s and into the 1990s, officials maintained that homelessness was no worse than it had been in previous decades. They argued that the number of homeless people only appeared to have increased drastically because homelessness was being covered more frequently by the media. The extent of homelessness would diminish over time, these policymakers claimed.

An April 1992 *Newsweek* article supported this view. The article reported that shelter populations in New York City; San Francisco; Philadelphia; Hartford, Connecticut; and Trenton, New Jersey, had stabilized or declined during the previous year. The same article quoted Martha R. Burt, author of *Over the Edge: The Growth of Homelessness in the 1980s*, who maintained that although homelessness was still increasing, it was doing so at a much slower rate: "You might be looking at 5 percent growth a year, but you're not looking at 20 percent."

However, other experts argued that homelessness was rapidly becoming a serious problem. According to a 1994 report by the U. S. Conference of Mayors, the number of homeless people was growing at a faster rate than 5 percent a year. The report found that in twenty-four of the thirty cities the conference surveyed, requests for emergency shelter had increased by 13 percent over the previous year.

Even those who agree that the extent of homelessness has grown in recent years disagree over the cause of the perceived increase. Suggested reasons include the economic recessions of the 1970s and 1980s; budget cuts that affected welfare and unemployment; personal choice; and the government policy of deinstitutionalization, a massive emptying of state mental hospitals that began in the mid-1950s and continued into the 1980s.

The theory behind deinstitutionalization held that many mentally ill patients did not need to be hospitalized; instead they could be treated at community mental health centers, which the government would establish. Few community mental health centers were built, however, and many released patients had nowhere to go for treatment. E. Fuller Torrey, a psychiatrist who has worked with the homeless mentally ill, contends that, due to the lack of treatment and follow-up care, many mentally ill people became homeless.

However, many homeless advocates disagree with Torrey's contention that deinstitutionalization is a primary cause of the perceived increase in homelessness. Opponents of the deinstitutionalization theory include Christopher Jencks, who argues in his book

The Homeless that "deinstitutionalization caused very little homelessness from 1955 to 1975," the time period when the majority of patients were released. Richard W. White Jr. maintains that most homeless mentally ill people are too young to have been hospitalized and released under the deinstitutionalization policy; instead, they became homeless after deinstitutionalization had run its course. Therefore, White contends, deinstitutionalization cannot be blamed for their homelessness.

Others believe that the homeless themselves choose to live on the streets. During the 1980s, President Ronald Reagan said homeless people were "homeless, you might say, by choice"; his former attorney general, Edwin Meese, contended that people ate in soup kitchens for a "free lunch." Conservative commentator Rush Limbaugh maintains in his book *The Way Things Ought to Be*, "The simple fact is that some—not all—of the homeless consciously choose their plight. They don't want to work." There are plenty of jobs and housing options available for those who do not want to live on the street, many politicians maintain, but a significant number of homeless people prefer to remain homeless.

Most advocates for the homeless argue that homelessness is not a personal choice. They contend instead that economic conditions force people into homelessness. For example, contradicting the view that homeless people do not want to work, the U.S. Conference of Mayors found that 23 percent of cities surveyed in 1994 reported that 25 percent or more of their homeless populations worked full- or part-time. Moreover, in her book *Out of Bedlam: The Truth About Deinstitutionalization*, Ann Braden Johnson argues that the homeless people who do work tend to be eligible only for nonskilled, low-paying jobs—jobs that often do not pay enough for rent. Compounding their difficulties, many homeless people who do not have marketable skills report that they are denied employment when their employers discover they are homeless or living in an emergency shelter.

Economic conditions, personal choice, deinstitutionalization, and other factors that may contribute to homelessness are among the topics examined in *The Homeless: Opposing Viewpoints*, which contains the following chapters: Is Homelessness a Serious Problem? What Are the Causes of Homelessness? What Housing Options Would Benefit the Homeless? How Can Society Help the Homeless? How Can Government Help the Homeless? In these chapters, the social, political, legal, and medical issues associated with homelessness are discussed and debated.

1 CHAPTER

Is Homelessness a Serious Problem?

THE HOMELESS

Chapter Preface

Since the early 1980s, when the issue of homelessness became the focus of national attention, homeless advocates, social scientists, and policymakers have tried to obtain an accurate count of homeless people. From the beginning, each group had its own reasons for wanting to count the homeless: Advocates wanted to prove homelessness was a serious problem that needed immediate attention from policymakers; social scientists wanted to know if the recession of 1980–81 was behind the perceived increase in homelessness; and politicians (especially Republicans) hoped to find low numbers that would show the problem was not the result of Ronald Reagan's economic policies.

The first salvo in the war of homeless statistics was fired by Mitch Snyder and Mary Ellen Hombs in 1980. In a congressional hearing, these two homeless advocates contended that 2.2 million Americans were homeless. They later raised that figure to 3 million in their 1983 book *Homelessness in America*. This figure eventually was accepted as fact by many advocates and the majority of the media and was reported widely, even after Snyder's admission that it was pure fabrication:

> Everybody demanded it, everybody said we want a number.
> . . . We got on the phone, we made lots of calls, we talked to
> lots of people, and we said, "Okay, here are some numbers."
> They have no meaning, no value.

Snyder and Hombs wanted to draw the country's attention to the plight of the homeless, and they succeeded. Their exaggeration made homelessness a household word.

In the years that followed, the government published more conservative estimates of the number of homeless people. In 1984, the U.S. Department of Housing and Urban Development (HUD) reported 250,000 to 350,000 people homeless, and in 1990 the U.S. Census Bureau counted 228,621. While advocates such as Snyder and Hombs insisted that these numbers were far too low, others argued that the government figures proved that the homeless problem had been grossly exaggerated by homeless advocates and the media. In 1987, Martha R. Burt and Barbara E. Cohen of the Urban Institute estimated that 500,000 to 600,000 people were homeless, but their study did nothing to bring the two sides closer together.

Even in the mid-1990s, the battle over homeless statistics goes on as new studies continue to present conflicting statistics. No matter which figure is cited in the debate, those with an opposing viewpoint find a way to discredit it. The question of how many people are homeless is one of the issues debated in the following chapter on whether homelessness is a serious problem.

"[Link et al.] estimate that 7.4% of all *adult Americans (13.5 million) have experienced . . . homelessness."*

Homelessness Is a Serious Problem

Robert Rosenheck

In the fall of 1990 Bruce Link and five other professors at Columbia University directed a study to count the number of people who had been homeless during a five-year period (1985–1990) and during their lifetimes. In the following viewpoint, Robert Rosenheck argues that the conclusion of Link's study—that 8.5 million Americans experienced homelessness between 1985 and 1990—proves the magnitude of homelessness is much greater than previously reported. Rosenheck is a clinical professor of psychiatry at Yale University and a psychiatrist with the Northeast Program Evaluation Center of the Department of Veterans Affairs Medical Center in West Haven, Connecticut.

As you read, consider the following questions:

1. How are the results of the study by Bruce Link and his colleagues different from those of other studies on the homeless, according to the author?
2. What does the rise in the number of homeless indicate, in Rosenheck's view?
3. How does the change from a national economy to a world economy affect Americans and homelessness, according to the author?

Robert Rosenheck, "Editorial: Homelessness in America," *American Journal of Public Health,* vol. 84, no. 12 (December 1994), pp. 1885–86. Copyright ©1994 American Journal of Public Health. Reprinted with permission.

The study by Bruce G. Link, Ezra Susser, Ann Stueve, Jo Phelan, Robert E. Moore and Elmer Struening: "Lifetime and five-year prevalence of homelessness in the United States" (*American Journal of Public Health*, December 1994), uses an innovative household sampling method to estimate that 8.5 million Americans experienced homelessness between 1985 and 1990. This figure is two to three times that of previous estimates. Furthermore, the risk for homelessness does not appear to be concentrated among residents of large cities, men, or African Americans, as has been indicated in prior studies. Rather, it is far more evenly distributed among low-income people across the country.

When homelessness first surfaced in public awareness in the early 1980s, it was viewed as a tragic but temporary aberration affecting particularly vulnerable segments of the population. The deep recession of 1982 to 1983 had brought a precipitous but temporary rise in unemployment. Accordingly, many people expected the crisis of homelessness to be short-lived and to be largely resolved by the next upward turn of the business cycle.

It was also widely understood that some homeless people would not be able to work. These people were likely to be medically or psychiatrically disabled and would need emergency shelter and special services. The deinstitutionalization of the mentally ill [the massive emptying of state mental hospitals that began in the 1950s], in particular, had failed to provide adequate community supports for patients discharged from state mental hospitals. Early research reports showed that a large number of homeless persons suffered from schizophrenia; that single mothers and their children were the fastest growing subpopulation of the homeless; and that, unlike single homeless persons of previous eras, those of the 1980s were mostly young, unemployed African-American men. These reports reinforced the widely held view that homelessness is a temporary problem that is confined to the fringes of society and does not affect the societal core.

A Peripheral Issue?

Although, in the late 1980s, the United States experienced the longest sustained period of economic growth of the postwar period, homelessness did not disappear, nor did its growth abate. While the paradox of expanding homelessness amid unprecedented economic growth gained widespread attention, homelessness was still seen as a peripheral issue and a problem of marginal populations. Study after study highlighted the fact that many homeless persons were mentally ill, that they often suffered from substance abuse disorders and severe social isolation, and that many were members of racial minority groups. President Ronald Reagan reassured the American public that the federal safety net was operational and effective for those who sought its help. Persistently homeless street people, he suggested, were deviants who chose their homeless lifestyles voluntarily. He pointed to the vast number of jobs available in the want ads of the typical Sunday paper, jobs that were presumably available to any motivated homeless worker who made the effort required to apply. A prominent commentary in a leading news magazine echoed the chief executive's perspective and portrayed the homeless as rebels, voluntary exiles who *could* but *would not* participate in the social mainstream. When large numbers of veterans were observed among the homeless, researchers emphasized that their presence was probably yet another manifestation of the Vietnam War, whose legacy tragically extended across the decades to the present. The sense that homelessness is an aberration affecting Americans who have distinct personal histories or who are situated on the fringes of society was further supported by the sense that homelessness is an urban problem that mostly affects large cities, especially those in the industrial Northeast.

A National Phenomenon

Unlike previous research, the study of Link and his colleagues challenges the perception that homelessness is limited in its reach. Basing their study on a telephone survey of a representative sample of US households, they estimate that 7.4% of *all* adult Americans (13.5 million) have experienced *literal* (i.e., street and shelter) homelessness in their lives, and that 3.1% of adult Americans (5.7 million) experienced it between 1985 and 1990. Again, this is a far larger estimate than previous ones based on surveys of currently homeless people. Even more striking than these large numbers (which the authors show to be conservative estimates) is that the incidence of homelessness appears to be no greater among men than among women, among Blacks than among Whites, or among urban than among rural populations. Homelessness, these data suggest, affects a broad spectrum of Americans and, not surprisingly, is most likely to affect those who have low incomes or are poorly educated.

The discrepancy between these findings and those of previous studies is striking. Homeless people are most visible in large cities, where they draw attention because they are an irritant to those with whom they share public spaces. As a result, most survey research has been conducted in such settings, with limited attention paid to the broader national picture. Link et al.'s study is the first to look at homelessness as a truly national phenomenon, and, as a result, it may be the first to approximate the true magnitude of homelessness in our society.

The rise in homelessness, it appears, may be less an aberrant phenomenon affecting the margins of urban society than an indicator of major changes in American society as a whole. Like the proverbial miner's canary, the homelessness of the 1980s may have been a harbinger of broad social changes that would affect the health and welfare of a wide range of low-income Americans and, ultimately, the quality of life of all Americans.

A 3-Percent Trend

A recent analysis of turnover rates in two large shelter systems by Dennis Culhane at the University of Pennsylvania found that 3 percent of Philadelphia's population had spent some time in its shelters in a three-year period; in New York, the same 3 percent showed up in its shelters, this time over a five-year period (roughly co-terminous with the period asked about by Bruce Link). Similarly, in an independent investigation of shelter turnover rates in a number of jurisdictions, Martha Burt of the Urban Institute found that an annual count was anywhere from five to eight times higher than of an average night. If one applies this turnover rate to the 1990s shelter occupancy figure compiled by the Census Bureau (178,828), one arrives at a range of 4.5 to 7.2 million people, over a five-year period.

Kim Hopper, *Safety Network*, July/August 1994.

By the end of the decade, it had become clear that during the 1980s and for the first time since the end of World War II, the United States had experienced a regressive change in distribution of wealth: the lowest quintile of the population experienced a 13% decline in income while the highest quintile experienced an 8% increase. With the deindustrialization of the American economy, employment opportunities for less well educated workers declined substantially, and African Americans living in large cities in particular found their neighborhoods to be increasingly characterized by concentrated poverty. Unemployment rates were higher in rural areas than in urban settings, and many small farmers were displaced from their land.

A Change in Commitment

In one view, the core commitment of Americans to one another was eroded by the change from a national economy that depends on American workers to a world economy centered on international corporations that may be based in the United States but that owe allegiance to workers of no particular nation. To the extent that Link et al. show homelessness to be a national problem of broad scope, it may be understood as reflecting these deep structural changes that cut across all of American society. From an even broader perspective, the continuing erosion of domestic life in America, of which homelessness is but one symptom, may be understood to be a consequence of the commitment of resources to defense policies that may benefit the nation by protecting the security and stability of international trade, but that restrict our investment in social welfare at home.

Homelessness is a serious public health issue in its own right. In addition, homeless people suffer from associated conditions such as mental illness, alcoholism, tuberculosis, and a substantial excess of deaths. After a decade of trying, we know that emergency approaches to this problem have not worked. Link et al. show us why. Homelessness is not an isolated problem that can be resolved through emergency interventions with currently homeless persons. One cannot fix a leaky boat by bailing out the water. One must find the holes and patch them.

Homelessness is a symptom of much deeper and more serious changes in American society. How we would reverse these changes is not easy to specify in policy recommendations that are both empirically based and politically acceptable. Effective action is urgently needed in the areas of housing, health care, employment, and education. The alternative of continued social disintegration will have grave consequences for the national health and welfare and makes this a problem on which we cannot turn our backs.

"There aren't 7 million homeless people in America. Or 5 million. Or 3 million."

The Extent of Homelessness Is Exaggerated

Jon Katz

While the Clinton administration and others cite figures estimating that as many as 7 million Americans were homeless at some point during the late 1980s, the true figure is about one-twentieth of that, charges Jon Katz in the following viewpoint. Katz maintains that the figures have been exaggerated by homeless advocates and repeated by journalists until the numbers became "facts." Katz is a writer on the media for *New York* magazine.

As you read, consider the following questions:

1. Why are erroneous figures concerning the homeless and other social causes continuously printed in the press, according to Katz?
2. Why do advocates for the homeless and other causes inflate their figures, in the author's view?
3. Where, according to Katz, can government policy makers and the media find reliable data on the number of homeless in the United States?

Well, it turns out that there aren't 7 million homeless people in America. Or 5 million. Or 3 million. And it seems that the de-institutionalization of the mentally ill is not the primary cause of the increase in homelessness; and hard as it is to swallow, it seems that Republican housing policies were only marginally responsible for leaving the streets littered with the destitute.

The real figure is more like 300,000 to 400,000, says Christopher Jencks in his book, *The Homeless.*

How is it that a 57-year-old sociology professor can transcend hyped-up numbers, ideological cant, and government obfuscation to tell us roughly how many homeless there are and where they come from? Our biggest and best news organizations have been unable to perform this simple task since Ronald Reagan became president.

More than a decade after large numbers of people began living on our streets, the public generally knows little about homelessness, let alone what to do about it. Nor do we have accurate figures on a host of other hot-button issues: how many or what kinds of people are HIV-positive, how many people are raped, how many children and spouses are abused, how frequently kidnapping occurs. These numbers are hard but not at all *impossible* to come by. So what's the problem?

Statistics have become ideological and political weapons—pump up the figures enough and society must start taking notice. Reporters, hemmed in by outdated notions of objectivity, their Rolodex stuffed with the names of statistics-bearing advocates, are surprisingly easy prey for this sort of numerical manipulation. They rarely have the time or appetite to pore over government documents, nor can they expect much recognition for doing so.

It's easier to take ready-made figures from self-serving activists, therapists, and advocates—social-service flacks, in short—who routinely hustle the media into passing along as fact wildly varying and usually inaccurate figures.

Distorted Numbers

Remember how in the early eighties, children's-rights organizations claimed that at least 50,000 American kids a year—sometimes the cited number was much higher—were being abducted by strangers? The press dutifully reported the numbers, milk cartons became ubiquitously unsettling "wanted" posters, and a generation of kids received rigorous instruction in how to be phobic. Today, federal officials responsible for tallying the data report that a few hundred children at most each year are victims of classic kidnappings. Not that the media needed the government to tell us that the 50,000 figure was wrong: Simple intuition would have sufficed.

Needless to say, the child-abduction distortions prompted little change in journalistic practices. As Jencks's book demonstrates anew, journalism is too daily a business to have even a rudimentary sense of history or statistics.

It's also full of bleeding hearts. The press is continually accused of insensitivity, but the opposite is true: Though owners tend to be bloodless and nonideological corporate Pooh-Bahs, the journalists who work for them are, overwhelmingly, squishily sensitive, socially conscious, eager to prove their humanity.

Reprinted by permission of Chuck Asay and Creators Syndicate.

This homogeneity seems to have blunted the media's traditional and necessary skepticism. "If you're a conservative, or if you differ from the prevailing conventional liberal wisdom, you keep your mouth shut about it, or you get very isolated," says a metropolitan editor at a New York newspaper. "If somebody says there are 10 million homeless people in America, you don't challenge that, even if you know it's bullshit, because people will see you as not caring about the homeless. So these numbers are just passed on to the public even though everybody in the newsroom, left or right, knows they're probably not true."

Advocates for the homeless have learned how to play on the media's sympathies. Mere tens or hundreds of thousands of victims won't move the political agenda, they've learned; it takes millions. And these millions must be more than just pathetic; they must be pathetic for reasons entirely beyond their control. You can see these stereotypes in movies like *With Honors*, in which Joe Pesci plays a hardworking shipbuilder who breathes asbestos for decades, gets too sick to work, is fired, and ends up living in the basement of a Harvard library.

Jencks's *The Homeless* is a rebuke to this sort of sloppy, feel-good flabbiness. It is a book a journalist could have written, and should have, years ago.

There for the Taking

"In the absence of official statistics," Jencks writes about the early eighties, "both journalists and legislators turned to advocacy groups." These activists—especially the late and very media-savvy Mitch Snyder—came up with estimates of between 2 million and 3 million. Lacking better figures, says Jencks, journalists repeated Snyder's figure, usually without attribution. "In due course," he writes, "it became so familiar that many people treated it as an established fact."

James K. Glassman, the former editor of *Roll Call*, points out in *Forbes Media Critic* that news organizations from CNN to the Memphis *Commercial Appeal* to the Baltimore *Sun* have all invoked the 3 million figure. Not content to stop there, the Clinton administration was preparing a report in the spring of 1994 endorsing recent estimates that as many as *7 million* Americans were homeless at some point during the late eighties.

The Clintonites and the media have failed to avail themselves of actual, *reliable* data. The information, it seems, has been there for the taking, from Census Bureau and Labor Department studies to the findings of scores of foundations, urban-policy centers, local governmental agencies, authors, and sociologists. After crunching more objective numbers, Jencks came up with the almost certainly accurate 300,000-to-400,000 figure—a whole order of magnitude less catastrophic than Americans had been taught for a decade.

The number gap between Jencks and the homeless lobby has large implications for urban policy. Huge numbers allowed homeless advocates to persuasively argue that the phenomenon was primarily linked to unemployment (and thus could befall any number of Joe Pescis), Glassman notes, rather than to drugs, mental illness, and other factors. Journalism contributed to this misunderstanding, making it even more unlikely that intelligent solutions would emerge.

In sorting through extensive surveys on consumer expenditures, housing and income, drug treatment, jobless claims, shelter enrollments, mental-health programs, and scores of other statistical material, Jencks found that the left and the right have misperceived the causes and nature of homelessness—not only its scope. Certainly, the deinstitutionalization of the mentally ill during the seventies contributed to some of the increase in homelessness; so did the gentrification of so-called skid rows.

Most of the people who end up sleeping on the streets or in public buildings are not the lazy and the shiftless but the addicted, the unskilled, the profoundly luckless, and the disconnected—often in toxic combination. Married couples rarely end up homeless, Jencks found. Joblessness by itself is unlikely to lead to the streets. And Republican housing policies—spending went up, not down, under Reagan—had only a marginal effect. Housing units were abandoned not by government but by private landlords. . . .

Conclusions Supported by Facts

Christopher Jencks is seen as a brilliant academic, his work worthy of front-page reviews in *The New York Times Book Review*. But he would serve far better as a journalistic role model. (And not for the first time, either. In his previous, contrarian work, *Rethinking Social Policy: Race, Poverty and the Underclass*, Jencks explored difficult questions about crime, affirmative action, and welfare in much the same way.) He is fearless about reporting his conclusions, even when they fly in the face of conventional wisdom. Those conclusions are shaped and supported by facts. And he is willing to advocate.

Jencks seems to understand that people would rather hear the truth than weigh conflicting, carefully concocted versions of it. "There is a certain kind of knee-jerk liberal and conservative position on almost every subject," he told the New York *Times*. "But the number of people who actually take these positions is relatively modest; most people pause to think about things."

Given half a chance.

"Viewing homelessness as intractable is simply wrong."

Homelessness Can Be Limited

Henry G. Cisneros

In November 1993 a homeless woman named Yetta Adams died on a park bench in Washington, D.C. Her death occurred right across the street from the offices of Henry G. Cisneros, the secretary of the U.S. Department of Housing and Urban Development (HUD), who had said relieving homelessness was HUD's top priority. In the following viewpoint, Cisneros examines the history and causes of homelessness. He proposes the "D.C. Initiative," a program to help the homeless in the District of Columbia, and maintains that such a program, if successful, could serve as a model for cities across the nation.

As you read, consider the following questions:

1. What evidence does Cisneros cite to show the war against homelessness is not lost?
2. What is required from the homeless and those trying to help get them off the streets, in the author's opinion?
3. What are the four goals of the D.C. Initiative listed by Cisneros?

Henry G. Cisneros, "A Death on the Nation's Doorstep," *Washington Post National Weekly Edition*, December 13–19, 1993. Reprinted with permission.

On the last Sunday in November 1993, as the temperature plummeted into the low 30s, a woman lay down on a bus bench in the nation's capital covered only by an old blanket and the cloak of night. She was alone. She was homeless. When she lay down to sleep that cold night, she was anonymous.

We know her name today—Yetta Adams. She was 43, the mother of three adult children. We know these things about her because, sometime in the night, as she lay on that bench, she died.

Yetta Adams was not the first person to succumb to death on a cold street in a big city, and she will not be the last.

But her death has marked us more than others, because she died across the street from the U.S. Department of Housing and Urban Development. She died across the street from my office, just weeks after I said that relieving homelessness would be HUD's top priority.

The temptation is strong to see Yetta Adams' death as an indictment of a callous, uncaring people, or as a sign that the problem has become so intractable that efforts to help the homeless are doomed to failure. But indicting each other is too easy. And viewing homelessness as intractable is simply wrong. While Yetta Adams' death jarred me and all of my colleagues at HUD, reminding us that our society is becoming an increasingly hostile environment for the homeless, I know there are success stories—model programs that have lifted people out of homelessness, programs from which we can learn.

But the successes aren't visible enough, and we have hardened ourselves to the pain of the homeless; we defensively brush by them in the streets and brush off their entreaties for help. We are resigned to the homeless as fixtures of the urban landscape, and we wish we did not have to see them among us. The simple fact that we now call these men, women and children "the homeless" labels them as a new, permanent statistical category.

Compassion Fatigue

It is not surprising that Americans feel this way about homeless people today. But this fatigue in the battle against homelessness means that the nation's leadership—in Washington, in our state capitals and in our local communities—has to ensure that in their weariness, Americans do not turn this fight into a war on the homeless themselves.

It is important to understand the source of this weariness. For more than 12 years, Americans have watched in dismay as the number of homeless people on street corners, in doorways, in vestibules, in parks, in libraries and in every other conceivable public place and space has grown.

We know why the ranks of the homeless have swollen: Mental

institutions have shut down and thrown people into the streets; drug and alcohol addiction has sent others to join them there. Recession and unemployment have added still others to the homeless population.

1988 Estimates of the Number of Homeless Persons in Different Metropolitan Areas

Place	Number Homeless	Place	Number Homeless
Albuquerque	543	Little Rock	300
Atlanta	3,000	Los Angeles	30,000
Baltimore	700	Louisville	620
Baton Rouge	155	Miami	4,500
Birmingham	1,000	Minneapolis	500
Boston	3,000	New York	18,050
Charlotte	225	Pittsburgh	1,500
Chicago	3,750	Phoenix	1,155
Cincinnati	925	Portland	2,000
Cleveland	550	Philadelphia	2,100
Colorado Springs	100	Raleigh	225
Davenport	312	Richmond	350
Dayton	238	Rochester	90
Detroit	5,250	San Diego	1,900
Fort Wayne	475	Salt Lake City	489
Grand Rapids	110	San Francisco	1,670
Hartford	500	Scranton	75
Honolulu	800	Seattle	2,250
Houston	5,000	Syracuse	425
Kansas City	275	Tampa	500
Las Vegas	1,500	Worcester	900

Deborah Judith Devine, *Homelessness and the Social Safety Net*, 1988.

Meanwhile, Americans who have traditionally been considered "better off" have wrestled with their own economic demons: stagnant or falling real wages, the growing threat of unemployment, the soaring costs of sending their kids to college or caring for their aging parents. And during this time, they have watched as public agencies and private groups have fallen steadily behind the ever-growing need for emergency shelter—often despite increased public outlays and exertions in behalf of the homeless. Overwhelmed by the seeming enormity of the homeless issue, increasingly preoccupied with their own problems and even fearful that they are themselves only one or two paychecks removed from the streets, Americans have become more skeptical of government's ability to deal with this problem.

We have witnessed this evolution in the District of Columbia, and the District's experience has been mirrored in other major American cities.

A Growing Problem

In 1975, the District was able to keep up with the needs of homeless people with two city-run emergency shelters and the help of several private service providers. At that time, there were virtually no people living on the streets of the nation's capital.

Six years later, the District had 15 shelters, including four operated by the city government, housing 600 people a night. Another 200 families received temporary vouchers for hotel and motel rooms. That winter, despite the increased assistance, nine homeless people died of exposure on the District's streets.

The problem continued to worsen, and in 1984 District voters demonstrated their desire to do something about it by giving their overwhelming approval to a ballot initiative guaranteeing the "right to adequate overnight shelter." The law significantly expanded the District's emergency shelter effort.

Five years later, the District was sheltering more than 11,000 single adults and 2,400 families, at an annual cost of $40 million. But despite this enormous public investment, the number of homeless people on the city's streets continued to increase.

In 1990, the voters' attitude changed. As expenditures mounted to no visible effect, District voters repealed the right-to-shelter initiative by a 51-to-49-percent vote.

This brings us to the night of Nov. 28, 1993, when Yetta Adams died on a bus bench opposite HUD headquarters.

Indictment of a System

Yetta Adams' death is not an indictment of her fellow Americans; it is an indictment of a system that evolved haphazardly to treat the symptom of homelessness and failed to address its underlying causes. This broad indictment should not be taken to mean that all of our efforts to help the homeless have been failures. There have been successes:

• Miami has a new tax on restaurants and hotels to create more emergency and transitional beds for homeless people.

• In Minnesota, a transitional housing facility is creating jobs for residents through a painting and decorating business it owns.

• In Yonkers, New York, a family inn provides transitional housing for residents and jobs in a bakery and other businesses it owns.

• In Los Angeles, a nonprofit group is rehabilitating dilapidated, single-room occupancy hotels to house elderly people, people who are chronically and mentally ill, substance abusers and people with active tuberculosis that is no longer contagious.

These success stories give us cause for hope and strong reason to believe that we can come to grips with this problem, provided we truly understand it.

Homelessness is not a condition; it is an outcome of mental illness, drug abuse, alcoholism, disability, chronic illness and just plain hard times. The problems that drive the Yetta Adamses of this nation into its streets are profound, complex and persistent. They cannot be solved by a hot shower, a warm meal and a bed. Yetta Adams, as we now know, suffered from disabling mental depression, compounded by a serious health problem: diabetes. She had been in and out of shelters over the past decade. According to press accounts, a network of shelter operators, caseworkers and doctors tried repeatedly to help her. She had $300 in cash with her when she died. Nevertheless, Yetta Adams dropped off the system's radar scope.

Tens of thousands of homeless Americans—no one knows the exact number—disappear from the system's cluttered screens every day. If we are to truly help these people, we must address the problems that have rendered them homeless in the first place—and that means we need to encourage and enable homeless people, as much as possible, to take responsibility for their own destinies.

The D.C. Initiative

The approach that HUD has developed with the strong support of President Clinton addresses a broad range of needs: psychiatric care; substance abuse counseling; training; housing, be it temporary, transitional or permanent; and, of course, jobs. Although it is HUD's responsibility to provide leadership and resources, it is up to our local partners to translate our support into locally designed actions and services. The tragic irony of Yetta Adams' death in the shadow of HUD is that it came at a time when we were ready to begin testing this approach in the District of Columbia.

HUD's assistant secretary of community planning and development, Andrew Cuomo, has worked with other federal agencies, the District government and with community homeless advocates on this effort, which we call the "D.C. Initiative." Cuomo has secured the support of Congress and engaged the White House and all of the concerned domestic departments and agencies of the federal government in this initiative for which HUD has earmarked $20 million in federal funds.

The D.C. Initiative will:

• Shift the focus of homeless assistance from simply getting people off the streets for the night to solving the problems that drive them into the streets. It will enable them to make a transition from the streets, to shelter, to permanent housing.

• Require the homeless to take responsibility for themselves. It will offer them help in exchange for their commitment to make the most of that help. The homeless must agree to accept the services and housing offered to them and strive to become self-sufficient.

• Seek to end the use of public spaces by homeless persons as residences.

• Increase affordable housing for low-income District residents and develop a fair and effective means of allocating those housing units, outside the homeless system.

The D.C. Initiative will be coordinated and implemented by a new, public-private entity that will bring together government agencies, community-based, nonprofit service providers and the business and foundation communities. . . .

All of this would be happening even if Yetta Adams had not died as she did. But her death has underscored—for all of us involved in the D.C. Initiative—the urgent need to move forward.

Expanding the Approach

The D.C. Initiative's success is critical to the entire country. We want to expand this approach to more cities. . . . But before we can ask Congress for money to expand this program, we must demonstrate there is a will to carry it out. We must show that the federal government, local government and community groups can work together.

Many people have told me that HUD is making a mistake in committing such substantial resources to the District. But as someone who drives through the District's streets every day, as the administration official most directly responsible for confronting homelessness in America, I cannot turn my back on homeless people sleeping in doorways and on benches and steam grates at the center of the nation's government. If we cannot deal with homelessness on our very doorsteps in Washington, where can we deal with it? And if we cannot deal with it now, when can we deal with it?

"There will always be a sliver of society . . . who will be more than desperately poor. They will drop off the edge."

There Will Always Be a Homeless Problem

Robert J. Samuelson and William Raspberry

In Part I of the following viewpoint, economist Robert J. Samuelson, a columnist for *Newsweek*, argues that there have always been and will always be homeless people, no matter what steps individuals or government agencies take to solve the problem. Samuelson maintains that the homeless of the past were relegated to skid row where they were "out of sight and out of mind." Today, he contends, the homeless are more visible because there are more of them and because they have been driven out of downtown areas by urban renewal and other policies. In Part II, William Raspberry, a columnist for the *Washington Post*, writes that because most efforts to help the homeless have failed, he has concluded that homelessness is a problem that may lack a solution.

As you read, consider the following questions:

1. What can be done about the homeless, in Samuelson's view?
2. At what level of government should solutions to homelessness be developed, according to Samuelson?
3. What is Raspberry's attitude toward the homeless and what made him change it?

No problem better highlights the limits of collective compassion than that of the homeless. The Clinton administration proposed raising federal spending on the homeless to $2.2 billion in 1995—double the 1993 level and more than four times what it was in 1987. Even the administration does not claim that its program will reduce homelessness by more than a third, and this may be optimistic. All the federal spending to date has barely dented the problem.

We Americans are eternal optimists. We think that all problems are solvable. We believe in the "indefinite perfectibility of man," as De Tocqueville put it. But people are permanently imperfect, and all problems are not solvable. Some will endure forever. There will always be a sliver of society—especially in a nation as big, diverse and individualistic as ours—who will be more than desperately poor. They will drop off the edge.

Many of these people used to be called "vagrants, tramps, bums," as the writer Tom Wolfe once put it. Homelessness is a blander term, implying that the homeless bear no responsibility for their plight. All labels simplify the human condition, and if homeless is too forgiving for some, "bums" may not be forgiving enough for others. But whatever the labels, some people will always fall to the bottom.

Why, then, is homelessness so conspicuous now when it wasn't 15 or 20 years ago? The main explanation is that the problem we now call homelessness existed before in other forms and other places. In a new book, *The Homeless*, sociologist Christopher Jencks of Northwestern University has meticulously reviewed the various studies and concludes that a large part of today's problem results from the destruction of "skid rows" and the "deinstitutionalization" of mental patients.

Out of Sight, Out of Mind

Skid rows were rarely visited by the middle class. The homeless were out of sight and out of mind; they slept on the streets or in flophouses. In 1958, Chicago's so-called "cage hotels"—which offered single, windowless rooms for less than $1 a night—housed 8,000. By 1992, only one similar hotel remained with, perhaps, 200 rooms. Skid rows were regarded as disgraces. They often became sites for urban renewal, or strict enforcement of building codes put hotels out of business. In the process, the down-and-out lost their most reliable form of housing.

That loss, writes Jencks, "combined with changes in the laws about panhandling and vagrancy, encouraged destitute single adults to spread out over the entire city, turning every doorway into a potential flophouse." Homelessness increased and became a lot more visible, though the numbers were never huge. A 1958 survey in Chicago found about 1,300 homeless; three decades later, the number was about 2,800 in a city of 2.8 million.

Other Causes

"Deinstitutionalization" has had a similar effect. It transformed an invisible problem into a visible one. People who had no place to go were released from state hospitals; involuntary commitment became almost impossible. Slightly less than a quarter of today's homeless have been in mental hospitals. But as Jencks points out, this does not cover those homeless with recent mental problems who might have been hospitalized under previous policies. Including these, he reckons that perhaps a third of today's homeless are mentally ill.

There are other causes of higher homelessness. Jencks says that crack addiction (cheaper than cocaine), more long-term unemployment and a decline in welfare benefits all mean that people with the most precarious lives stand a greater danger of landing in the streets. What Jencks does not think caused homelessness is a drop in government-subsidized housing. Between 1979 and 1989, he points out, the number of tenants in subsidized housing rose from 2.9 million to 4.2 million. Though the Reagan and Bush administrations disliked these programs, previous spending commitments kept construction expanding.

Nor has housing for the poor generally deteriorated, though obviously much of it remains below middle-class standards. "The low-rent housing available in 1973 often lacked amenities, such as central heat and hot water," Jencks reports. "Many poor tenants who came of age before World War II saw these amenities as luxuries. . . ." By 1989, surveys showed tenants had more rooms, more "complete bathrooms, complete kitchens . . . modern plumbing, central heat and air conditioning" than in 1973.

A Largely Insolvable Problem

What remains is a small, highly visible and largely insolvable problem. Jencks thinks that the homeless at any one time tripled or quadrupled in the 1980s to 300,000 or 400,000; the Clinton administration uses a figure of 600,000, which seems on the high end of reasonable estimates. Some people experience brief periods of homelessness, so that in the late 1980s, as many as 1.2 million people annually might have been on the streets sometime. All estimates are rough; all seem large but are relatively small in a nation of 260 million.

What can be done? Families with children deserve the most help. But they account for less than a fifth of the homeless, and most already use shelters and tend to move fairly rapidly out of homelessness. Many of the rest (mostly single men) are barely employable. Many are alcoholics or drug users. Many have chosen panhandling as a way of life. The odds of helping them are long. If we had no other social problems, we might still spend heavily to beat the odds. But there are many demands on limited public funds for other pressing needs: to control crime, reduce welfare dependency, improve schools or provide more health care. Spending more for the homeless crimps spending for something else.

Is the extra effort worth it? The hard questions are best settled locally. People can weigh their own conditions, competing needs and moral sensibilities. Homelessness is mainly a local problem. Transforming it into a national issue is convenient for advocates, because it provides the most government money for the least amount of lobbying. But this is ultimately a corrupt and delusional bargain. It makes people less responsible for local problems and imposes a moral burden on the federal government to try to solve problems that it can't.

II

I've found a lovely cure for social-responsibility smugness. Whenever I'm tempted to dismiss someone else as selfish, bigoted or socially irresponsible—all because he doesn't share my enthusiasm for a particular policy—I think of my own changing attitude toward the homeless. Brings me back down to earth every time.

No, I haven't turned against the homeless. It's just that I no longer see homelessness as a problem that's likely to be solved anytime soon, and as a result, I find it hard to sustain much interest in it.

That must sound cold—as cold, perhaps, as people used to sound to me when they complained about public spending for inner-city education, or job training or whatever policy happened to make sense to me at the time. Now I'm a little more tolerant thanks to waning interest in the homeless.

Maybe I ought to explain a little of what I'm talking about. I'm talking about homelessness as a rather recent phenomenon: not the hobos of the Depression, not the people who show up at the shelters for battered women.

Growing Numbers

The homeless I refer to didn't seem to exist until "deinstitutionalization" dumped them out of the mental hospitals and onto the streets. The reasonable-sounding notion was that mental patients should have their illness treated in the least restrictive environment. For the non-dangerous schizophrenics and others who needed only regular medication, that meant outpatient care at neighborhood clinics.

It turned out—surprise!—that mental patients don't always

36

show up for the medication. A lot of those who didn't wound up sleeping on benches and in cardboard boxes, joining those we used to call the "street people" in a new category known as the homeless. Their numbers have been growing ever since.

And, I confess, my openness to the appeals from homeless advocates has been declining.

Little Has Changed

I used to get excited about the prospect of clean, well-managed shelters, run by saints such as the late Mitch Snyder. Surely such facilities were within the fiscal means of the local governments, particularly if ordinary citizens would pitch in to help. But the shelters didn't seem to stay clean or well-managed very long, and even many of the homeless preferred to take their chances on the streets and steam grates.

The Incurability of Human Suffering

When New York mayor Edward Koch attempted to clean up the streets and institutionalize the mentally ill for the benefit of all New Yorkers, including the homeless, the ACLU [American Civil Liberties Union] declared a civil right to live on busy thoroughfares. One of Koch's "captives," an obviously deranged woman, was even invited to lecture at Harvard, while others gave the woman a job and a new set of clothes, all apparently to show that what the homeless merely needed were a "chance" and a "break." Before *60 Minutes* could even get this "success story" on the air, the woman had traded in civility for a return to her previous calling: defecating on the streets of Manhattan. . . .

There is, of course, no long-term answer to homelessness. There will always be drunkards, addicts, slackers, and the insane who will end up on the streets either by choice or circumstance. What advocates for the homeless actually despise is not the homelessness itself, but what homelessness mirrors about humanity's darker side: about the incurability of human suffering and sin and the fatuousness of modernity's promise of the perfectibility of man and his social institutions. We think it tragic that a society capable of placing a man on the moon is one incapable of curing homelessness; but what is tragic is our inability to see the inanity of the comparison.

Theodore Pappas, *Chronicles*, November 1991.

It once seemed reasonable to me that a lot of the homeless could find work if only they had access to shower facilities, a clean set of clothes and a mailing address. Churches and other organizations started to provide these basics of human dignity, and I'm sure a few once-homeless men and women are now gainfully employed and snug in their modest apartments. Very few. What's more likely is that very little has changed, even for those who found their way to the showers and free clothing centers.

At one time it seemed plain to me that the growth in homelessness was a direct result of discrete societal changes: a troubled domestic economy, a skyrocketing real estate market and a Reagan administration cut in housing subsidies for the poor. But while these things were going on during the surge in homelessness, I doubt that they caused the surge in homelessness. A more likely culprit is growing (and untreated) addiction to drugs and alcohol and what might be called "noninstitutionalization."

Nothing Has Made a Difference

The relevant point, though, is this: Nothing, no matter how promising it seemed at the time, has made any difference. Things keep getting worse, and it gets harder to respond to each new proposal, each new attempt at conscience-pricking.

And finally, decent people like me—who used to lay homelessness at the feet of the authors of the Vietnam War and Reaganism and neo-heartlessness—start to doubt that there really is a solution to the problem. We don't say it out loud; we simply stop hearing the pleas of the advocates.

Something very much like that may be happening with regard to the causes I still care deeply about: public education, criminal-justice reform, the plight of the inner-city underclass. How could anyone be so cold-hearted as to walk away from crack babies, pitifully uneducated children, hopeless adolescents and boys so bereft of positive role models they are virtually destined to wind up in prison or dead?

Can't we see that we all have a responsibility for this tangle of problems, and even if we don't, can't we see that it's in our interest to help make things better?

I once believed that anyone who didn't see it that way was, almost by definition, a bigot. But when I think of my frustration over the question of homelessness, I see another possibility: You don't have to be mean-spirited to walk away from social problems. All it takes is the certainty that nothing can be done to solve them.

"Families are the fastest growing segment of the homeless population."

Homelessness Increasingly Affects Families

Lisa Mihaly

Homeless families are the fastest growing subgroup of the homeless population, writes Lisa Mihaly, an expert on national policy affecting homeless children, youth, and families. In the following viewpoint, Mihaly discusses the numbers and characteristics of homeless families. Mihaly is a senior program associate in the Child Welfare and Mental Health Division at the Children's Defense Fund in Washington, D.C., and the author of *Homeless Families: Failed Policies and Young Victims.*

As you read, consider the following questions:

1. According to the author, what ratio of the homeless population consists of families with children?
2. Why are homeless families hard to count, according to Mihaly?
3. In the author's opinion, why is a high percentage of homeless families headed by parents under the age of 30?

Images of families living in campgrounds and sleeping on cots in crowded shelters are joining those of disheveled men sleeping on park benches and women pushing their belongings through bus stations in shopping carts.

Throughout the country, families are the fastest growing segment of the homeless population. Because counting the homeless is difficult and has become highly politicized there is no single, accepted count of homeless families. There is virtual unanimity, however, that the 1980s have produced a homeless population—and a rate of homelessness among families—far larger than at any other time since the Great Depression of the 1930s. Estimates of the total number of homeless persons range from 250,000 to 3 million; it is generally thought that members of homeless families with children make up about one-third of this population. Every night, according to a 1988 estimate by the Institute of Medicine, 100,000 American children go to sleep homeless.

Families are homeless today primarily because there is a shortage of affordable housing. The number of homeless families will continue to grow unless the country addresses the pressures that are forcing more and more families out of their homes. By the year 2000, if current trends continue, millions of American children will have spent at least a part of their childhoods without a place to call home. Throughout their lives, these youngsters will bear the physical, educational, and emotional scars that result from a childhood punctuated by cold, hunger, sporadic schooling, and frequent moves among temporary shelters and "welfare hotels" riddled with violence and drugs. . . .

Counting Homeless Families and Children

Counts of homeless families with children often are hindered by some of the special characteristics of this population. First, afraid that they will be charged as neglectful parents and their children taken from them, parents are often particularly hesitant to identify themselves as homeless. Second, families in unconventional forms of shelter, such as campgrounds and cars, may not be counted. Third, families that have been separated by homelessness are not likely to be captured in surveys. They may have members in different shelters, some with friends or relatives, or children in foster care.

Perhaps the most complete pictures of the homeless family population to date have come from the annual surveys conducted by the U.S. Conference of Mayors. The surveys, conducted since 1982, collect information about the number and characteristics of homeless persons served in approximately 28 cities around the country. Since 1986, the reports have estimated that, on average, one-third of the homeless population nationwide are parents and children. This proportion has been rising steadily. In 1985, homeless families were about one-fourth of the homeless population. In the 1989 report, families were estimated to comprise 36 percent of the homeless population in the sites studied. Other reports have confirmed these findings. For example, one-third of the homeless population in Delaware shelters in 1988 were members of families with children, as were 26 percent of those in Colorado shelters that same year.

More Families on the Street

Families constituted an increasingly larger part of the urban homeless population in 1993 and almost a third of families seeking emergency shelter were turned away, according to a survey of 26 cities released by the U.S. Conference of Mayors.

While single men once constituted the bulk of the homeless population, their numbers are now equaled by members of families, the survey found. Each group represents about 43% of the homeless population, while single women represent 11% and unaccompanied children the remainder. . . .

The Conference of Mayors, which publishes the survey on homelessness every year, stressed that the most disturbing news in the latest report was the growing percentage of families without homes and the failure of government and private services to address the shift.

"Previous years' estimates have shown families accounting for about one-third of the population seeking help," said St. Louis Mayor Freeman Bosley Jr., a co-chairman of the task force. "But this year [1993], cities put families with children at 43% of this population."

Elizabeth Shogren, *Los Angeles Times*, December 22, 1993.

Based on such findings, national estimates of the number of homeless persons in families most often are calculated as one-third of various national estimates of the total homeless population. To obtain counts of homeless children, further manipulations are necessary. It generally is assumed that the average homeless family includes one parent and one or two children. Thus, children are estimated to make up between one-half and two-thirds of the members of homeless families. Using estimates of homeless persons ranging from 250,000 to 3 million, the Children's Defense Fund estimated that between 50,000 and 500,000 children were homeless in 1988. A 1988 study by the Institute of Medicine, which used other figures, estimated that a minimum of 100,000 children are homeless on any given night.

In 1988, the General Accounting Office (GAO), using indirect estimates, conducted the first national study of the number of homeless children. The GAO first surveyed shelters and hotels in forty randomly selected urban counties; it counted all the children under age sixteen who were residing there with their families. To those counts were added the estimated numbers of homeless families presumed not sheltered and those living in suburban and rural communities. It finally estimated that 68,000 children were homeless on any given night in 1988 and that an estimated 310,000 children were served by homeless shelters during the course of that year.

It is agreed widely that families with children currently make up the fastest growing segment of the homeless population. Cities surveyed by the Conference of Mayors have had greater increases in requests for shelter by families than by individuals. For example, in 1987, cities surveyed reported an average 32 percent increase in shelter requests by families, while overall requests (including families) rose only 21 percent. In 1988, family requests for shelter rose 22 percent while requests by all homeless persons rose 13 percent. Some local sources have confirmed particularly dramatic growth. Washington, D.C., experienced a 500 percent increase in the number of sheltered families during 1986. Charleston, West Virginia, reported a 144 percent increase during that same period.

Homelessness plagues rural areas and smaller cities as well as large cities. Campgrounds and state parks in many rural areas report homeless families living in them. Reports to the Federal Department of Education on the number of homeless school-age children provide some interesting statistics on homeless families outside of the largest cities. For example, Oklahoma City reported more than 2,500 homeless children. Montana reported 1,600 homeless children. Arkansas reported 800 homeless children outside of Little Rock.

The Hidden Homeless Families

Because the numbers of homeless families are used as a backdrop for discussions about the problems they face and the services they need, families who are among the "hidden homeless" also should be counted and considered. Hidden homeless families include families living "doubled up" or "camped out" with friends and family because they have no home of their own, those living in cars and other unconventional settings, and families in which parents and children have been separated due to homelessness.

Many homeless families are hidden in doubled-up households, where two or more families share housing intended for only one. This is not the same as shared housing, in which two or more families choose to share adequate living space and utility expenses, and often help each other with child care and other needs.

Doubled-up families often suffer many of the consequences of homelessness, such as lack of privacy, instability, and overcrowding. In many communities today, there are almost as many doubled-up families as there are other homeless families. The 1988 GAO national study estimated that on any given night, while there are 68,000 homeless children, there are 186,000 precariously housed, as defined by shelter providers. In 1988, over 5 million children lived doubled up in the homes of friends or family, a 36 percent increase since 1980. Although not all of those children are in overcrowded or precarious housing, this dramatic rise is an indication of the growing inability of many families to find affordable housing of their own.

To avoid going to emergency shelter when they lose their own homes, families often first choose to move in with family or friends. In fact, research by Kay Young McChesney indicates that the lack of family or friends with whom to stay may be a key factor in determining which poor families become homeless.

Doubling up is a precarious housing alternative, as illustrated by the significant proportion of homeless families that come to shelters from friends' or families' homes: 27 percent of the families in Alameda County, California, shelters, 30 percent of the shelter families interviewed by the Philadelphia Committee for Children and Youth, and 71 percent of the families applying for shelter in a New York City study.

Avoiding Traditional Shelters

Homeless families also may be hidden because they are not in traditional shelters. These are usually families that either have chosen not to approach a shelter or have been turned away for lack of space. Families may choose not to seek formal shelter for a variety of reasons. There may be no facilities that can accommodate two-parent families or teen-age parents with children. Parents also may fear that the shelter will report them to city child-protection officials as neglectful, and that their children will be taken from them and placed in foster care. Others may be concerned that conditions in the local shelters are unsafe for women and children or fear that an abusive spouse will be able to find them. They may be forced to seek shelter instead in cars, vans, abandoned buildings, public parks, and campgrounds.

Also among the hidden homeless are families whose members have been separated from each other by homelessness. In 62 percent of the cities surveyed by the Conference of Mayors, families sometimes must be separated to find shelter. In some cases, shelters cannot house two-parent families at all, or will do so only if the parents provide a marriage license or birth certificates. Many shelters cannot accommodate boys over the age of ten, so that a mother may go to one shelter, while men and older boys go to another. Sometimes parents, anticipating separation, may send their children to stay with friends or relatives. In some cases, homelessness may result, directly or indirectly, in the placement of children in foster care.

Some communities report substantial numbers of children placed in foster care solely because of housing problems. A New Jersey study reported that homelessness was the primary cause of placement in 19 percent of the placements studied and a contributing factor in an additional 40 percent. Similarly, a 1989 report issued by the National Black Child Development Institute found that housing problems, including homelessness, were a significant and contributing factor in placement in 38 percent of the cases they reviewed in six major cities. Often, housing problems exacerbate other family problems, such as child abuse, which then may precipitate the placement of children in care.

Who Are the Homeless Families?

Homeless families are a diverse population. No systematic national research describes them. What is known about them comes primarily from surveys and studies of families using services in specific communities. The findings from these studies have limited general applicability because they usually include only families that seek help (and often a fairly small number). They do, however, provide some useful information. Not surprisingly, the studies report that the families most likely to be homeless look very much like families most likely to be poor. They also describe several problems, in addition to poverty, that seem to put families at increased risk of homelessness.

Single-parent families, most often headed by women, represent almost four-fifths of all homeless families nationwide, according to the U.S. Conference of Mayors. In Pennsylvania, for example, 90 percent of all homeless families are headed by single women. This phenomenon, however, is not universal. In the West, for example, about 25 percent of the homeless families in cities such as Denver, Portland, and Seattle are two-parent families. Two-parent families are also the majority of homeless families in some rural areas.

Female-headed families are often at increased risk of homelessness because they are more likely to be poor. They lack a second wage earner, and women's wages are generally lower than men's. In addition, those who become single parents as adolescents often have limited education and job skills. Those who become single through divorce may experience a very sudden decline in family resources.

Young families, those headed by parents under thirty, also are heavily represented among the homeless. In Delaware, for example, in 30 percent of the homeless, female-headed families the mother was between twenty and twenty-nine years old and another 8 percent were under twenty. Among single-parent homeless families in Pennsylvania, 13 percent of the parents were between sixteen and twenty, 30 percent were between twenty-one and twenty-five, and another 29 percent were between twenty-six and thirty.

Young families have been hit very hard by the economic changes since the mid-1970s. Their earnings declined by an average of 39 percent between 1973 and 1986. Not surprisingly, the poverty rate among young families almost doubled, from 12 percent to 24 percent, in that same period, increasing their risk of homelessness.

Young parents tend to have young children, who also often make up a significant proportion of the homeless-shelter residents. In Alameda County, California, 21 percent of the children in shelters in 1987 were younger than five. In Colorado, 35 percent of the children in shelters in 1988 were younger than three. It is possible that the predominance of young children is due in part to regulations in some shelters that exclude older children, especially males. Parents also may be more reluctant to send young children off alone to family or friends, which they may do with older children to spare them the horror of shelter life and the disruption of schooling.

"The problem of chronic homelessness is essentially a problem of single adult men."

Homelessness Mostly Affects Single Men

Peter Marin

Although homeless women and children are becoming more numerous in the United States, homeless men still make up the biggest portion of the homeless population, maintains Peter Marin. In the following viewpoint, Marin explores how society's expectations of and attitudes toward men's roles contribute to their homelessness. Marin is an essayist and novelist who has been researching and writing about the homeless since the late 1980s.

As you read, consider the following questions:

1. Why are more men homeless than women, in the author's opinion?
2. According to Marin, how does the welfare system affect family relationships, particularly between women and men?
3. How do society's beliefs about men make and keep men homeless, according to the author?

Excerpted from Peter Marin, "The Prejudice Against Men," *Nation*, July 8, 1991. This article first appeared in the July 1991 *APF Reporter* and is reprinted by permission of the Alicia Patterson Foundation, ©1991.

For several years advocates for the homeless have sought public support and sympathy by drawing attention to the large number of homeless families on our streets. That is an understandable tactic. Americans usually respond to social issues on the basis of sympathy for "innocent" victims—those whose blamelessness touches our hearts and whom we deem unable to care for themselves. Families, and especially children, obviously fill the bill.

But the fact remains, despite the claims of advocates, that the problem of chronic homelessness is essentially a problem of *single adult men*. Far more single adults than families, and far more men than women, end up homeless on our streets. Until we understand how and why that happens, nothing we do about homelessness will have much of an impact.

Most figures pertaining to the homeless come from limited studies or educated guesses that tend, when examined, to dissolve in one's hand. The most convincing figures I know can be found in James Wright's book *Address Unknown: The Homeless in America*. According to Wright's data, out of every 1,000 homeless people in America, 120 or so will be adults with children, another hundred will be children and the rest will be single adults. Out of that total, 156 will be single women and 580 will be single men. Now break that down into percentages. Out of all single homeless adults, 78 percent are men; out of all homeless adults, more than 64 percent are single men; and out of all homeless people—adults or children—58 percent are single men.

But even those figures do not give the full story. Our federal welfare system has been designed, primarily, to aid women with children or whole families. That means that most of the families and children on the streets have either fallen through the cracks of the welfare system or have not yet entered it. They will, in the end, have access to enough aid to get them off the streets and into some form of shelter, while most men will be left permanently on their own.

A Male Problem

I do not mean to diminish here the suffering of families or children, nor to suggest that welfare provides much more than the meanest alternative to homelessness. It is a form of indentured pauperism so grim it shames the nation. But it does in fact eventually get most families off the streets, and that leaves behind, as the chronically homeless, single adults, of whom four-fifths are men. Seen that way, homelessness emerges as a problem involving what happens to men without money, or men in trouble.

Why do so many more men than women end up on the streets? Let me begin with the simplest answers.

First, life on the streets, as dangerous as it is for men, is even

47

more dangerous for women, who are far more vulnerable. While many men in trouble drift almost naturally onto the streets, women do almost anything to avoid it.

Second, there are far better private and public shelters and services available to women.

Third, women are accustomed to asking for help while men are not; women therefore make better use of available resources.

Fourth, poor families *in extremis* [in extreme circumstances] seem to practice a form of informal triage. Young men are released into the streets more readily, while young women are kept at home even in the worst circumstances.

Fifth, there are cultural and perhaps even genetic factors at work. There is some evidence that men—especially in adolescence—are more aggressive and openly rebellious than women and therefore harder to socialize. Or it may simply be that men are allowed to live out the impulses women are taught to suppress, and that they therefore end up more often in marginal roles.

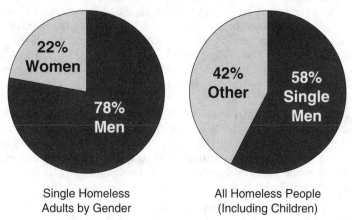

Percentage of Men Among the Homeless Population

Single Homeless Adults by Gender — 22% Women, 78% Men

All Homeless People (Including Children) — 42% Other, 58% Single Men

Peter Marin, *The Nation*, July 8, 1991.

More important, still, may be the question of work. Historically, the kinds of work associated with transient or marginal life have been reserved for men. They brought in crops, worked on ships and docks, built roads and railroads, logged and mined. Such labor granted them a place in the economy while allowing them to remain on society's edges—an option rarely available to women save through prostitution.

And society has always seemed, by design, to produce the men who did such work. Obviously, poverty and joblessness forced men into marginality. But there was more to it than that. Schools produced failures, dropouts and rebels; family life and its cruelties produced runaways and throwaways; wars rendered men incapable of settled or domestic life; small-town boredom and provinciality led them to look elsewhere for larger worlds.

Now, of course, the work such men did is gone. But like a mad engine that cannot be shut down, society goes right on producing them. Its institutions function as they always did: The schools hum, the families implode or collapse, the wars churn out their victims. But what is there for them to do? The low-paying service-sector jobs that have replaced manual labor in the economy go mainly to women or high school kids, not the men who once did the nation's roughest work.

Remember, too, in terms of work, that women, especially when young, have one final option denied to men. They can take on the "labor" of being wives and companions to men or of bearing children, and in return they will often be supported or "taken care of" by someone else. Yes, I know: Such roles can often constitute a form of oppression, especially when assumed out of necessity. But nonetheless, the possibility is there. It is permissible (as well as often necessary) for women to become financially, if precariously, dependent on others, while such dependence is more or less forbidden to men.

The Welfare System

Finally, there is the federal welfare system. I do not think most Americans understand how the system works, or how for decades it has actually sent men into the streets, creating at least some male homelessness while aiding women and children. Let me explain. There are two main programs that provide care for Americans in trouble. One is Social Security Disability Insurance. It goes to men or women who are unable, because of physical or mental problems, to work or take care of themselves. The other is Aid to Families with Dependent Children (AFDC). It is what we ordinarily call "welfare." With its roots early in this century, it was established more or less in its present form during the Depression. Refined and expanded again in the 1960s, AFDC had always been a program meant mainly for women and children and limited to households headed by women. As long as an adult man remained in the household as mate, companion or father, *no aid was forthcoming*. Changes have recently been made in the system, and men may remain in the household if they have a work history satisfying certain federal guidelines. But in poor areas and for certain ethnic groups, where unemployment runs high and few men have a qualifying

49

work history, these changes have not yet had much of an impact and men remain functionally outside the welfare system.

When it comes to single and "able-bodied," or employable, adults, there is no federal aid whatsoever. Individual states and localities sometimes provide their own aid through "general assistance" and "relief." But this is usually granted only on a temporary basis or in emergencies. And in those few places where it is available for longer periods to large numbers of single adults—California, for instance, or New York—it is often so grudging, so ringed round with capricious requirements and red tape, that it is of little use to those in need.

Depriving Men of Their Homes

This combination of approaches not only systematically denies men aid as family members or single adults. It means that the aid given to women has sometimes actually deprived men of homes, even as it has provided for women and children. Given the choice between receiving aid for themselves and their children and living with men, what do you think most women do? The regulations as they stand actually force men to compete with the state for women; as a woman in New Orleans once told me: "Welfare changes even love. If a man can't make more at a job than I get from welfare, I ain't even gonna look at him. I can't afford it."

Everywhere in America poor men have been forced to become ghost-lovers and ghost-fathers, one step ahead of welfare workers ready to disqualify families for having a man around. In many ghettos throughout the country you find women and children in their deteriorating welfare apartments, and their male companions and fathers in even worse conditions: homeless in gutted apartments and abandoned cars, denied even the minimal help granted the opposite sex.

Is it surprising, in this context, that many African-Americans see welfare as an extension of slavery that destroys families, isolates women and humiliates men according to white bureaucratic whim? Or is it accidental that in poor communities family structure has collapsed and more and more children are born outside marriage at precisely the same time that disfranchised men are flooding the streets? Welfare is not the only influence at work in all of this, of course. But before judging men and their failures and difficulties, one must understand that their social roles are in no way supported or made easier by the social policies that in small ways make female roles sustainable.

Is this merely an accidental glitch in the system, something that has happened unnoticed? Or does it merely have something to do with a sort of lifeboat ethic, where our scarce resources for helping people are applied according to the ethics of a sink-ing ship—women and children first, men into the sea?

I do not think so. Something else is at work: deep-seated prejudices and attitudes toward men that are so pervasive, so pandemic, that we have ceased to notice or examine them.

To put it simply: Men are neither supposed nor allowed to be dependent. They are expected to take care of both others *and* themselves. And when they cannot do it, or "will not" do it, the built-in assumption at the heart of the culture is that they are *less than men* and therefore unworthy of help. An irony asserts itself: Simply by being in need of help, men forfeit the right to it.

Think here of how we say "helpless as a woman." This demeans women. But it also does violence to men. It implies that a man cannot be helpless and still be a man, or that helplessness is not a male attribute, or that a woman can be helpless through no fault of her own, but that if a man is helpless it is or must be his own fault.

Try something here. Imagine walking down a street and passing a group of homeless women. Do we not spontaneously see them as victims and wonder that has befallen them, how destiny has injured them? Do we not see them as unfortunate and deserving of help and *want* to help them?

Now imagine a group of homeless men. Is our reaction the same? Is it as sympathetic? Or is it subtly different? Do we have the very same impulse to help and protect? Or do we not wonder, instead of what befell them, how they have got themselves where they are?

And remember, too, our fear. When most of us see homeless or idle men we sense or imagine danger; they make us afraid, as if, being beyond the pale, they are also beyond all social control—and therefore people to be avoided and suppressed rather than helped. . . .

Finally, I must add one more thing. Whatever particular griefs men may have experienced on their way to homelessness, there is one final and crippling sorrow all of them share: a sense of betrayal at society's refusal to recognize their needs. Most of us—men and women—grow up expecting that when things go terribly wrong someone, from somewhere, will step forward to help us. That this does not happen, and that all watch from the shore as each of us, in isolation, struggles to swim and then begins to sink, is perhaps the most terrible discovery that anyone in any society can make. When troubled men make that discovery, as all homeless men do sooner or later, then hope vanishes completely; despair rings them round; they have become what they need not have become: the homeless men we see everywhere around us.

"Homelessness is less visible in rural communities, though no less severe and tragic to those who experience it."

Homelessness Is Serious in Rural Areas

Kris Zawisza

Kris Zawisza is the director of the Washington Low-Income Housing Network, a statewide coalition that promotes the development of low-income housing. In the following viewpoint, she writes that homelessness is not just an inner-city problem, but is also a problem in rural areas. Because the rural homeless are less visible, they are often overlooked, she maintains.

As you read, consider the following questions:

1. What makes the rural homeless less visible, according to the author?
2. What economic factors of the 1980s contributed to rural homelessness, in Zawisza's opinion?
3. How does the rural homeless population differ from that of the urban homeless, according to the author?

From Kris Zawisza, "Rural Homelessness: The National Picture." This article appeared in the December 1991 issue and is reprinted with permission from *The World & I*, a publication of The Washington Times Corporation, copyright ©1991.

It challenges long-held notions of the peaceful and bountiful countryside, where people care about and for each other. But, yes, in small towns and villages throughout this country, homelessness exists. Like poverty and many other social problems, homelessness is less visible in rural communities, though no less severe and tragic to those who experience it. Its victims, as in urban areas, are often the most economically and socially vulnerable members of society.

Homelessness is not widely recognized as a problem of rural communities. Homeless is a word we associate with people living on the street or in shelters, and rural people are not often found in these situations. When they are in need of housing, they are more likely to be temporarily sheltered by family or friends or in motels, live in housing unfit for habitation, or find shelter in places such as abandoned buildings, sheds, vehicles, and shipping containers.

A shelter provider in downstate Illinois, quoted in "Rural Homelessness," captures the many ways in which rural homeless people find shelter:

> We are often asked, "Where are the homeless people? We never see them." They are out there. Some of these people stay with friends or family, financially draining both. They have to move frequently from one house to another because these people cannot afford to support them or they could lose their housing. . . . We housed a young man who had been living in an abandoned car during the month of December. . . . Another young man said he lived in a large wooden crate on the streets in Marion. When it was too cold to sleep in the crate, he would spend the night at a truck stop. Then he would sleep during the day in the park or in front of the Public Aid office. . . . One of our residents slept in an abandoned building in Herrin. Another one slept in ditches and under overpasses. We recently housed a woman who hasn't had an address for three years. These are just a few examples that illustrate the harsh life of the homeless.

Precariously Housed

Public officials are often reluctant to consider inadequate housing and doubling up as forms of homelessness; they prefer to use the term *precariously housed*. But clearly there are factors beyond the mere presence of a physical dwelling that determine whether or not someone is housed. People staying in shelters are temporarily housed—in fact, some shelters have no limits to how long a person can stay. Yet, people in shelters are considered "homeless" because they do not have an adequate place of their own. Being "housed" is tied to having a certain standard of housing and some degree of control over or stability in that housing. For many rural households, homelessness is a process

53

of moving from one inadequate dwelling to another with periodic stays with friends or relatives, in motels or shelters. . . .

Why Rural America?

The 1980s witnessed the decline of entire sectors of rural economies, particularly in farming, energy, and manufacturing industries. Replacement of industry and farm-related jobs by low-paying and often part-time service-sector employment does not enable working people to afford decent housing at current prices. The well-paying jobs that are available require higher skills than in the past, thereby excluding many of the working poor who are less highly educated or skilled. Recovery of rural economies has been erratic. While some communities have prospered in recent years, others have not regained their vitality. The economic outlook remains grim.

Economic problems have contributed to a persistently high poverty rate in rural areas. The nonmetropolitan poverty rate rose steadily throughout the early 1980s, peaking at 18.3 percent from 1983–85. In those years nearly one-fifth of all people in nonmetropolitan areas lived in households with incomes below the poverty level of $10,989 for a family of four. Though the poverty rate dropped to 15.7 percent by the end of the decade, it increased to 16.3 percent in 1990. . . .

Doubling and Tripling Up

In poverty-stricken rural areas, particularly in southern states and Appalachia, inadequate incomes and poor housing conditions have been exacerbated by collapsing local economies and insufficient housing production. For example, in 1988, public hearings on homeless in Kentucky revealed that "in some parts of the state, there is no decent basic shelter at any price. In other areas of the state there is plenty of housing for those who can afford it, but a drastic shortage for those with limited means."

In these areas, people frequently double and triple up, or live in homes without heat and water, and with faulty and exposed wiring, collapsed roofs, or gaping holes in the walls. Those less fortunate seek shelter in places such as chicken coops, caves, and utility sheds.

Doubling and tripling up are frequently referred to as the most common way of coping with homelessness in rural communities. The traditions of "taking care of our own" and extended families often take the place of a more formal social service network. The lack of landlord/tenant law and housing code enforcement in many rural areas also contributes to housing inadequacies, sudden rent increases, and evictions. Unfortunately, code enforcement would further reduce the already minimal housing options available to low-income households.

The combination of economic decline and problems of housing affordability and availability has made it impossible for some people to find and retain stable housing. For a segment of the population, income is simply too low or housing costs too high.

How Many Are Homeless?

Few studies address the extent of homelessness in rural or nonmetropolitan areas. Those that do tend to focus on people who receive shelter or other types of assistance. Since services are scarce in rural communities, the results are more likely to reflect the availability of services than the numbers and needs of people who are without stable and adequate housing.

Who Are the Rural Homeless?

One cannot separate the growing rural homelessness during the 1980s from the farm crisis of that period. For the period between 1980 and 1988, the U.S. government has estimated that the number of farms that disappeared was 271,000. For the same period, the number of people living on farms dropped from 6 million to 5 million. Meanwhile, the Public Voice for Food and Health Policy, a Washington consumer education and research group, has determined that the number of rural people living in poverty, between 1978 and 1986, increased by one-third to 9.7 million.

Among some of the more selective findings on the rural Midwest homeless populations of the 1980s are these:

• In 1987 more than three-quarters of community agencies responding to a Housing Assistance Council survey reported increases in rural homelessness from 1981–82 to 1986–87, and 38 percent reported the increases to be significant.

• A 1985 study in Ohio reported that the proportion of women among the rural homeless was twice that of urban homeless populations.

• The percentage of married people among the rural homeless is higher than the percentage of married urban homeless, 18.5 and 6.7, respectively. . . .

• An Iowa study found that one of the larger groups in danger of losing homes was farm widows, many of whom were living on just a few hundred dollars a month.

Gregg Barak, *Gimme Shelter*, 1992.

Studies that provide some useful estimates suggest that 5 to 14 percent of the nation's homeless population is in nonmetropolitan areas. Although estimates of the size of the homeless population vary, using the Urban Institute's national estimate of 567,000 to 600,000 homeless people in a one-week period, we would expect 32,000 to 75,000 people to be homeless in non-metro areas. Over the course of the year, the number would be at least two to three times larger.

The rural homeless population is diverse, though families—particularly female headed—and elderly women on their own are believed to be increasingly at risk. Data available on the sex, age, ethnicity, and family status of homeless households in non-metropolitan areas indicate that there tend to be fewer men, more women and families, and fewer minorities than among the urban homeless population, and some research has found the nonmetro homeless population to be younger than its urban counterpart. Some of these differences may be due to the nature of homelessness, but some are typical of urban-rural population differences.

In some parts of the country, migrant workers represent a significant portion of the homeless population. Farm workers have unique problems and needs. Their homelessness results from inadequate temporary housing and employment, as well as the absence of permanent housing and jobs for migrants who settle out. The use of seasonal labor creates large variations in housing needs of rural communities at different times of the year.

Part of the homeless population in many rural communities consists of people in transit to another location or relocating in search of employment. In some areas, these people are the majority of the homeless population. This appears to be particularly true of towns on major interstate highways.

Migration of homeless rural households to urban areas in search of employment or assistance from family or friends may also contribute to urban homelessness. Likewise, some homeless or near-homeless people in urban areas move to rural areas for similar reasons.

Demographics of the rural homeless population can differ significantly from one part of the state to another. A statewide survey in Wyoming, for example, found 60 percent of persons in need of shelter were adults and 40 percent children; at the county level, however, estimates ranged from 90 percent single men to 79 percent children. Similarly wide variation was found in Vermont's counties in 1987.

1990s Homelessness

The lack of in-depth knowledge about the recent history of rural homelessness makes it difficult to predict its future course. Rural homelessness is similar to urban homelessness in the sense that people lose their housing when incomes are not adequate to meet housing costs or when personal difficulties become overwhelming, regardless of where they reside. Thus, national indicators of economic well-being are perhaps as good a predictor as any in determining the direction that rural homelessness will take. The particular nature of economic and housing problems and the resources available to help people cope with those problems are different, however, not only in rural and urban areas, but also from one community to the next. The little that is known about rural homelessness suggests that the communities most likely to be affected are ones that are chronically depressed, poverty-stricken, or suffering major downturns in the local economy or—ironically—those that are growing rapidly. Given the state of affairs in rural America, many of them are at risk of increased homelessness.

It has been reported, both anecdotally and in some research, that families are representing an ever-larger segment of the rural homeless population. Those most at risk are likely to be female heads of families with small children, since the poverty rate of these families in nonmetro areas exceeds 40 percent. Single women, particularly displaced homemakers and senior citizens, also have been identified as at risk of homelessness. About one-third of them are poor, and opportunities for improving their economic situation are much more limited than for young persons.

But whether more rural people will become homeless and whether there will be more homeless people in rural communities are entirely different questions. The resources available to help people cope with homelessness are very limited in rural areas; little of the federal funding available for homeless-assistance programs reaches these communities, and small local governments cannot support these services. People who cannot find work, food, and shelter in their own community often move into towns and cities. Some of these people then become part of the urban homeless population.

Periodical Bibliography

The following articles have been selected to supplement the diverse views presented in this chapter.

Linda Burnham   "And of the Heart It Took," *Crossroads*, February 1993. Available from PO Box 2809, Oakland, CA 94609.

Betty Liu Ebron   "We Must Seize Opportunity to Address Homelessness," *Liberal Opinion Week*, March 13, 1995. Available from PO Box 468, Vinton, IA 52349-0468.

Guy Gugliotta   "The Ways That Homelessness Counts," *Washington Post National Weekly Edition*, May 23–29, 1994. Available from 1150 15th St. NW, Washington, DC 20071.

Kim Hopper   "Notes of a Slow Learner," *Health/PAC Bulletin*, Summer 1993. Available from 853 Broadway, Suite 1607, New York, NY 10003.

Bob Levin   "The Crime of Making Children Disappear," *Maclean's*, December 5, 1994.

Bruce G. Link et al.   "Lifetime and Five-Year Prevalence of Homelessness in the United States," *American Journal of Public Health*, December 1994. Available from the author, Epidemiology of Mental Disorders, 100 Haven Ave., #31D, New York, NY 10032.

Mary McGrory   "Homeless Women Find a Compassionate Chronicler," *Liberal Opinion Week*, August 30, 1993.

Moody   "Missions Report New Surge of Homeless," January 1993. Available from 820 N. La Salle Blvd., Chicago, IL 60610.

Peter H. Rossi   "Troubling Families: Family Homelessness in America," *American Behavioral Scientist*, January 1994. Available from Sage Publications, 2455 Teller Rd., Thousand Oaks, CA 91320.

John Tuohy   "There's No Such Thing as a Childhood on the Streets," *U.S. Catholic*, March 1993.

Pastor Urbanus   "For Pete's Sake: Our Homeless Parishioner," *America*, April 10, 1993.

What Are the Causes of Homelessness?

THE HOMELESS

Chapter Preface

Despite the fact that homelessness has been a major national issue since the early 1980s, homeless advocates and analysts still do not agree on what causes homelessness.

The debate about the causes of homelessness centers primarily around the question of whether social and economic conditions are responsible for homelessness or whether the homeless themselves are responsible for their plight. Proponents of the personal responsibility philosophy contend that people are homeless because of moral failing or personal choice. According to a 1993 study, 83 percent of the homeless suffer from drug addiction, alcoholism, mental illness, or a combination of all three. Taking these factors into account, the personal responsibility theorists argue that the solution to homelessness is for homeless people to give up drinking and abusing drugs, seek treatment for their mental and physical health problems, secure employment, and move off the streets.

On the other hand, opponents of the personal responsibility theory maintain that the homeless are average people who have become homeless because of the social and economic conditions in which they live: Poverty, a lack of affordable housing, high unemployment rates, or other problems beyond their control have forced them into homelessness. Robert Hayes, one of the nation's most prominent homeless advocates, maintains that if social and economic conditions are improved—for example, if more jobs and affordable housing are made available—homelessness will disappear.

The question of who or what is responsible for homelessness—the homeless people themselves or the conditions in which they live—is an issue of fervent debate. In the following chapter, the authors examine and discuss the different theories of what causes homelessness.

> "Homeless people are homeless because they do
> not have a place to live."

A Lack of Affordable Housing Causes Homelessness

Elliot Liebow

Elliot Liebow volunteered at a soup kitchen and shelter for homeless women near Washington, D.C. He writes about the women he met and their efforts to get off the streets in his book *Tell Them Who I Am: The Lives of Homeless Women*. In the following viewpoint, taken from his book, Liebow argues that people are homeless because they cannot afford a place to live. Liebow contends that persistent joblessness and substandard wages prevent a large number of poor Americans from adequately providing themselves and their families with homes. While he concedes that many homeless people may need psychological treatment, Liebow insists that the first order of business is to provide them with appropriate and affordable housing.

As you read, consider the following questions:

1. On what basis does the author maintain that people are not homeless because of their mental or physical disabilities?
2. According to Liebow, what are the benefits of providing the homeless with appropriate and affordable housing (besides reducing the number of homeless people)?
3. How has free enterprise failed the homeless, according to the author?

There are many homeless people in America and that is a shame. Shame on you, shame on me, shame on America. Shame because it is the result of choices we have made; shame because it does not have to be.

To begin at the beginning, let me offer Proposition No. 1: Homeless people are homeless because they do not have a place to live. I do not offer this as a tautology but as a statement of cause.

People are not homeless because they are physically disabled, mentally ill, abusers of alcohol or other drugs, or unemployed. However destructive and relevant these conditions may be, they do not explain homelessness; most physically disabled people, most mentally ill people, most alcoholics and drug addicts, and most unemployed persons do have places to live. Moreover, when mentally ill or physically disabled or alcoholic homeless persons do get a place to live, they are no longer homeless but they remain, as they were before, physically or mentally disabled, drug addicts, or whatever. Clearly, then, there is no *necessary* connection between these conditions and homelessness. Homeless people are homeless because they do not have a place to live.

Homelessness and Poverty

My second proposition derives from the most fundamental fact about homelessness: Homelessness is rooted hard and deep in poverty. Homeless people are poor people, and they come, overwhelmingly, from poor families. Proposition No. 2 holds that homelessness is no longer a matter—if it ever was—of a few unfortunate winos or crazy people falling through the cracks of our vaunted safety net. Indeed, homelessness is not an individual matter at all. Homelessness today is a social class phenomenon, the direct result of a steady, across-the-board lowering of the standard of living of the American working class and lower class. As the standard of living falls, individuals and families at the bottom are plunged into homelessness.

The connection between homelessness and poverty points to major system failures at the lower and sometimes middle levels of our wage-labor hierarchy. The major failure is the inability of the system, even in the best of times, to provide jobs for all who are able and willing to work. Every day, many millions of would-be workers are told that our society has nothing for them to do, that they are not needed, that they and their dependents are surplus.

Another major system failure, equally destructive, is the fact that a growing number of men and women—individuals and heads of families—are workers but remain poor. They work or seek work year-round, full-time. They work as salesclerks and checkers and servers in Ames and Kmart, in McDonald's and

Roy Rogers; they clean houses and mop floors in hospitals and nursing homes; they work as casual laborers, telephone solicitors, receptionists, delivery men and women, file clerks, even as data-entry clerks at IBM. What should no longer come as a surprise, however, after all is said and done, is that even if they can get these jobs, many workers cannot live on what they earn. These workers file the papers, mop the floors, clean the tables, or guard whatever needs guarding. At the end of the day, they say, "OK, I've done what you asked me to do. What am I worth?" And our society answers, through the employer, "Not much. Not even enough to live on."

What goes on here? How can this be? Are these workers not entitled to an honest day's pay for an honest day's work? Admit-

---

The Importance of Affordable Housing

In 1988, together with our colleague James Knickman, we interviewed 700 New York City families who requested shelter and 524 New York City families randomly drawn from the public assistance caseload as a comparison group. . . .

In these two samples with comparable incomes, housing conditions were the major predictors of homelessness. Over two fifths (44%) of shelter requesters, compared to one eighth (12%) of housed families, had never been able to break into the housing market in New York City. That is, they had never had a place of their own for as long as a year. Four fifths of the shelter requesters (81%), compared to 38% of housed families, had doubled up with others; only 37% (vs. 86% of housed families) had been the primary tenant at the place they stayed the longest in the year before requesting shelter. Families becoming homeless lived in poor and crowded conditions: 47% reported having lived in a place with two or more serious building problems, such as rats or lack of heat in winter or lack of running water for a week or more; 45% reported there were three or more people per bedroom in the place they lived the longest in the past year. Of families who were primary tenants, only 20% of homeless families, compared to 38% of housed families, lived in public subsidized housing. The immediate precipitants of families' requests for shelter varied according to their housing situation. Families who had been primary tenants in the past year most often cited eviction and rent problems, followed by building problems, as reasons for entering a shelter. Families who were doubled up with others were asked to leave by the primary tenant, felt that they could impose no longer, or cited other problems with the doubled-up situation. (Over half of these households had three or more people per bedroom.)

Marybeth Shinn and Beth C. Weitzman, *American Behavioral Scientist*, January 1994.

---

tedly, "an honest day's pay" is a very fuzzy term. At the very least, however, can an honest day's pay be less than it takes to live on?

"Don't look at me," says the employer. "I'm paying them what they are worth. If you force me to pay my employees more than they are worth, I will have to go out of business." In the long run, he is probably right.

A Matter of Perspective

Perspective is critical. Unemployment, underemployment, and substandard wages are system failures only when viewed from the bottom. Looking from the top down, they are seen as "natural" processes essential to the healthy functioning of a self-correcting market system. From that perspective, it is as if the market system requires human sacrifice for its good health.

One result of these system failures is wide and deep poverty and a growing number of working poor, of working yet homeless men, women, and families, and a lot of discouraged workers. Then, through welfare programs, through shelters and soup kitchens and vouchers and a wide variety of purchased goods and services, our whole society goes about the business of subsidizing those employers who are unable to pay their employees enough to live on. As if by magic, however, the onus of welfare and dependency is lifted from the system of work and the employers and placed on the workers and the unemployed right in front of our very eyes, and no one is any the wiser.

Most profoundly affected by the falling standard of living are those who would be dependents if their families could continue to support them. Among the homeless women in shelters and on the street, for example, are many women who would probably not be sufficiently productive to command a living wage under any conditions of wage labor. Many of them are homeless because their relatives and friends, under the gun themselves because of their worsening economic situations, can no longer afford to care for still another dependent. . . .

What Is Actually Needed

We talk increasingly about an "underclass" as we try to put more and more distance between ourselves and the very poor. "Underclass" suggests that they live outside (under) the system in which the rest of us live. But homeless women do live in the same real world that most of us live in, where security and housing and jobs are major concerns. Perhaps because we do not know how to deal with jobs and housing for the poor and homeless, or do not want to deal with them, we excuse our do-nothing job and housing policies by telling ourselves that homelessness is Oh, such a complex problem! whose many causes lie deep within the homeless people themselves. What is needed first and foremost, we say, is an array of treatment programs to help them straighten out their heads or their habits.

Since most homeless women are much like everyone else, many of them would agree that that is what the other homeless women need, but most homeless women would also agree with Claude, a bright young man in his early 30s. Claude had just moved into a subsidized high-rise after years of living in shelters. We had just finished watching an account of the October 1989 "Housing Now" March on Washington on television news.

"That 'Housing Now' march was right on the ball," he said. "Those people know what they're talking about. The homeless need housing, not that psychological bullshit that puts the blame on the homeless themselves." He slapped the brace on his withered leg. "Sure, some of us are imperfect, but we live in an imperfect world, so what's the big deal?"

Claude is mainly right, but he may be overstating the case. Some homeless people could probably benefit from what he calls "psychological bullshit," and it may even be an essential first step for a few of them. For most homeless people, however, even those who could benefit from them, such services are not necessarily the first order of business. Trying to deliver services to people on the run is typically inefficient if not futile. For most homeless people, the first order of business is to help them stop running. The first order of business is to get homeless people out of the crazy-making and destructive world of homelessness. The first order of business is housing.

Crazy-making homelessness produces a world of paradoxes and contradictions: citizens with homes are afraid of the homeless and the homeless are afraid of the citizens and one another and everyone is right to be afraid; people in situations they cannot tolerate another day find they have no alternatives; problems abound that have no solutions. . . .

The Benefits of Housing

We seem to accept or ignore conditions of homelessness that mock the values we claim to hold: people who work full time and cannot live on what they earn; people who have no place to live; people who are put in jail because they have no place to live; people who feel safer living on the street than in public shelters; people in shelters who walk 11 blocks to use the toilet in Union Station rather than use the toilets in the shelter; shelters in neighborhoods in which the homeless are not permitted to walk, but are bussed in at night and bussed out in the morning; and on and on and on.

Appropriate and affordable housing for individuals and families—houses, apartments, single room occupancy hotels, group homes—would do more than simply reduce the number of homeless persons. It would go a long way toward making life on the bottom more rational, more coherent, especially for workers who could once again support themselves and their families. Appropriate and affordable housing would also contribute importantly to the treatment and prevention of a variety of social ills and individual tragedies, including homelessness itself. Surely homeless children who are moved into decent housing are less likely to become parents of homeless children than children who grow up homeless. Surely people who are mentally ill or alcoholic or drug-addicted and have a place of their own are more likely to stand still long enough to profit from a program of treatment than someone living in shelters and on the street.

A Transition from Outcast to Citizen

Most important of all, for most homeless persons and families there is no more therapeutic environment than a place of one's own—a place that is safe and warm, that allows wounds to heal, that allows you to choose your associates rather than have them thrust upon you, that gives you your own unique address, your own place in the world. Indeed, as one looks at the handful of women described in *Tell Them Who I Am* who were homeless and now have a place to live, it is probably no exaggeration to see the transition from homelessness to a place of one's own as a transition from outcast to citizen.

A very few women were able to make this transition entirely on their own efforts. More women made this transition with the assistance of subsidized housing. Unfortunately, very few homeless women can expect to get jobs that will allow them to support themselves, and very few can expect to come to the top of the list for housing assistance.

"Housing Now" must be the principal goal of public policy for dealing with homelessness. But until permanent and affordable housing for the poor becomes a reality, we need more and better shelters. Many will argue that building more shelters will further institutionalize homelessness. Not so. Failure to provide minimally decent shelters institutionalizes homelessness. Pushing people onto the street full time—perhaps beyond the point of no return—institutionalizes homelessness far more than giving people a safe place to sleep. To do nothing, then, is to deepen the institutionalization of homelessness; but to close down shelters, as is being done in Washington, D.C., and other cities around the country in the name of economy, is plainly and simply criminal, self-defeating, and dumb. . . .

Not just any shelter will do. An armory or dormitory or other barn of a shelter that thrusts hundreds of strangers into impersonal intimacy will not do. Shelters that cannot ensure the safety of their occupants, or cannot treat them with minimal decency and respect, will not do. The homeless women themselves point the way for public policy in this respect. The best shelters, they say, are those operated by nonprofit organizations (mainly religious, and mainly local rather than national), and the more volunteers and pro-bono professionals the better. The worst shelters are those operated by municipalities or private for-profit organizations on contract with the city or county. . . .

Victims of Free Enterprise

To summarize: In an important sense, homeless men and women and families are victims of the same system of free enterprise that has been so extraordinarily productive and generous to others. Viewed from the bottom, two of the most obvious system failures are the abject failure of the free market to provide minimally decent jobs and affordable housing for poor people. The recent historical record offers clear evidence that the free market, left to its own devices, cannot and will not do the job.

All along the line then, from the world of jobs and housing to the very shelters themselves, the free market has failed the great majority of homeless persons. Indeed, while capitalism has worked in spectacular fashion for many Americans, it has created many poor people and treated them badly. If we cannot change the rules of the marketplace, then the federal government, the government of all Americans, must itself become a much more active and vigorous player in the job and housing markets on behalf of the poor.

Not Everyone Can Be a Hero

For these things to happen, there must be a wider and deeper understanding of the nature of poverty and its destructiveness. We must stop blaming the poor for being poor and the homeless for being homeless. There will always be people at every level of society whose intelligence, ability, and determination will lift them high above the stations they were born into. But it makes no sense to say, "If they can do it, why can't the others?" Not everyone can be above average. Not everyone can be a hero. By definition, most people are of average intelligence, ability, and determination. It is by its ability to make possible a decent life for the masses—for average people and for those who are below average—that a society is to be judged.

"Providing housing is not *the primary solution to the problem of homelessness because the lack of affordable housing is* not *the primary cause."*

A Lack of Affordable Housing Does Not Cause Homelessness

Alice S. Baum and Donald W. Burnes

Homelessness is not caused by a lack of housing, argue the authors of the following viewpoint, Alice S. Baum and Donald W. Burnes. According to their research, most homeless persons are either mentally ill or substance abusers, or both, and are therefore incapable of keeping themselves housed. The answer to homelessness is not more affordable housing, but treatment for mental illness and substance abuse, they maintain. Baum and Burnes, who have both worked in programs for the poor and homeless, are the authors of *A Nation in Denial: The Truth About Homelessness*, from which this viewpoint is taken.

As you read, consider the following questions:

1. What reasons do the authors give for the increased demand in the housing market during the 1980s?
2. What evidence do Baum and Burnes provide to support their opinion that merely providing housing for the homeless is not the answer to the problem?
3. Why do homeless advocates support the theory that there is not enough affordable housing for the homeless, according to the authors?

There can be no doubt that the 1980s was a period of major changes in America's housing market. First, in 1976 the leading edge of the baby boom began to turn thirty. Most of the boomers began to settle down, marry, take jobs, and start families, and they needed housing. The absolute numbers of the baby boom generation put enormous demands on the American housing supply between 1970 and 1990; in 1970, there were only 63 million households in the United States, but by 1990, there were 93 million, making for an increase of almost 50 percent over the twenty-year period. The increased demand for housing units was compounded by a number of life-style patterns characteristic of the baby boom: fewer young married couples were living with their parents than in past decades; divorce increasingly turned one household into two; single-parent families became more common; and more single adults left their parental homes to set up their own households.

Interestingly, the major increase in demand was not in the rental market. In 1970, 64.3 million people lived in 23.6 million rental units; by 1980, 65.1 million people occupied 28.6 million units. This increase in renters of slightly less than one million suggests that most people were buying instead of renting during this period. In their study "The Baby Boom—Entering Midlife," Leon F. Bouvier and Carol J. De Vita calculated that, during the 1970s, 32 million Americans turned thirty, the typical age for buying a first home, and another 42 million turned thirty during the 1980s. Bouvier and De Vita maintained that "the number of new *homebuyers* was a prime factor in pushing up the cost of housing in the late 1970s and early 1980s" (emphasis added). . . .

Housing Costs and Homelessness

Housing costs skyrocketed. The increases were fueled by several factors, including the size of the aging baby boom cohort, life-style choices, the new definition of what constituted acceptable space, and increased construction costs, which resulted from the OPEC [Organization of Petroleum Exporting Countries]-driven inflationary cycle of the 1970s. The resulting increases gave pause to the entire population, especially first-time homebuyers, newcomers to the rental market, and not incidentally, their middle-class parents, who found their baby boom children returning home after an initial foray into the housing market. The rhetoric of the homelessness movement, therefore, found fertile ground in the middle class and played on this very real concern about housing. By portraying the homeless as ordinary people, the advocates successfully tapped into the national anxiety about the rising cost of housing in the 1980s.

Despite the claims of the homelessness movement, analysts have never established a definitive causal linkage between the increased demand for housing, along with the rise in costs, and the rise in homelessness during the 1980s. Instead, they have cited information about the high cost of housing, the numbers of poor and middle-class people paying larger and larger proportions of their incomes for housing, and the declining government subsidies for housing and implied that all these factors account for the increase in homelessness.

A Complex Issue

If the strategy of the homelessness movement was to play upon the fears of the many Americans confronted by rising housing costs, its success derived not from the public's gullibility but from the sheer complexity of the issue of affordable housing. Because government subsidies—tax deductions for mortgages, construction subsidies to builders, and direct housing grants for rent subsidies in both government-owned and private-sector housing—are an integral part of most affordable housing programs, the debate has focused in large measure on making changes in these various governmental subsidies. There is considerable disagreement, however, over the question of whether government assistance has declined since the late 1970s, and if so, how much it has declined and what effect this has had on housing for the poor. For example, how much has the rehabilitation of existing housing, as opposed to the development of new housing, affected the supply of housing for the poor? Did budget appropriations for the major federal housing programs show the same degree of decrease as authorizations for those programs? Did outlays for subsidizing low-income housing in future years change housing opportunities available under current expenditures? Has there been an actual increase in the number of people being subsidized, and if so, has the rate of increase in the number of new people being subsidized declined during the 1980s? Should housing subsidies be in the form of Section 8 certificates, which guarantee that the renter pay only 30 percent of income, or should they take the form of vouchers, which permit renters to search on the open market and make decisions about what percentage of their income they are willing to pay?

In summarizing all of the often contradictory data about affordable housing, Martha Burt concluded that, even though federal outlays for future subsidized housing decreased by more than 80 percent during the Reagan years, these decreases would not affect low-cost housing until the 1990s and that the impact of these funding decreases on homelessness in the 1980s was "not as straightforward as it might seem." Michael Carliner agreed:

> There has been no . . . extraordinary deterioration in the national housing supply or affordability in recent years. By many

measures, the housing situation actually appears to have improved. Construction has accelerated, vacancy rates have increased, overcrowding has diminished, and, despite sharp cutbacks in new budget authority for housing programs since 1979, the number of households benefitting from federal assistance has continued to increase.

For most people the issue of affordable housing is an enormously confusing puzzle, and the arguments made on each side of the debate are almost as arcane as those used in the controversies surrounding the research methodologies employed to count the number of homeless people. Despite the difficulty in untangling these arguments, there is no doubt that changes in government subsidies for housing affect the poor and the very poor, but as Grace Milgram pointed out, "It is not clear . . . that homelessness results from a physical lack of housing units rather than from other social ills."

Housing Will Not Cure Homelessness

In truth, homelessness is a symptom of many complex problems: mental illness, emotional instability, chronic substance abuse, illiteracy, unemployment (largely due to a lack of job skills) and, most basic of all, breakdown of the family structure.

The vast majority of homeless in the United States are individuals who are unable to function successfully in society and who require intensive rehabilitation. And while they may not fit the stereotypes of the older, alcoholic male, neither are they mostly young families thrust out onto the streets by a soured economy and a stingy Administration. . . .

What's more, the majority of the chronically homeless would be hard pressed to keep a home if they received one. Because of emotional problems, substance abuse and low self-esteem—which is more the cause of their plight than the result of it—they generally do not have the wherewithal to manage their lives successfully.

Mark Holsinger, *Los Angeles Times*, March 6, 1990.

Those who argue that the lack of affordable housing is the primary cause of homelessness imply that the main problem confronting the homeless is their lack of resources to participate in the American housing market, either because they cannot earn enough money or because the cost of housing is beyond their reach. For those who take this position, the solution is simple— provide housing that does not overtax their financial resources. One way of testing the effectiveness of such a solution is to examine what would happen if housing units for all the homeless were provided. On one level, of course, the problem would be solved and homelessness would be eliminated; all the homeless would now be living in their own houses. The real question is how long the problem would stay solved.

The story of Jacqueline Williams, the woman with fourteen children who obtained housing from Washington, D.C., authorities after appearing on *The Donahue Show*, provides some indication of the answer. Mrs. Williams' family needed much more than housing. They were not able to maintain the housing that was provided, child welfare officials eventually removed her children under the age of eighteen to foster care, and after one year's occupancy, the house was condemned as being unfit for human habitation. Further evidence is provided by statements from others who have studied or worked with homeless people. The New York City Commission on the Homeless reported in their 1992 study that fully half of all homeless families placed in permanent housing returned to the shelter system. The social worker at the Capitol City Motor Inn in Washington, D.C., reported similar recidivism rates for families placed in housing.

In short, simply providing housing is *not* the primary solution to the problem of homelessness because the lack of affordable housing is *not* the primary cause. Without help for their many disabling conditions, most of the homeless will continue to be unable to maintain themselves in permanent housing. The futility of simply providing housing is underscored by the data about the long-term chronicity of homelessness among the single homeless population and its episodic nature. Those disabled by addictions and mental illness or both, who drift in and out of homelessness, staying intermittently in shelters, hospitals, jails, detox units, transitional programs, and back on the streets in a continuous cycle, are particularly at risk of not being able to maintain independent housing.

Affordable Housing Is Political

The absence of affordable housing as a primary cause of homelessness is advanced by advocates for mainly political reasons—to promote consideration of systemic macroeconomic problems that they believe need to be addressed. For example, Kim Hopper and Jill Hamberg asserted that, because the shortage in affordable housing results from profit-driven housing policies that produce a declining proportion of low and moderate rent units, "anything short of a massive public subsidized housing effort" will not address the problem; "only if housing is recognized as a social good and its provision seen as a necessary public service [will] appropriate action be taken." By first mobilizing for the right to shelter for the homeless, advocates were actually pushing for a national entitlement to housing, an entitlement that extends well beyond helping the homeless. Hopper and Hamberg admitted: "A right to shelter is not the same thing as a right to housing—much less a right to appropriate housing—although it may be an opening wedge."

We are not suggesting that the issue of housing is irrelevant to the homeless. Instead, we would argue that policymakers and the public must address the disabilities that make maintaining stable housing impossible before making the issue of affordable housing the central issue for today's homeless. Appropriate, affordable, and often specialized housing for homeless people with different types of problems will eventually be required; before then, space in various types of treatment programs, followed by structured living arrangements that support continued recovery, where appropriate, are necessary. It is only when individuals have made substantial progress in overcoming their disabilities that independent living in affordable housing will become relevant.

Focusing solely on affordable housing without first addressing the disabling conditions of the vast majority of the homeless is analogous to simply providing a walking cane to someone who has suffered a broken foot without first resetting the bones in the foot and encasing the foot in a cast. In the case of a broken foot, the use of a cane is only appropriate after the broken bones have been treated; providing a cane without first treating the broken bones will only make future recovery more difficult. In the case of homelessness, permanent, affordable housing is appropriate only after the immediate disabling conditions that prevent independent living have been treated. Failure to treat the disabling conditions will only make recovery from them and emergence from homelessness more difficult. In the meantime, the indiscriminate call for affordable housing, especially when it is used by advocates as an "opening wedge" to solve all of America's housing problems, is not helpful.

"Aspects of mental illness appeared to have contributed to the subjects' becoming and remaining homeless."

Mental Illness Contributes to Homelessness

H. Richard Lamb and Doris M. Lamb

In the following viewpoint, H. Richard Lamb and Doris M. Lamb present the results of their study of homelessness among fifty-three psychiatric patients. Because all fifty-three subjects were severely mentally ill before and during their homelessness, the authors argue that the symptoms of mental illness—such as disorganization and paranoia—helped put them on the streets and kept them from seeking assistance. Based on these findings, the authors conclude that mental illness is a contributing factor in homelessness among the mentally ill. H. Richard Lamb is a professor of psychiatry and Doris M. Lamb is an associate clinical professor of psychiatry at the University of Southern California Medical School in Los Angeles.

As you read, consider the following questions:

1. On what basis do the authors conclude that a lack of effective care contributes to homelessness among the mentally ill?
2. Why is homelessness among the mentally ill not primarily a housing problem, in the authors' view?
3. How do substance abuse, family, and youth affect homelessness among the mentally ill, according to Lamb and Lamb?

Excerpted from H. Richard Lamb and Doris M. Lamb, "Factors Contributing to Homelessness Among the Chronically and Severely Mentally Ill," *Hospital and Community Psychiatry*, vol. 41, no. 3 (March 1990), pp. 301–305. Copyright ©1990, the American Psychiatric Association. Reprinted by permission.

There has been much speculation about why a sizable and visible segment of the chronically and severely mentally ill become and remain homeless. Many concerned with the problem postulate that a shortage of housing contributes to or causes homelessness among the mentally ill. Others point to problems within the mental health delivery system. Such factors as the problems of youth, dual diagnosis, the combination of severe mental illness and substance abuse, and narrowly drawn commitment laws have been thought to contribute to homelessness.

Still others have suggested that mental illness itself plays a part. If that is the case, in what ways does mental illness contribute to homelessness? These are the issues addressed in this study. . . .

The purpose of this study was to examine a sample of homeless persons with major mental illness in a setting where clinicians could get to know them and their life situation, verify the data obtained, and gather additional information from family and other third parties in order to better understand how and why the mentally ill become homeless.

Method and Subjects of the Study

The subjects were 53 consecutive admissions of homeless patients who were treated during 1987–88 in the Alternatives to Hospitalization Program, a residential program for acute and subacute psychiatric treatment operated by the University of Southern California in Los Angeles. To qualify for the study, patients had to have been homeless for a week or longer immediately before entering the program or the hospitalization that had preceded it.

For the study, homelessness was defined as living on the streets, on the beach, in parks, or in such places as cars or abandoned buildings; time spent in shelters was not included. This definition eliminated the ambiguity of the housing status of some persons who have extended stays in shelters. This is not to say such persons are adequately housed, but that it is not clear that they are, strictly speaking, undomiciled. Thus the study addressed itself to those completely undomiciled persons who are of such great concern to mental health professionals and the general public.

All of the patients were interviewed by one of two psychiatrists (the authors). A structured interview format was used. In the interviews, a history was obtained, and a diagnosis was made. Particular emphasis was placed on inquiring how and why the patient became and remained homeless, and on assessing the patient's functional status during the period of homelessness. . . .

The 53 subjects ranged in age from 19 to 53 years (median, 31 years). Forty (75 percent) were men, and 13 (25 percent) were women. Their education ranged from seventh grade to four years of college (median, four years of high school). The subjects had been homeless (completely undomiciled) for one week to nine years (median, 60 days) immediately before entering the alternatives program or the hospitalization that preceded it. . . .

In every case, severe mental illness was present when the homelessness that immediately preceded the present admission began. Moreover, aspects of mental illness appeared to have contributed to the subjects' becoming and remaining homeless. . . .

Mental Illness and Homelessness

Present clinically were disorganization and poor problem-solving abilities resulting from the illness, severe paranoia that interfered with or prevented the subjects from accepting help, and the depression that immobilized many patients. Thus we can only conclude that these disabling functional deficits of mental illness were important contributing factors to the homelessness of this group of severely mentally ill persons. In addition, however, the mental illness of a large proportion of the subjects clearly was worsened by the stress of homelessness.

Only 4 percent of the sample had case managers [social workers who monitored their condition], and none were known to be in any other outpatient mental health treatment during their periods of homelessness. These findings are not surprising in view of the generally inadequate and disorganized systems of mental health care in our largest cities. There is no escaping the conclusion that lack of a comprehensive and effective system of care for the chronically and severely mentally ill is also an important contributing factor to homelessness for this group. For instance, although many of the homeless mentally ill subjects were too depressed and disorganized to mobilize themselves to find help, when they were discovered and help was offered, they accepted it voluntarily.

A 31-year-old single man had been hospitalized four times since age 20 for major depression with psychotic features. The patient had come to California four years earlier; all his family continued to live in a city on the Eastern seaboard. He had held occasional brief jobs over the past four years, but for the most part had lived on the streets, obtaining enough money for food and illegal drugs by panhandling.

He had been chronically and severely depressed, and when not panhandling, he spent most of his time sitting on the streets, staring into space, and listening to voices saying derogatory things about him. Though he made some friends when he first came to California, he was not able to mobilize himself to contact them or to apply for general relief funds, which he knew about, or even to go to nearby shelters and missions. In describing his life on the streets, he said, "Things that would normally have occurred to me didn't occur to me." Finally, he was found by a friend who brought him, without resistance, to a psychiatric emergency room.

The Effect of Deinstitutionalization

A massive and precipitous emptying of state mental institutions, [called] deinstitutionalization, . . . is thought to be the major cause of homelessness among the mentally ill. Thousands of patients were discharged to unprepared and unreceptive urban communities before any support systems could be put into place. From 1955 to 1987, the patient population in public mental hospitals dropped from 560,000 to about 116,000. In New York state alone, from an inpatient census of 93,000 in 1955 the institutionalized population dropped to about 20,000 in 1987. At the same time, due to the coming of age of 64 million babies born between 1946 and 1961, the absolute number of people at risk for developing schizophrenia increased dramatically. Thus, the impact of these policies can be seen not only in the many patients that have been discharged from institutions without aftercare plans or support, but in the many mentally ill patients that are denied access to long-term care in hospitals because of strict policies of admission.

Unable to negotiate the complexities of the mental health and social welfare systems, and in the face of minimal resources of the communities, particularly supportive housing, thousands of mentally ill joined the ranks of the homeless.

Paula F. Eagle and Carol M. Caton in *Homeless in America*, 1990.

It has been observed that just providing housing may not adequately resolve the problem of homelessness. Indeed, for the group of severely mentally ill patients in this study, homelessness was not primarily a housing problem per se, especially if housing means mainstream housing such as an apartment where the patient lives alone. Clinical experience, both ours and that of others, has shown that for most chronically and severely mentally ill persons, living alone in their own apartment is not a viable option. In such a situation, they become very lonely, neglect their nutrition, stop their medications, and in time, sometimes a very brief time, find their way back to the hospital or to the streets. They need supervised housing with varying amounts of support and structure.

At the time of this study, Los Angeles County had no shortage of empty beds in licensed board-and-care homes. In fact, at discharge from the alternatives program, 53 percent of the previously homeless patients were placed in board-and-care homes and community rehabilitation facilities. A primary problem, then, is the lack of mental health resources as part of a comprehensive system of mental health care to engage homeless persons and facilitate their placement in such facilities, or in some cases their placement back with their families.

Mental Illness and Substance Abuse

The issue of substance abuse is an important one. The high incidence of dual diagnoses of substance abuse and mental illness among the homeless has been noted in the literature. In this study, 68 percent were known to have a history of serious substance abuse, and 13 percent were known to consistently spend what money they had on alcohol and drugs rather than on housing. These percentages may well be higher. Substance abuse makes many of these persons unwelcome in their families' homes and in most community residential facilities for the mentally ill. Thus substance abuse appears to play a part in homelessness in this group of severely mentally ill people.

Emergency 72-hour detention had been used to bring 53 percent of the sample to hospital emergency rooms, most to be involuntarily hospitalized and some to be transferred directly, as voluntary patients, to the alternatives program. These patients had met the criteria of being dangerous to others, dangerous to self, or gravely disabled. It should be noted that all of the subjects came to the alternatives program voluntarily, either directly from the emergency room or after hospitalization; thus this is not a random sample of involuntarily detained homeless persons, many of whom refuse referrals of any kind after their period of involuntary detention expires. Nevertheless, these study subjects had been unable to do on their own what was necessary to extricate themselves from homelessness and in most cases a dangerous and chaotic situation. After varying, though usually brief, periods, they were willing to voluntarily enter a community treatment program. Thus emergency involuntary hospitalization would appear to have a place in the initial treatment of many of the homeless mentally ill.

A number of patients had lived at home with their families until the significant caretaking person died or moved to another city. Often they were patients whom only the family seemed able to tolerate and were willing to try to manage in the community. Usually the caretaking person was the mother, but in some cases it was a grandmother, father, aunt, or sibling.

A 32-year-old man was first hospitalized at age 20. He had had multiple hospitalizations since then because of delusions, hallucinations, and severe depression. He lived at home until age 26, when his mother died. His behavior was bizarre when he did not take his medications, but his mother had monitored him

closely, dispensed each dose, and most of the time was successful in having him take it. Further, although the patient tended to
be isolated, what companionship he had was with his mother.
She had considered her son to be her primary responsibility
since her husband's death, and to the patient the loss of his
mother was beyond comprehension.

The patient had been in a variety of placements since his
mother's death, including halfway houses and board-and-care
homes, but he repeatedly had been asked to leave because he
constantly put his hands on women and he masturbated in public. (His mother had closely monitored his behavior as well as
his medications.) He steadfastly refused to take medications. For
the past year he had lived on the streets. He had been beaten
and robbed twice. Because he openly masturbated, he had even
been thrown out of soup kitchen lines—the ultimate rejection.

In the past year the patient had been hospitalized with increasing frequency because of delusions, hallucinations, and suicidal
ideation. In the hospital his symptoms would quickly disappear,
and he would no longer meet the criteria for ongoing involuntary treatment. He refused long-term hospitalization or treatment in any other locked facility, and open facilities continued
to refuse to take him. He was usually discharged to the streets.

Resistant to Treatment

According to their histories, a large proportion of the subjects in
this study had been treatment resistant; they tended to not take
their prescribed medications, to impulsively and precipitously
leave their supervised housing arrangements, and to become lost
from the system. Hardly any of these patients had had the benefit of aggressive case management, which might have engaged
them and prevented them from becoming homeless. It also
seemed probable that some of these persons, even with aggressive case management, would need some form of ongoing involuntary treatment in the community such as conservatorship, outpatient commitment, or simply assignment of a payee. Moreover,
some patients, as illustrated by the preceding case, appeared to
need a period of prolonged structured residential treatment.

Significantly more subjects 30 years of age and under left the
program against medical advice or [escaped] compared with
those over 30 years of age. This finding is consistent with observations that younger mentally ill persons are less likely than
those who are older to go along with treatment in the mental
health system and recommendations for residential placement.
Schizophrenic patients, especially when they are young, have
life goals like others their age, and without the guidance of a
therapist or case manager, they may pursue these goals in an
unrealistic or irrational way, which may result in homelessness.

A 25-year-old woman had been living in a board-and-care home for three years. Her diagnosis was schizophrenia, chronic undifferentiated type, and she was treated only with neuroleptic medications, monitored by a psychiatrist whom she saw for 15 minutes once a month. She brooded about her failures in school, in not being able to hold a job, in not being able to relate to men, and in not being able to live independently. She rationalized that her medications were preventing her from leading a normal life. She stopped the medications and within a month had decompensated. She was delusional and hallucinating and had very loose associations. She told her roommate she was going to make a success of her life by becoming a rock star, and she precipitously left the board-and-care home.

By this time she was quite disorganized and began living on the beach. She had vague thoughts that she should find another place to live, but could not focus on this idea and instead spent her time listening to the "voices." She ate by stealing food from supermarkets. Six months later her condition was noticed by a woman who had known her when they had been patients together in a psychiatric hospital. This woman pointed the patient out to a passing policeman, who brought her to the hospital.

A Great Challenge

The homeless mentally ill present us with one of our greatest challenges: the younger among them are perhaps the greatest challenge of all. The younger persons are more apt to still have life goals, to deny their dependency and their illness, and to be unready to come to terms with living in a sheltered, segregated, low-pressure environment. They may have a greater need for a highly structured living situation, in some instances on an involuntary basis. It may be that this is the group that most cries out to us to set aside our preconceived ideologies, to come face to face with clinical reality, and to do what is necessary to provide them with support, protection, treatment, and rehabilitation.

"Various disabilities such as alcoholism and mental and physical illnesses are not the causes of homelessness."

Mental Illness Does Not Cause Homelessness

Doug A. Timmer, D. Stanley Eitzen, and Kathryn D. Talley

In the following viewpoint, Doug A. Timmer, D. Stanley Eitzen, and Kathryn D. Talley argue that personal disabilities such as mental illness, alcoholism, drug abuse, and physical or mental handicaps are not the primary causes of homelessness. While these conditions make people more vulnerable to homelessness, they maintain, the main causes of homelessness are structural economic factors that result in extreme poverty and a shortage of affordable housing. Timmer and Talley are associate professors of sociology at North Central College in Naperville, Illinois. Eitzen is a professor of sociology at Colorado State University in Fort Collins.

As you read, consider the following questions:

1. According to the authors, what percentage of the homeless are mentally ill?
2. Explain the authors' views regarding class bias and homelessness.
3. What do the authors say about the cause and effect of mental illness and homelessness?

Excerpted from chapter 2 of *Paths to Homelessness: Extreme Poverty and the Urban Housing Crisis* by Doug A. Timmer, D. Stanley Eitzen, and Kathryn D. Talley. Copyright ©1994 by Westview Press. Reprinted by permission of the Association for Humanist Sociology.

A recurrent belief among politicians, journalists, social scientists, and the public is that homelessness is a consequence of personal disabilities. That is, homeless persons tend to suffer from chronic alcoholism or from chronic physical or mental disorders and these disabilities explain their homelessness. This is a myth with damaging consequences. Although some homeless persons suffer from alcoholism, most do not. Some suffer severe mental or emotional disturbances, but most do not.

Typically, the recent rise in homelessness is seen as a consequence of the deinstitutionalization of mental patients that began in the 1950s. The data appear to support this notion, since the average daily census of psychiatric institutions dropped from 677,000 in 1955 to 151,000 in 1984. The numbers of former mental patients swelled as a result of deinstitutionalization, but this does not necessarily explain the increased numbers of the homeless in the 1980s. Almost all of the reduction in mental patients had occurred by 1978, yet the homeless did not begin overflowing the streets and shelters until 1983.

Several other cautions must be raised concerning the emphasis on the homeless as mentally ill. First, although it is undeniable that some homeless people are mentally disturbed and incapable of sustaining personal relationships and steady work, most of the homeless are *not* mentally ill; most are quite capable of functioning in society. There is solid research evidence to indicate that no more than 10 to 15 percent of persons living on the street are mentally impaired in some way. Researcher James Wright, using data from the national Health Care for the Homeless (HCH) program, has concluded that as many as one-third of the homeless probably are mentally ill. But more recent research has confirmed the 10 to 15 percent estimate. Irving Piliavin, Herb Westerfelt, and Elsa Elliot have found Wright's higher figures to be biased by his sample, which was limited to homeless persons who used health clinic services. These researchers have found the homeless who use these services to have significantly higher rates of mental illness than those homeless persons who do not use them. Yet the myth is perpetuated in the media that the majority of the homeless have a history of chronic mental illness.

Deviant Behavior or Class Bias?

A second caution concerns context. Elliot Liebow, in his description and analysis of homeless women, argues that judgments about the homeless often involve descriptions of them as deviant—mentally ill, alcoholic, drug addicted—descriptions that would receive more positive judgments if they were in another setting.

Like you, I know people who drink, people who do drugs, and bosses who have tantrums and treat their subordinates like dirt. They all have good jobs. Were they to become homeless, some of them would surely also become "alcoholics," "addicts," or "mentally ill." Similarly, if some of the homeless women who are now so labelled were to be magically transported to a more usual and acceptable setting, some of them—not all, of course—would shed their labels and take their places with the rest of us somewhere on the spectrum of normality.

In short, there is a class bias involved here. When homeless people do have mental difficulties or problems with alcohol, these situations are identified as the cause of their homelessness. But when well-housed middle-class and upper-middle-class people are mentally ill or alcoholic it is identified as an unfortunate situation requiring attention and treatment. Clearly, then, the source of homelessness is not behavior—mental illness or alcoholism—but the different social or class context for the behavior.

Cause and Effect

A third caution has to do with cause and effect. Does mental illness cause homelessness or do the stresses induced by extreme poverty and homelessness cause mental illness? Although some argue that mental illness is a cause of homelessness, there are no data to support this claim. The much stronger argument is that mental illness is a probable consequence of homelessness. This is based on the assumption that a stable life leads to mental stability and an unstable one to mental instability. In Jonathan Kozol's words:

> Many pregnant women without homes are denied prenatal care because they constantly travel from one shelter to another. Many are anemic. Many are denied essential dietary supplements by recent federal cuts. As a consequence, some of their children do not live to see their second year of life. Do these mothers sometimes show signs of stress? Do they appear disorganized, depressed, disordered? Frequently. They are immobilized by pain, traumatized by fear. So it is no surprise that when researchers enter the scene to ask them how they "feel," the resulting reports tell us that the homeless are emotionally unwell. The reports do not tell us we have made these people ill.

Blaming the Victim

A fourth caution is that the emphasis on the personal sources of homelessness blames the victims for their problem and deflects attention away from its structural sources. To do so leads to faulty generalizations and public policies doomed to fail. In the words of David Snow and his colleagues, leading researchers on the presumed connection between mental illness and homelessness:

It is demeaning and unfair to the majority of the homeless to focus so much attention on the presumed relationship between mental illness, deinstitutionalization, and homelessness. To do so not only wrongfully identifies the major problems confronting the bulk of the homeless. It also deflects attention from the more pervasive structural causes of homelessness, such as unemployment, inadequate income for unskilled and semi-skilled workers, and the decline in the availability of low-cost housing.

In this regard, sociologist Michael Sosin's 1992 study of homeless persons in Chicago is instructive. Comparing a sample of homeless persons to a sample of "vulnerable" persons—not homeless but impoverished and precariously close to losing their shelter—Sosin found the lack of access to various social and institutional supports and resources to be a much better predictor of homelessness than any personal disabilities or "deficits."

Doubts About Deinstitutionalization's Role

The passage of time and better current behavior add to the doubts about the relationship between homelessness and previous institutionalization. Although 22 percent of the homeless population had been institutionalized in one Berkeley study, slightly less than half had been released five or more years before. Deinstitutionalization may have made them vulnerable, but it was other events that made them homeless. Similarly, while 29.9 percent of an Ohio study had spent time in an institution, interviewers judged less than 5 percent to be currently in need of hospitalization. The coincidence of homelessness and deinstitutionalization is indisputable, but a causal relationship of real significance is hard to detect.

Joel Blau, *The Visible Poor*, 1992.

We must stress that various disabilities such as alcoholism and mental and physical illnesses are not the causes of homelessness. As James D. Wright has summarized:

Some of the homeless *are* broken down alcoholics, but most of them are not. Some *are* mentally impaired, but most of them are not. . . . In a hypothetical world where there were no alcoholics, no drug addicts, no mentally ill, no deinstitutionalization movement, no personal or social pathologies at all, there would *still* be a formidable homelessness problem.

Structural Causes, Not Disabilities

People are homeless not because of their individual flaws but because of structural arrangements and trends that result in extreme impoverishment and a shortage of affordable housing in U.S. cities. We believe that Wright's analysis is correct. The extent to which the homeless population is made up of the mentally ill, the physically handicapped and disabled, alcoholics, and drug abusers and addicts results from their being more vulnerable to the kind of impoverishment that excludes them from the urban housing market. Their vulnerabilities mean that they may be the first to lose permanent shelter. But the absolute shortage of low-income, affordable housing in the United States ensures that even if no one were plagued with these personal disabilities, the size of the homeless population would be roughly the same. Only then we would not be able to identify the homeless population as drunk or crazy and therefore identify the causes of homelessness as these personal defects. The homeless would be like everyone else (as they, in reality, are now) except that they would not have a home.

In short, the homeless are not deficient and defective. We found them to be much the opposite. The homeless people we came to know [through case studies] are much like those that David A. Snow and Leon Anderson encountered in their study of homeless street people—resilient and resourceful.

> What has impressed us most about the homeless we came to know and whose stories we have endeavored to tell is their resourcefulness and resilience. Confronted with minimal resources, often stigmatized by the broader society, frequently harassed by community members and by law enforcement officials, and repeatedly frustrated in their attempts to claim the most modest part of the American dream, they nonetheless continue to struggle to survive materially, to develop friendships, however tenuous, with their street peers, and to carve out a sense of meaning and personal identity. To emphasize this is not to romanticize the homeless and their lives but simply to recognize the many ways they confront their often brutalizing circumstances.

"Government has intentionally sided with the interests of elite groups at the expense of low- and moderate-income people."

The Government Contributed to the Homeless Problem

Susan Yeich

Homelessness in the United States has grown phenomenally due to massive changes in the economy, housing market, and political system, writes Susan Yeich in the following viewpoint. She argues that these changes are due to policies advocated by the federal government—beginning with the administrations of Ronald Reagan and George Bush—to benefit the wealthy elite at the expense of the poor. Yeich also contends that Reagan and Bush adopted the "victim-blaming tradition" (blaming the homeless for their condition instead of government policies that made them that way) to divert the public's attention from the growing inequality in American society. Yeich was involved for three years with the Homeless Person's Union in Michigan and is the author of *The Politics of Ending Homelessness*, from which this viewpoint is excerpted.

As you read, consider the following questions:

1. According to the author, what four changes in government policy contributed to the epidemic of homelessness?
2. List the three groups given by Yeich who participated in the "victim-blaming tradition."

Homelessness can be most accurately understood as one symptom of changing social conditions in the U.S. Changes in society since the 1960's and 1970's have dramatically altered the social class structure and given rise to the current epidemic of homelessness. Trends that began in the 1960's and intensified in the 1980's have resulted in a dramatic redistribution of wealth which has considerably widened the gap between the rich and poor. . . .

The following viewpoint discusses how trends in the economy, housing market, and political system have transformed the social structure and resulted in this dramatic redistribution of wealth and the corresponding epidemic of homelessness. While trends in these three areas are presented separately, they are in fact integrally related.

Economic Trends

At the core of the changing social class structure are economic trends which have resulted in a dramatic shift in income distribution. There is an increasing concentration of jobs at the extremes of the country's range of earnings. In previous decades, the country had few jobs at the extremes and many in the middle; in today's economy, many of the middle positions are disappearing. Because of the polarization of job earnings, the U.S. is losing its middle class, and there is a corresponding widening gap between rich and poor.

At the root of these changes in job opportunities is the massive economic transformation which has taken place since the 1960's and 1970's. The country has been undergoing a major shift from an industrial base to an information and service base. While the effects of this transformation began to be felt in the mid-1970's, the effects were intensified throughout the 1980's.

Advances in technology have played a major role in spurring this transformation. Innovations in such fields as computers and robotics have allowed companies to restructure their production process and develop more efficient, automated production techniques. Such innovations have eliminated the need for many manufacturing jobs. . . .

Corporations began moving production sites to other countries when they were faced with intensifying global competition and a series of organized labor victories over management. Third World countries have often been a favorite relocation site for multinational corporations. Transferring production sites to these countries has allowed multinationals to maximize their profits by exploiting cheap labor, avoiding union demands, reducing taxation, and avoiding environmental and other regulatory restrictions. . . .

This changing pattern of job opportunities is an issue distinct from problems of poor economic growth. Enhanced economic growth will not alter this trend toward a polarized wage distribution. Economic growth may lead to higher employment rates and more profit for the rich, but will not curtail the structural trend which is keeping many people in low-paying jobs. The issue today is not merely how much capital the country has, but how the resources are distributed among social classes. . . .

These structural economic changes are integrally related to the diminishing supply of low-cost housing. Deindustrialization of cities in fact is the primary cause of the low-cost housing shortage. Service- and information-based cities require a different physical environment than manufacturing-based cities and create a demand for high quality housing adjacent to business districts. . . .

© Swann / Rothco. Used with permission.

The current epidemic of homelessness has been caused by an economic transformation, not merely a decline in economic growth. It is often assumed that economic growth will help alleviate homelessness. This belief may be a carry-over from the previous period of "mature industrialization." As stated above, the issue today is not economic growth per se, but how the resources are distributed among social classes. With the changing structure of the economy, economic growth can in some ways actually exacerbate the problem of homelessness. Increased economic growth can create greater demand for property, which leads to more gentrification.

Gentrification can be defined as a process by which people with higher incomes reclaim low-income neighborhoods, resulting in the displacement of existing residents. Gentrification not only involves a "household-driven" process, where individual higher-income households move back into the city, but also a "developer-driven" process, which includes condominium conversion and other revitalization efforts. Gentrification has typically been viewed as merely a "back to the city" movement by suburbanites. Such a simple explanation does nothing to expose the economic and political causes behind the process. The public and private sectors actually operate together to create gentrification.

Two stages are necessary in order for gentrification to occur. First there must be a disinvestment of resources from low-income neighborhoods, which leads to deterioration and makes the area an undesirable place to live. This often serves to persuade current residents to leave and results in lowering property values. Residents who do not choose to leave can be forced out by procedures such as condemning buildings or other legal action. Once property values are sufficiently low, the second stage occurs as developers purchase the property and construct more profitable structures. This second stage is made possible by a reinvestment of resources in the area. . . .

Gentrification of low-income neighborhoods is a process created by certain groups who benefit economically and politically from it. The transformation of the economy has made the revitalization of cities desirable for these groups, and their power over other groups in society has made the process feasible. . . .

Political Trends

Changes in the political system which began in the late 1960's and culminated in the "Reagan Revolution" of the 1980's, have played a major role in the redistribution of wealth and the corresponding epidemic of homelessness. To some extent, these changes encompass the trends in the economy and housing market. As Donald L. Barlett and James B. Steele described it, the economy operates under the framework of a "government rule book"—a system of rewards and penalties set by Congress and the president that influences business behavior and, in turn, has profound effects on the lives of all individuals within the system. During the 1970's and 1980's, the rule book was dramatically altered to serve the interests of the privileged few at the expense of all others. . . .

With the inauguration of Reagan in 1981, the capitalist heyday was fully under way. Similar to other heyday periods, the Reagan administration made sweeping changes in government policies, which included less regulation of business, changes in tax policy, conservative financing, and limited government. As Kevin Phillips has outlined, these four areas of policy changes are major factors in the redistribution of wealth.

Less Regulation of Business

Reduced government regulation of business played a fundamental role in the redistribution of wealth in the 1980's. With the foundation for deregulation set by the Carter administration in 1980, the Reagan administration maintained and intensified deregulation of business, discarding decades worth of regulations and restraints. . . .

Throughout the 1980's, it became increasingly apparent that wealthy individuals and financial institutions were the beneficiaries of deregulation. Low- and moderate-income people were actually being hurt by deregulation policies. Deregulation resulted in thousands of firms disappearing and a loss of 200,000 jobs from the trucking and airline industries alone. The corporate debt explosion and resulting bankruptcies led to the loss of even more jobs. As in all conservative deregulation periods, the power of organized labor was undermined. Three million union workers in airlines, telecommunications, trucking, bus transportation, and other areas, suffered wage cuts. . . .

Tax Policy and Conservative Financing

A fundamental component of Reagan economic policy involved changes in federal income taxation. The Reagan administration was successful in passing two pieces of legislation that dramatically altered the existing tax structure: the 1981 Economic Recovery Tax Act and the 1986 Tax Reform Act. While the rhetoric of the time claimed that these new taxation policies would bring relief to the middle classes, it later became apparent that the changes actually hurt middle- and low-income classes, while they helped the wealthy. . . .

Under Reagan, the tax rate for the top personal tax bracket dropped from 70% to 28%, the top rate on capital gains was reduced to 20%, and taxation on unearned income (including rental and interest income) was capped at 50%. Corporate tax rates were also reduced. By 1983 income tax revenue from corporations accounted for only 6.2% of all federal tax receipts, down from 32.1% in 1952 and 12.5% in 1980.

These tax policy changes have dramatically affected the distribution of wealth in this country, and in turn the extent of homelessness. One other very significant change which was made in the 1986 tax reform has had perhaps an even more direct effect on homelessness. The 1986 Act removed many tax and investment incentives for real estate developers to build low-cost housing, thus further encouraging the gentrification of cities and contributing to the low-cost housing shortage.

The economic and fiscal policies of the Reagan administration were major factors in the redistribution of wealth in the 1980's. Reagan combined a supply-side economic theory—which Budget Director David Stockman admitted was the Republicans' latest version of "trickle-down" theory—with a tight money policy which severely limited the rate of money expansion. . . .

The Reagan and Bush administrations' conservative fiscal policies resulted not only in increasing economic disparity among social classes, but also in an enormous federal debt and decreased U.S. competitiveness in the global economy. These developments will have serious long-term ramifications for the U.S. economy, and ultimately, for the U.S. workforce. In the end, it will be middle- and low-income people who will suffer the consequences of failed policies which they did not create.

Perhaps the area of policy changes most visibly associated with the redistribution of wealth and the corresponding increase in homelessness is the reallocation of government spending which arose from the Republican philosophy of limited government in domestic affairs. The Reagan administration dramatically altered the pattern of federal funding—making severe cuts in domestic programs and huge increases in military defense. From 1980 to 1987, spending for human resources decreased from 28% of all federal allocations to only 22%, while spending for defense rose from 23% to 28%. Under the Reagan administration's policies, people in poverty suffered cuts in government spending two and a half times greater than those of all other groups combined. . . .

Funding Reductions for Housing

While in office, the Reagan administration eliminated most housing programs existing in 1980. For example, the component of Section 8 which provided for construction of new low-cost housing was terminated in 1983, and the budget of the Department of Housing and Urban Development (HUD) was reduced from $30 billion in 1980 to $10 billion in 1987.

This reduction in housing programs has been directed at low-income households, not to the public in general. In 1989, 52% of all housing subsidies went to households with incomes greater than $50,000, while only 16% of the housing subsidies went to households with incomes less than $10,000. Nationwide, only 36% of the 75 million low-income renters in 1989 received a rental subsidy from a federal, state, or local housing program or lived in public housing.

This trend of the federal government's withdrawing its responsibility for low-cost housing began in 1979. In that year, Congress began approving reductions in federal funding for housing and left the issue to the states. The Reagan administration coined the term "devolution" to describe the new trend of transferring responsibility from the federal government to states, cities, and counties.

This trend has also occurred in U.S. welfare policies. Eligibility requirements for federal assistance programs became much more restrictive under the Reagan administration. Millions of people had their benefits reduced or eliminated during the 1980's. Between 1981 and 1986, 442,000 people were dropped from federal programs. Food Stamps were cut $6.8 billion from 1982 to 1988, with 1 million people losing eligibility and 20 million more receiving reductions. Only by late 1988 was legislation passed to restore the level of food stamp benefits.

From 1970 to 1987, the average value of Aid to Families with Dependent Children (AFDC) benefits fell by 35% to only 44.2% of the poverty line. In 41 states in 1988, the combined value of AFDC and Food Stamps was less than 75% of the poverty level, and the AFDC housing allowance in all but seven states covered less than half of the federally defined "fair market rent." In 1987, the percentage of unemployed citizens receiving unemployment insurance benefits reached a record low—only 31.5% received any, leaving 5.1 million jobless people without benefits. By the recession of 1991, this percentage had increased to only 42%, and the emergency unemployment compensation program enacted in November of that year has fallen far short of returning unemployment insurance protection to adequate levels.

Devastating Funding Cutbacks

Federal government policies have also hurt the working poor. The real value of the minimum wage was $2.30 per hour in 1977; it had dropped to $1.88 per hour in 1988. The low minimum wage, raised in April 1990 for the first time since 1981, has left many working families in poverty. In 1992, full-time, year-round work at the minimum wage of $4.25 paid only 78% of the poverty line for a family of three, and only slightly more than 60% of the poverty line for a family of four. . . .

Funding cutbacks in government programs to serve the poor have been especially devastating because they have occurred in conjunction with other structural changes in the economy, housing market, and political system. Trends in these areas have converged to create a dramatic transformation of the U.S. social structure—one which is resulting in growing disparity between rich and poor and a lack of affordable housing for people living in poverty.

An awareness of the structural changes which have transformed our society reveals that homelessness can be viewed as one symptom of those changes. The fact that homelessness can be traced to structural sources attests to the political nature of the issue. Changes in the economy, housing market, and political system have directly benefitted those in elite classes, and this is precisely the reason the changes have occurred. The interests of those victimized by the changes have been overlooked in the process. Government has intentionally sided with the interests of elite groups at the expense of low- and moderate-income people.

Government has catered to the interests of elite groups not only by implementing conservative policies, but by propagating conservative ideology which has served to justify inequality and keep impoverished people docile and self-blaming. The response to homelessness is an example of these efforts. Throughout the 1980's and early 1990's, a common response by policy-makers has been to try to minimize the problem by attributing blame to homeless people themselves. Such a victim-blaming strategy serves to protect the interests of elite groups by diverting attention from the structural sources of social problems and encouraging the public to view victims of the problems as irresponsible or deficient in some way.

The Victim-Blaming Response

The victim-blaming response to homelessness has in fact been very successful at deluding the public into believing that homeless people are to blame for their own condition. Social science research has played a major role in propagating this idea. Numerous research studies have examined "deviant" characteristics of homeless people, such as mental illness and substance abuse, and defined these characteristics as the cause of homelessness. These research findings provided policy-makers with a rationale for the growing homelessness problem and a justification for ignoring the structural conditions giving rise to the problem. The media also played a role in propagating victim-blaming ideas by promoting similar characterizations of homeless people. The result of this victim-blaming ideology has been a widespread lack of awareness about the structural sources of homelessness and a corresponding lack of awareness about the politics of the issue.

The point being made here is not that characteristics such as mental illness and substance abuse do not exist in the homeless population. Rather, the point is that focusing on these characteristics misrepresents the homelessness problem. There is no question that changes in U.S. social structure have increased the poverty rate, lowered the incomes of people in middle-income and impoverished classes, and dramatically reduced the supply of low-cost housing. Many kinds of people have been affected by these structural changes. One reason that people exhibiting "deviant" characteristics exist in the homeless population is because it is often the most vulnerable groups in our society which are first to fall victim to such changes. Another reason is that the reality of being homeless can create such "deviant" behavior in people. Living on the street is probably as much a cause of mental illness and substance abuse as it is an effect. But perhaps the most significant point to be made is that these groups constitute only a portion of the homeless population. There are many other homeless people whose condition cannot be similarly "pathologized." These are the people that victim-blaming researchers and policy-makers disregard in their accounts. There is no way to explain their presence in the homeless population using a victim-blaming perspective.

The victim-blaming tradition served the interests of the Reagan and Bush administrations by providing a justification for the homelessness problem and by diverting attention from structural sources of growing inequality. Under this tradition, responding to homelessness became a matter of charity, as revealed by former President Bush's call for "1000 points of light" to solve problems of poverty and inequality. People in poverty came to no longer be seen as an oppressed group with rights, as they were regarded by many in the 1960's and 1970's, but as inferior individuals who were at best pitied, and at worst despised.

"The two statistical linchpins of the Reagan-did-it hypothesis stand as frauds . . . and Mr. Reagan ought to stand exonerated."

The Government Is Not Responsible for the Homeless Problem

Carl F. Horowitz

Liberals and Democrats often blame Ronald Reagan for a dramatic increase in homelessness beginning in the 1980s. But Reagan is not to blame, argues Carl F. Horowitz in the following viewpoint. He writes that the theory that "Reagan did it" is based on two falsehoods concerning the number of homeless and the availability of affordable housing. Horowitz contends that since the number of homeless people in the United States is exaggerated and that since spending for housing programs actually increased during Reagan's presidency, Reagan is blameless. Horowitz is a policy analyst at the Heritage Foundation, a conservative think tank in Washington, D.C.

As you read, consider the following questions:

1. How can government spending increase for housing programs if the authorizations have been cut, according to Horowitz?
2. According to the author, the housing stock grew by what percentage from 1981 to 1989?
3. What precipitated the visibleness of homelessness in the 1980s, in the author's opinion?

Carl F. Horowitz, "Inventing Homelessness," *National Review*, August 31, 1992, ©1992 by National Review, Inc., 150 E. 35th St., New York, NY 10016. Reprinted by permission.

"Mr. Reagan and Congress's housing cutbacks are directly responsible for the homeless problem," announced the late grand provocateur Mitch Snyder on the eve of the October 1989 Housing Now! march in Washington, D.C. Representative Charles Schumer (D., N.Y.) was also getting in his licks: "The Reagan Administration systematically decimated the nation's [low-income] housing supply." Homelessness, as much as AIDS, became during the Eighties an issue fully engaging Left-collectivism's passions for attaching guilt to the accumulation of wealth, rejecting empiricism, and projecting political explanations onto personal problems.

Homelessness was destined to become a national problem during the 1983–89 economic boom, precisely because it was a political, rather than an economic, phenomenon. By anointing derelicts as "homeless," overstating their presence, and attributing their status to the false consciousness of people in a rat race for success, activists found an effective strategy to encourage Americans to disavow the values that lead to prosperity (including good housing). Consider this comment by homeless activist Jeff Dietrich, in a guest editorial in the November 26, 1988, *Los Angeles Times*.

> We in the Catholic Worker Community believe that the problem of homelessness in America goes to the heart of our problems as a culture. And we believe that our country's culture is rotten because our system is rotten. . . . The driving force of our culture today seems to be the elimination of all those who do not have a degree in computer science, sell Tupperware, or teach aerobics.

Oh, that fiendish Tupperware!

With a few stray exceptions like Richard White, author of *Rude Awakenings*, almost no one understands how homelessness became a super-issue, and why the major media still present as "news" the fabrications of homeless activists. The case rests on two statistical falsehoods—one concerning the number of homeless people; the other, the availability of affordable rental housing.

Maestro of Homelessness

"The first thing a man will do for his ideals is lie," Joseph Schumpeter once wrote. It is 1982, and Mitch Snyder is about to "go national." Snyder had been known since the mid Seventies in the Washington, D.C., area as something of a zany. He and fellow members of the Community for Creative Non-Violence (CCNV), originally an anti-war group, having discovered the issue of homelessness, instigated hunger strikes, squatting, vandalism, and other happenings for the local homeless.

In 1980, Mr. Snyder, along with a colleague, Mary Ellen Hombs, conducted an informal nationwide survey of homeless-shelter operators. In 1982 they summarized the results in a monograph,

Homelessness in America: A Forced March to Nowhere. According to the authors, 1 per cent, or some 2.2 million, of all Americans lacked shelter. They added: "We are convinced the number of homeless people in the United States could reach 3 million or more during 1983." Mr. Snyder and Miss Hombs failed to explain how they arrived at such estimates. The General Accounting Office in 1988 reviewed 83 studies on homelessness, finding only 27 to be useful. *Homelessness in America* was not among them.

The major media, on the other hand, saw the CCNV survey as a springboard for a crusade against President Reagan. In short order, "3 million homeless" became enshrined in newspaper headlines and television feature stories. (Old habits are hard to break. On the March 26, 1991, *CBS Evening News*, Harold Dow reported: "In New York there are an estimated 70,000 homeless people, three million across America. A problem that got a lot worse during the boom times of the Eighties.")

The Department of Housing and Urban Development (HUD), for months on the hot spot, conducted a study of its own. Thorough and professional, *A Report to the Secretary on the Homeless and Emergency Shelters* (1984) concluded that the number of homeless probably ranged from 250,000 to 350,000, and that emergency shelters, far from bursting at the seams, were only about two-thirds full.

The Left, understanding the political cost if HUD's analysis were widely accepted, reacted with swift outrage. Mitch Snyder coaxed Congress to inquire into the "undercount." Though Mr. Snyder admitted in testimony that his own estimate was meaningless (in 1989 Miss Hombs told me the same thing), House Joint Committee Chairman Henry Gonzalez (D., Tex.) was moved to compare HUD's estimate with denials of the Nazi Holocaust.

Recklessly inflating the number of homeless on a local basis is also good sport. In the spring of 1992, former President Jimmy Carter observed that when he left office, the homeless in Atlanta numbered 1,200, but they now number 15,000. Carter did not cite his source of information.

Finally, the homeless can be redefined to include people "at risk" of losing their housing. In 1989, for example, David Schwartz and John Glascock, of the American Affordable Housing Institute at Rutgers University, authored a frequently cited study, *Combatting Homelessness*, which concluded that 4 million to 14 million American families are "living on the knife edge of homelessness." That's a lot like saying that millions of American married couples are "living on the knife edge of divorce."

Second String

The second element in the statistical charade was that there was a Reagan-inspired cut in federal rent subsidies by some 70 to 85 per cent, and that it forced people out of their dwellings. Richard Celeste, then Democratic governor of Ohio, speaking at the Housing Now! rally, denounced "the $24 billion that was denied to the poor and the powerless who depended on HUD for housing." Sociologist Richard Applebaum, of the University of California at Santa Barbara, referred to a "cut" in the federal housing budget from $32 billion to $6 billion and raised the possibility of housing riots at some time in the future.

Table 1: The Amazing Expanding HUD Budget

Year	HUD Outlays (Millions)	Low-Income Households Receiving Housing Subsidies
1980	$12,735	3,107,070
1981	14,880	3,297,451
1982	15,232	3,507,896
1983	15,814	3,663,328
1984	16,663	3,859,676
1985	28,720	3,943,238
1986	14,139	4,076,783
1987	15,484	4,151,252
1988	18,938	4,227,330
1989	19,680	4,315,317
1990	20,167	4,386,365
1991	22,751	4,432,077*
1992	24,159*	4,577,616*
1993	28,141*	4,703,625*

*Estimate.

Note: The unusually high outlay figures for 1985 resulted from HUD's buying back of loans from public housing authorities; the loans eventually were forgiven.

Sources: Executive Office of the President, Office of Management and Budget, *Budget of the United States Government: Fiscal Year 1993*, Supplement, Part Five, Historical Tables, February 1992, pp. 60–62; U.S. Department of Housing and Urban Development, *Expanding the Opportunities for Empowerment: New Choices for Residents*, Fiscal Year 1993 Budget, January 29, 1992.

Let the record show: The reduction in the HUD budget during fiscal years 1981–83 was from $34.2 billion to $16.6 billion (a little more than 50 per cent). More importantly, it was a cut in *authorizations*, not outlays. An authorization merely sets a spending limit, much as a Visa or a MasterCard account establishes a personal credit line. Money authorized reveals nothing about money spent. A federal agency conceivably can receive a zero-dollar authorization for a given year, and still raise its outlays by drawing upon unspent authorizations from prior years.

Table 1 reveals that HUD outlays went up during the Reagan years (fiscal 1981–89) by roughly one-third and increased even more rapidly under President Bush. Also going up substantially since the early 1980s has been the number of low-income households on the housing dole.

The anomaly of rising outlays and falling authorizations is attributable mainly to Congress's cancellation of programs committing HUD to subsidizing rents over several decades in new apartment projects, and its shift of funds toward the rent-certificate and voucher programs, which subsidize tenants of existing housing. Ironically, because of the backlog of construction projects approved during the Carter years, a great many federally subsidized apartments opened their doors under President Reagan anyway. Indeed, as William Tucker reported in September 1987, almost three times as many apartments were completed under the public-housing program during 1981–84 as during 1977–80.

Federal subsidies aside, the total year-round housing stock grew from 89.6 million dwellings in 1981 to 102.8 million in 1989 (14.7 per cent), according to the U.S. Census Bureau's *Housing Survey.* There was especially room at the inn for renters, presumably the population most at risk of becoming homeless. In 1981 the rental vacancy rate stood at 5.0 per cent; by 1989 the rate was 7.1 per cent, according to the Bureau.

Homelessness Visible

So the two statistical linchpins of the Reagan-did-it hypothesis stand as frauds. The statistical phase of the homelessness debate, by any reasonable expectation, ought to be over, and Mr. Reagan ought to stand exonerated. Yet the Left will not yield. They know the political value of making the homeless visible to as many random observers as possible.

Homelessness, Eighties-style, has its genesis in 1972, when the U.S. Supreme Court handed down its decision in *Papachristou* v. *City of Jacksonville*, overturning the convictions of several persons on vagrancy charges in Jacksonville, Florida. Writing for the majority, Justice William O. Douglas rationalized: "Persons 'wandering or strolling' from place to place have been extolled by Walt Whitman and Vachel Lindsay."

This radical redefinition of rights gradually acquired a deadly political force. Local governments found it difficult to evict vagrants from parks, sidewalks, bus terminals, and other public amenities. Indeed, fearing the bad publicity that now greeted attempts to evict, they allowed the problem to get worse, despite growing complaints from commuters and residents.

New Age liberalism, fulfilling its own prophecy, in turn described the highly visible street people as the castaways of Reaganism gone mad, people whom Snyder and Hombs called "surplus souls in a system firmly rooted in competition and self-interest."

Whether in San Francisco's Civic Center Plaza or in New York City's Tompkins Square Park (both of which experienced rioting during eviction attempts), whether on sidewalks or in subway stations, derelicts had become political love objects, all the better to be seen, so as to shame passers-by whose apathy had supposedly allowed the situation to happen. (A.M. Rosenthal likened tolerating homelessness to being a silent witness to the Kitty Genovese murder.)

Here one comes to the heart of the matter. Homeless activists' boilerplate was made possible by the integration of collective guilt into our political culture. By assigning blame for homelessness to nearly all housed, employed Americans, and by shoving the homeless into their full view, political activists transformed the homeless into "victims" of the pursuit of self-interest (i.e., Reaganism). Until collective guilt as an operational doctrine is defeated, "Reagan did it" will continue to serve as an explanation for homelessness regardless of the evidence that, in or out of the White House, Mr. Reagan is blameless.

"The group most responsible for the homeless being the way they are receives the least blame. That group is the homeless themselves."

The Homeless Choose to Be Homeless

L. Christopher Awalt

L. Christopher Awalt has worked with the homeless as a volunteer for the Salvation Army and a Texas soup kitchen. In the following viewpoint, Awalt argues that the homeless who do not want to be homeless quickly find a way to get off the streets and resume their normal lives. On the other hand, according to Awalt, the hard-core homeless—those who have been on the streets for long periods of time—remain on the streets because they prefer a life free of responsibility. Awalt is a writer and editor who lives in Austin, Texas.

As you read, consider the following questions:

1. What evidence does Awalt give that society is not to blame for chronic homelessness?
2. What must solutions to the homeless problem include, in the author's view?

L. Christopher Awalt, "Brother, Don't Spare a Dime," My Turn column, *Newsweek*, September 30, 1991. Reprinted by permission of the author.

101

Homeless people are everywhere—on the street, in public buildings, on the evening news and at the corner parking lot. You can hardly step out of your house these days without meeting some haggard character who asks you for a cigarette or begs for "a little change." The homeless are not just constant symbols of wasted lives and failed social programs—they have become a danger to public safety.

What's the root of the homeless problem? Everyone seems to have a scapegoat: advocates of the homeless blame government policy; politicians blame the legal system; the courts blame the bureaucratic infrastructure; the Democrats blame the Republicans; the Republicans, the Democrats. The public blames the economy, drugs, the "poverty cycle" and "the breakdown of society." With all this finger-pointing, the group most responsible for the homeless being the way they are receives the least blame. That group is the homeless themselves.

How can I say this? For the past two years I have worked with the homeless, volunteering at the Salvation Army and at a soup kitchen in Austin, Texas. I have led a weekly chapel service, served food, listened, counseled, given time and money and shared in their struggles. I have seen their response to troubles, and though I'd rather report otherwise, many of them seem to have chosen the lifestyles they lead. They are unwilling to do the things necessary to overcome their circumstances. They must bear the greater part of the blame for their manifold troubles.

The Temporarily Homeless Versus the Chronically Homeless

Let me qualify what I just said. Not everyone who finds himself out of a job and in the street is there because he wants to be. Some are victims of tragic circumstances. I met many dignified, capable people during my time working with Austin's homeless: the single father struggling to earn his high-school equivalency and to be a role model for his children; the woman who fled a good job in another city to escape an abusive husband; the well-educated young man who had his world turned upside down by divorce and a layoff. These people deserve every effort to help them back on their feet.

But they're not the real problem. They are usually off the streets and resuming normal lives within a period of weeks or months. Even while "down on their luck," they are responsible citizens, working in the shelters and applying for jobs. They are homeless, true, but only temporarily, because they are eager to reorganize their lives.

For every person temporarily homeless, though, there are many who are chronically so. Whether because of mental illness, alcoholism, poor education, drug addiction or simple laziness, these homeless are content to remain as they are. In many cases they choose the streets. They enjoy the freedom and consider begging a minor inconvenience. They know they can always get a job for a day or two for food, cigarettes and alcohol. The sophisticated among them have learned to use the system for what it's worth and figure that a trip through the welfare line is less trouble than a steady job. In a society that has mastered dodging responsibility, these homeless prefer a life of no responsibility at all.

Waste of Time

One person I worked with is a good example. He is an older man who has been on the streets for about 10 years. The story of his decline from respectability to alcoholism sounded believable and I wanted to help. After buying him toiletries and giving him clothes, I drove him one night to a Veterans Administration hospital, an hour and a half away, and put him into a detoxification program. I wrote him monthly to check on his progress and attempted to line up a job for him when he got out. Four months into his program, he was thinking and speaking clearly and talking about plans he wanted to make. At five months, he expressed concern over the life he was about to lead. During the sixth month, I called and was told that he had checked himself out and returned home. A month later I found him drunk again, back on the streets.

Homeless by Choice

There are two primary reasons that people are homeless. This is either by choice or by circumstances.

There are some individuals who, no matter what you say to them, or what you may offer them—be it money, food, or a roof over their heads, will still flat-out refuse to come in off of the streets. It seems that no inducements will change that. Some people simply categorize this group as mental. Yet clearly, there are some homeless individuals who are very independent in their thinking and actions and who have grown accustomed to living on the street. This is their way of life. They seem comfortable not having a permanent home and can find no reason to change their ways.

Eric Rubenstein, *Vital Speeches of the Day*, April 15, 1992.

Was "society" to blame for this man? Hardly. It had provided free medical care, counseling and honest effort. Was it the fault of the economy? No. This man never gave the economy a chance to solve his problems. The only person who can be blamed for his failure to get off the streets is the man himself. To argue otherwise is a waste of time and compassion.

Those who disagree will claim that my experience is merely anecdotal and that one case does not a policy make. Please don't take my word for it. The next time you see someone advertising that he'll work for food, take him up on it. Offer him a hard day's work for an honest wage, and see if he accepts. If he does, tell him you'll pay weekly, so that he will have to work for an entire week before he sees any money. If he still accepts, offer a permanent job, with taxes withheld and the whole shebang. If he accepts again, hire him. You'll have a fine employee and society will have one less homeless person. My guess is that you won't find many takers. The truly homeless won't stay around past the second question.

The Homeless Must Help Themselves

So what are the solutions? I will not pretend to give ultimate answers. But whatever policy we decide upon must include some notion of self-reliance and individual responsibility. Simply giving over our parks, our airports and our streets to those who cannot and will not take care of themselves is nothing but a retreat from the problem and allows the public property that we designate for their "use" to fall into disarray. Education, drug and alcohol rehabilitation, treatment for the mentally ill and job training programs are all worthwhile projects, but without requiring some effort and accountability on the part of the homeless for whom these programs are implemented, all these efforts do is break the taxpayer. Unless the homeless are willing to help themselves, there is nothing anyone else can do. Not you. Not me. Not the government. Not anyone.

"Street life must always be compared to the actual alternatives *available to the poor."*

Homelessness Is Sometimes a Legitimate Choice

David A. Snow, Leon Anderson, and David Wagner

Part I of the following viewpoint is excerpted from the book *Down on Their Luck: A Study of Homeless People*, in which authors David A. Snow and Leon Anderson examine the lives of several homeless people in Austin, Texas. Based on observations and interviews, they conclude that some people choose to be homeless because they consider it preferable to the few alternatives available to them. Part II is excerpted from *Checkerboard Square: Culture and Resistance in a Homeless Community*, a book in which author David Wagner profiles the lives of a group of street people in a New England city. Based on these profiles, Wagner argues that some people may prefer homelessness to living with an abusive family, in an institution, or in other unpleasant situations.

As you read, consider the following questions:

1. Why do policy makers so readily accept the theory that people choose to be homeless, according to Snow and Anderson?
2. Why do Snow and Anderson say they are skeptical about accepting voluntarism as a reason for homelessness?
3. How does being poor affect one's options, according to Wagner?

I

Anyone who consults with agency personnel who have contact with the homeless, listens to media discussions of the problem, peruses the social science literature on homelessness, or talks with the homeless themselves will quickly discern a host of answers to the question of why some individuals become homeless rather than others who seem equally at risk. Although the answers may vary considerably in terms of the specific locus of blame, such as mental illness, alcohol, wanderlust, or marital discord, nearly all of them constitute variants of several explanations regarding the biographic roots of homelessness. One is voluntaristic. . . .

Homeless by Choice

The voluntaristic explanation holds that people are on the streets largely by choice. Homelessness is regarded as a lifestyle that has been selected rather than forced upon someone. The question of why masses of individuals would opt for life on the streets is sidestepped in deference to the notion that, except in the rarest circumstances, people have options and are therefore partly responsible for the situation in which they find themselves.

Such voluntaristic reasoning often has considerable currency within the political arena, in part because it exempts political decisionmakers and the structures and trends with which they are associated from direct responsibility for some of the problems confronting them. Thus, it is not surprising that Ronald Reagan favored this voluntaristic explanation of homelessness during his presidency. "One problem we've had," he explained when commenting on this problem in 1984, "is the people who are sleeping on grates, the homeless who are homeless, you might say, by choice."

This voluntaristic theme can be found in some social science discussions of homelessness, and it resonates, as well, with some agency personnel who work with the homeless. The Benedictine brother in charge of Angels Kitchen, in Austin, Texas, likened the homeless to wayward souls who "are on a pilgrimage . . . in quest of a better life," thereby suggesting that for many people homelessness is a voluntary undertaking. Some of the Austin city police held a similar, although less charitable, view, attributing homelessness not to social forces, personal problems, or bad luck, but to ill-considered choice. In the words of one officer, "They have chosen their life-style" and are "content to be the way they are."

When we turn to the homeless themselves, however, we find little support for this voluntaristic explanation. It is not one of the favored or frequently articulated reasons the homeless give for being on the streets. Only 6.3 percent of the homeless with whom we discussed the reasons for their plight alluded to factors suggestive of personal choice, and fewer than 3 percent of all the reasons given fell into this category. But even if a greater proportion explained their homelessness by reference to voluntaristic assertions, we would be skeptical about attributing great explanatory power to these claims alone.

Choosing Homelessness

The element of personal choice as a causal factor in homelessness is often misunderstood. Some observers deny it completely; others inappropriately consider it the chief cause of homelessness. Some people do choose shelters and the streets over mental hospitals, boarding homes, SROs [single room occupancy hotels], and intolerable family situations. Similarly, some people choose to sleep on the streets rather than in shelters because of dehumanizing conditions in the shelters. The choice to become homeless, however, is not an affirmation of an ideal lifestyle but a means to obtain a sense of self-control and dignity when faced with a lack of meaningful, safe, and viable living alternatives.

Gary A. Morse in *Homelessness: A National Perspective*, 1992.

The reasons for our skepticism are twofold. First, voluntaristic attributions were typically made by outsiders who have been on the streets for an extended period of time. This suggests that such accounts may be subcultural artifacts or at least reflective of some level of acceptance of the situation. In this regard, it is worth recalling that not only did a sizable portion of our street sample give some indication of embracing their street identities, but that those who did so were mostly outsiders. The point is that voluntaristic accounts proffered by homeless who have spent appreciable time on the streets may tell us more about their current orientation than about their cognitive state before they landed on the streets.

The Lesser of Evils

Moreover, even if the recently dislocated attributed their homelessness to choice, it would be difficult to assess accurately the meaning of such assertions without an understanding of the range of options available. Homelessness may indeed be a matter of so-called choice for some people, but perhaps only when the few available alternatives are no more palatable than life on the streets. To the extent that this is true, the choice is of the lesser of evils and takes on a rather different meaning than if it were made in the face of more attractive options. Thus, to attribute homelessness to choice without an understanding of the context in which that choice is made is to engage in an insidious form of victim-blaming. For all of these reasons, both empirical and theoretical, we find the voluntaristic explanation of little value in understanding the biographic roots of homelessness.

II

The study of subjective behavior among the homeless and the very poor has been limited by the narrow range of the debate on poverty, which consists of blaming the victim on the conservative side of the debate and embracing the politics of compassion on the liberal side. When conservatives argued that people "choose" to be on the streets, as typified by former President Ronald Reagan's famous comments on the homeless, liberals and most social scientists responded by stressing the macro-level causes of homelessness [the housing crisis, the economy, and social benefit cutbacks]. This made sense in the context of the widespread American tendency to view public issues as personal troubles, to trivialize and individualize social problems, and to ignore economic causation.

Yet the macro-level, or social structural, approach holds the danger of "overdetermining" social causation to the point at which social actors become only what Harold Garfinkel calls "judgmental dupes." First, the reality of homelessness is usually far more complex than any single-cause explanation can address. Most often there is an interaction between the opportunity structure (the economy, the housing market, social benefits) and the particular social location of the family or individual. Second, if the poor are people with no choices, there is little room for resistance or social change. The poor are then only passive victims of social policies and the economic system. Third, as Charles Hoch and Robert Slayton note, if all choices are equally bad for the poor and all effects of poverty are seen as only pathological, then policymakers and analysts can be inactive as different aspects of low-income life are intruded upon. For example, in Hoch and Slayton's study, the tendency of liberal policymakers to support or ignore the destruction of single-room occupancy (SRO) hotels and their distinctive community is cited. Finally, the social structural arguments ignore all effects of culture and norms in low-income communities.

Changes Affect the Vulnerable

One way to explain the situation is to argue that the macro-level social changes of the 1980s interacted with personal problems and had their greatest impact on those most vulnerable to homelessness—such as the mentally ill, the physically ill, those isolated from family, and those with criminal convictions. This is a more sophisticated treatment than viewing all of the poor as equally affected by social policies, but it still does not address the subjective and cultural elements of life in low-income communities.

For example, although Mitch, Cora, Harry, Amy, and Nina [homeless people profiled in *Checkerboard Square*] can be understood to have been vulnerable to homelessness due to family problems, mental illness, or physical disability, it was their own resistance to institutionalization, family abuse, the foster care system, and landlords that caused each of them to incur periods of homelessness. Had Cora, Harry, and Nina tolerated physical abuse, as millions of Americans evidently do, they could have remained housed (although I cannot comment on their chances of physical survival). Had Joel and Mitch [others profiled] returned to their middle-class families of origin when they developed financial, health, or mental health problems, they may have never experienced homelessness. Yet Joel has at times chosen to live in his van (only in part because he cannot afford housing); Mitch left a veterans' hospital to live on the streets; Cora, Harry, Amy, and Nina all left, and refused to return to, their abusive or hostile homes. Cora's resistance to a slum landlord, to various low-paying employers, and to the city welfare department has also extended her periods of homelessness, as have Harry's criminal acts and refusal to apply for welfare because of its workfare (forced work in order to receive welfare benefits) requirement.

Street Life Versus the Alternative

The key difficulty in explaining subjective processes centers around the understanding of the word *choice*. As social scientists know well, few people choose to become poor, and this is the best counterpoint to the extreme voluntarism of Reaganite individualism. To be poor is to be without the options of daily life that are available to middle-class citizens, including securing an apartment separate from parents, getting away from home to work or to go to school, obtaining a divorce from an abusive spouse, and moving with one's children to a new household. Yet to acknowledge the closing off of options for the poor is not the same as denying that *any* choice exists among the socially structured alternatives available to the very poor. Street life must always be compared to the *actual alternatives* available to the poor. Although some subjects found the streets and the homeless experience to be devastating, others—fleeing family abuse, institutional arrangements, and other dysfunctional situations—told researchers they preferred the streets to their prior living arrangements. Of the six individuals profiled, Joel preferred the streets to shelters and institutions; Cora, Harry, Amy, and Nina preferred the streets to living with their families (Nina even left her apartment to live in tent city). Only Mitch described the streets as a completely negative experience to which under no circumstances would he ever return.

Sociological thought is based on the notion that the social structure limits and constrains choice to structural alternatives. It is a disservice to the poor to also deny them any choice within these structural alternatives. For example, the horrible alternatives of living literally on the streets, living within the shelter system, staying with friends or family, or living out of a car represent choices. So do decisions to stay in one city or region or to move, to lie and receive benefits or to be honest, to steal for food or to submit to institutional degradation in order to receive food, and so forth. Since all of these choices seem bizarre to a middle-class observer, these important realms of subjective behavior of the very poor are often misunderstood or completely ignored.

Periodical Bibliography

The following articles have been selected to supplement the diverse views presented in this chapter.

Keith R. Ablow — "Homeless, but Not Crazy," *Sun*, March 1993. Available from 107 N. Roberson St., Chapel Hill, NC 27516.

Stephen T. Asma — "The New Social Darwinism: Deserving Your Destitution," *Humanist*, September/October 1993.

Jean L. Athey — "HIV Infection and Homeless Adolescents," *Child Welfare*, September/October 1991. Available from 440 First St. NW, #310, Washington, DC 20001-2085

William F. Buckley — "The United States, Home of the Homeless," *Conservative Chronicle*, September 8, 1993. Available from PO Box 29, Hampton, IA 50441.

P. Chin — "Homeless No More," *People Weekly*, January 17, 1994.

Carl I. Cohen — "Down and Out in New York and London: A Cross-National Comparison of Homelessness," *Hospital and Community Psychiatry*, August 1994. Available from 1400 K St. NW, Washington, DC 20005.

David Handelman — "Unsettled Lives," *Vogue*, June 1994.

Dwight Hobbes — "Wrong Way to Help the Homeless," *Reader's Digest*, May 1993.

A. Hoffman — "Travels with Lizbeth: Three Years on the Road and the Streets," *Z Magazine*, July 1994.

Homewords — "Domestic Violence: A Leading Cause of Homelessness," June 1993. Available from 1830 Connecticut Ave. NW, 4th Fl., Washington, DC 20009.

M. Nemeth — "Life on the Mean Streets," *Maclean's*, February 22, 1993.

Elizabeth O'Connor — "Our Rag-Bone Hearts," *Sojourners*, January 1993.

Marybeth Shinn and Colleen Gillespie — "The Roles of Housing and Poverty in the Origins of Homelessness," *American Behavioral Scientist*, February 1994. Available from Sage Publications, 2455 Teller Rd., Thousand Oaks, CA 91320.

Ernest van den Haag — "Who Goes Homeless?" *National Review*, March 1, 1993.

Carol Walker — "Living on the Streets," *Essence*, January 1994.

What Housing Options Would Benefit the Homeless?

THE HOMELESS

Chapter Preface

Providing housing for the homeless is a crucial issue, yet experts disagree on which housing options would best serve the needs of the poor and the homeless. Many experts consider the unaffordability of housing as one of the primary causes of homelessness. In order to make housing more affordable, the government often regulates or subsidizes housing costs. One method of containing housing costs is rent control, which typically involves limits imposed by local governments on the amount landlords can charge for rent and the amount rent can increase during a given period of time.

John Gilderbloom and Richard Appelbaum, rent control advocates and authors of many articles about rent control, maintain that rent control helps to prevent homelessness by keeping housing costs affordable for low-income renters. They also argue that rent control creates stable neighborhoods because people do not move out of their low-rent apartments. Gilderbloom and Appelbaum contend that when renters pay a lower proportion of their income in rent, they have more money to spend, thus contributing to the economy and creating an increase in jobs.

Other housing experts, including William Tucker, author of *The Excluded Americans: Homelessness and Housing Policies*, argue that rent control actually hurts the very poor and the homeless. Tucker contends that cities with rent control have higher rates of homelessness than cities without rent control. He maintains that rent control causes a scarcity of low-income housing precisely because people will not move out of their cheap apartments. According to Tucker, as people earn more money, they typically move up into more expensive housing, thus freeing cheaper housing for those with lower incomes. In cities that have rent control measures, Tucker asserts, renters are unwilling to give up their rent-controlled apartments even as they earn higher incomes, making it extremely difficult for low-income workers to find affordable housing.

As this debate about rent control illustrates, there are no easy solutions to the housing difficulties of the homeless. The authors in the following chapter discuss some housing alternatives for the homeless.

"Service providers should transform . . . emergency shelters . . . into education-based facilities that truly address the needs of homeless families."

Shelters Can Help the Homeless

Ralph Nunez

Ralph Nunez is president and chief executive officer of Homes for the Homeless, a private, nonprofit provider of transitional housing for homeless families in the New York City area. In the following viewpoint, Nunez maintains that homeless shelters should be transformed into facilities that provide comprehensive services designed to help homeless families get back on their feet and into permanent housing. Many homeless parents and children lack education and independent living skills, he contends, and by teaching them these vital skills, shelters can give them a chance to get and stay off the streets.

As you read, consider the following questions:

1. How have the characteristics of the average homeless family changed since the late 1980s, according to Nunez?
2. What are some of the obstacles that keep homeless families homeless, in the author's opinion?
3. According to Nunez, what education programs and workshops are taught at the residential educational training centers?

As we move toward the year 2000, the assumption of national health care, education and safety for all Americans is that together we will strengthen families and bolster communities. But sadly, too many families find themselves disenfranchised from our nation's social and economic structure. Poverty, with its recognizable symptoms—unemployment, drug use, violence and crime—has become an expected part of the American landscape. In the 1980s, however, poverty took on a new and alarming dimension, that of homeless families.

A New American Poverty

Family homelessness—far different from individual panhandlers on the street—is a complex phenomenon that represents a new American poverty. For families, homelessness is linked with the intertwined problems of poor education, welfare dependency, inadequate health care, domestic violence, substance abuse, child abuse and foster care. Narrowly focused attempts to resolve the issue since the mid 1980s consistently have fallen short and have failed to address these interlinked causes. The challenges are many, while easy solutions are few.

Past policy responses to the homeless family crisis have been hindered by the ever-changing size and makeup of the population. Throughout the 1970s, family homelessness was synonymous with temporary displacement caused by fire, illness or short-term financial crisis. But by the early 1980s, homeless families began to multiply as never before, thanks to sweeping cuts in social service and benefit programs, changes in the housing and job markets and an apathetic political climate.

Unfortunately, limited initiatives during the early 1990s failed to stem the swelling number of families who fell through the social safety net into homelessness. Today, the number of homeless families is growing at a rate that far outpaces that of the homeless single population.

The Bush administration found that the number of individuals residing in shelters and on the street during one week in 1988 was approximately 500,000 to 600,000, of which 23 percent were members of family units, according to Martha Burt of the Urban Institute. Their ranks are joined by several thousand new families each month. In New York City alone, this population has grown by more than 500 percent since the mid 1980s. Because of such rapid growth and the sheer size of this group, government has been forced to respond with emergency measures that meet only immediate needs. This approach would be sufficient if housing and food were enough to help families out of homelessness. However, this response has been inadequate, because it does not begin to address the true needs of this population.

A review of demographic changes in New York City since the

mid 1980s produces a composite portrait of the new American poverty, typified by a young, homeless, single mother with several children. Plagued by domestic violence, substance abuse and poor health, she has little education, a low literacy level and virtually no work history. Whereas in the late 1980s the average age of a head-of-household was 35, today it is 22.

Profile of the Homeless of New York City: Comparison of 1987 and 1993 Demographics

Characteristics	1987	1993
Head of Household		
Female	92%	97%
Average Age (years)	35	22
Age Range		
Under 25	27%	56%
25 and over	73%	44%
Marital Status		
Single	60%	87%
Married	40%	13%
Education and Employment		
High school graduate	62%	37%
Have work experience	60%	40%
Social Welfare Indicators		
Substance abuse history	23%	71%
Domestic violence history	32%	43%
Pregnant or recent birth	15%	49%
In foster care as child	5%	20%
Children		
Age Range		
Under 6	15%	78%
6 and over	85%	22%

Source: Institute for Children and Poverty, New York, NY.

This profile signals the arrival of a new generation of homeless families headed by single women who have never been married. Lacking the support of a traditional family structure, nearly three-quarters of these families grapple with histories of substance abuse and more than half suffer from domestic violence.

Since the late 1980s, the number of high school graduates has plummeted. Today, only one-third of homeless heads-of-household have a diploma. Worse, the average literacy level is fifth grade. Almost none have significant work experience; only one in five has ever worked for more than one year. Moreover, their lack of self-sufficiency is demonstrated by turbulent housing histories. Presently, just half have ever lived in their own apartments; in fact, the overwhelming majority lived doubled or tripled up with friends or relatives prior to becoming homeless. More than ever before, homeless heads-of-household have grown into parenthood without the skills for independent living.

The Hidden, Silent Homeless

And for the children born into such unstable environments, chances for a future beyond poverty are slim. While they constitute the largest and fastest growing segment of the homeless population and account for nearly two-thirds of all homeless individuals, children are the hidden, silent homeless. Today's homeless children are younger and more vulnerable than ever. In 1987, the majority were adolescents; today, the average age is 3, and close to 80 percent are under 6. These young victims suffer early on from a host of challenges, particularly a lack of adequate health care. In 1993, almost half of all homeless women either were pregnant or recently had given birth, and 6 out of 10 had received virtually no prenatal care. It is not surprising that the infant mortality rate among the homeless is more than double that of the general population.

As they grow up, these children continue to face threats to their physical, mental and emotional health. In 1993, nearly half of the children in the New York shelter system did not have up-to-date immunizations. More than one-third of homeless families had open cases for child abuse or neglect with the city's Child Welfare Administration. In addition to malnutrition and emotional and physical neglect, these children face grave educational deprivation—perhaps most devastating to their long-term success. Few homeless children have the opportunity to attend preschool, and school-age children fare no better. In comparison to nonhomeless children, homeless children are nine times more likely to repeat a grade, four times more likely to drop out and three times more likely to be placed in a special education program.

A Nationwide Trend

The problems described above are not isolated to urban centers. Confirmed by similar reports from around the country, the changes seen in New York since the mid 1980s serve as indicators of trends nationwide. The greatest tragedy of this new American poverty is that young children, true victims of circumstance, bear its long-lasting effects. Without a strong national policy initiative—one that truly addresses these complex issues—America risks having the cycle of homelessness claim the futures of yet another generation of poor children.

Government strategies that have treated homelessness in a fragmented, static and costly fashion have failed. Policies must be comprehensive and flexible to meet the changing needs of the homeless population. While divisions continue to exist among advocates, service providers and policymakers as to what is the solution to the homeless problem, most would agree that the solution is not simply housing. As the majority of homeless families lack the independent skills necessary to face the challenges of poverty, it is education, rather than housing, that holds the greatest potential to ameliorate this crisis.

By prioritizing the education of society's most vulnerable children and families—those at the lowest rung of the welfare ladder—we invest in the future of our nation's social infrastructure. With the lowest estimate at 46,000 families and more than 90,000 homeless children nationwide, the magnitude of the challenge is great. However, the potential of the children and families who are inspired to adopt education and independence as a way of life is even greater.

Addressing the Needs of the Homeless

What should be done? Government officials and service providers should transform the infrastructure of emergency shelters built across America during the 1980s into education-based facilities that truly address the needs of homeless families. Homes for the Homeless, a private nonprofit transitional housing provider, has operated several such shelters—residential educational training, or RET, centers, in the New York area since 1987.

Though the components of RET centers are simple, their goals and impact are great. While families reside in RET centers, shelter administrators refer parents and children to a combination of programs aimed at meeting these families' multiple needs. On average, each family stays at a RET center for one year before being placed in permanent housing.

With the primary focus on education, on-site programs at the RET centers foster the idea of learning as a lifelong family value and enable parents and children to build skills essential for independence: Alternative high schools enable parents to return to their education by offering adult basic education and general equivalency diploma preparation and testing; early childhood development centers provide preschoolers with a jump-start on their education; accelerated after-school learning centers supplement the education of school-age students; and family literacy programs encourage parents' participation in their children's learning.

This focus on education is continued through on-site job training programs. Families become better prepared through job readiness and workplace skills training not only to end their homelessness, but also to end their welfare dependency. Other support programs help prepare families for lives beyond homelessness. Workshops teach young mothers independent living skills, such as parenting, budgeting and nutrition; substance abuse and domestic violence counseling helps families overcome crippling and life-threatening issues; health care, including prenatal and pediatric care, addresses physical well-being; and family support and preservation programs help prevent foster care placement. The last essential component is a community-based effort to continue the integrated services of RET centers once families move to permanent housing.

A Successful Approach

Homes for the Homeless has developed and refined the RET model since 1987 and has served more than 7,300 families and 17,600 children. This comprehensive, education-based approach has proved successful in helping families begin the path to independent living; once placed in permanent housing, 94 percent of participating families have maintained their residences for at least four years. By comparison with New York's return-to-shelter rates of roughly 50 percent, the RET model offers a viable method for ending family homelessness.

Although this may sound costly, it isn't. The overall price tag for housing a family in a RET center is approximately equal to the cost of housing the same family in an emergency shelter or welfare hotel ($30 per person per day in New York). However, dollar for dollar, RET centers provide at least six times as many services available in emergency shelters.

The problem is that government is not set up for one-stop shopping for families at risk. Homes for the Homeless applies for funding from more than 12 agencies at the federal, state and municipal level, with each agency demanding its own unique reporting requirements. The application and reporting demands are daunting. Currently, the majority of the RET centers' operation costs—residential and social services, child care and debt service—are funded through Aid to Families with Dependent Children. However, the core programs are financed through interlocking public and private grants, including those from the departments of Health and Human Services, Housing and Urban Development (HUD), Agriculture and Energy, as well as more than eight other government agencies at the federal, state and municipal levels.

The federal government must respond boldly to the homeless crisis by streamlining the application process for nonprofits seeking to provide multiple services to families at risk. It should waive distribution restrictions on federal money for states that are experimenting with their welfare delivery systems. Such experimentation is aimed not only at gaining the flexibility to pay for managed services, but also, more importantly, moving families off welfare entirely. Money available to combat homelessness must be organized with the flexibility to allow nonprofit organizations to tailor existing services and experiment with new ones, and with the firm intent of moving families from welfare dependence to independent living.

Expanding the Program

The opportunity for replicating the RET model nationwide never has been greater. The federal Resolution Trust Corp. holds tens of thousands of properties that could be converted to RET centers. At the same time, HUD is spending millions of dollars each year to acquire and rehabilitate properties to house homeless people. By converting some of the properties held by the RTC to RET centers, government could harness hundreds of millions of dollars spent for debt service and retarget those funds to essential educational and training programs. Moreover, RET centers offer attractive sites for other government and private parties to build on an existing economy of scale. Start-up, administrative and lease or capital costs are foregone by converting traditional shelters into RET centers: The physical space is a given, the program participants live on-site and all programs mutually reinforce the overall goals.

The RET model is not merely an effective policy option with a sound financial rationale; it is a gateway to a real and promising future for children and their families. While such an approach in and of itself proposes a reformulation of the homeless welfare system as we know it, it offers a far greater probability of successfully removing families from both homelessness and welfare dependency. The opportunity and times have never been greater for the federal government to seize the moment and expand this new concept nationwide.

By leaving the system as it is, we will continue to warehouse families. By narrowly focusing on the provision of permanent housing, we surely will find ourselves warehousing families in poverty. In the end, when everyone understands that the majority of the homeless in America are children with their futures at stake, there is no question about what must be done.

"*Shelters may in fact harm those they intend to serve.*"

Shelters Harm the Homeless

Doug A. Timmer, D. Stanley Eitzen, and Kathryn D. Talley

During the 1980s, one response to the problem of homelessness was the creation of homeless shelters. In the following viewpoint, Doug A. Timmer, D. Stanley Eitzen, and Kathryn D. Talley contend that shelters may actually contribute to the homeless problem by labeling the homeless as deviant or as passive, needy victims; by siphoning off funds that could be used for housing; and by creating an environment of dependency. Timmer and Talley are associate professors of sociology at North Central College in Naperville, Illinois. Eitzen is a professor of sociology at Colorado State University in Fort Collins.

As you read, consider the following questions:

1. List some of the ways the authors say homeless persons may be perceived as "deviant" by homeless advocates and social service providers.
2. What are some of the common complaints the homeless have about staying in emergency shelters, according to the authors?
3. What is the real solution to homelessness, in the authors' opinion?

Excerpted from *Paths to Homelessness: Extreme Poverty and the Urban Housing Crisis* by Doug A. Timmer, D. Stanley Eitzen, and Kathryn D. Talley. Copyright ©1994 by Westview Press. Reprinted by permission of Westview Press.

The overriding societal response to the problem of homelessness has been the provision of emergency shelters and shelter services, including job training, health care, education, and substance abuse counseling. These programs have been funded primarily through the Stewart B. McKinney Homeless Assistance Act, passed by Congress in 1987. Once shelters and their services are assumed to be the answer to homelessness, social service professionals operating these institutions are defined as the experts who know best how to proceed. But do they? Are shelters and their services necessary stopgaps (if not perfect, at least benign) or debilitating, dependency-creating institutions? We often ask what shelters do *for* the homeless; perhaps we should ask, what do shelters do *to* the homeless?

Shelterization as a solution to homelessness is at best a temporary necessity—emergency food and a bed when there is no other alternative. At its worst, the shelter contributes to the further victimization of the homeless by labeling these persons as deviants. Shelters may in fact harm those they intend to serve.

The Negative Impacts of Shelterization

In his critique of human services and the social work bureaucracy, John McKnight offers one route to such a conclusion. McKnight's analysis rests on two basic premises: (1) Human service interventions have negative effects as well as positive benefits and (2) human service interventions are only one of many ways to address the condition of "disadvantaged" persons. This critique of negative effects concentrates on four characteristics of the human services approach to problem solving.

1. Emphasis on "deficiencies": Persons with *specific* needs are labeled as *generally* deficient and incapable.
2. Unacknowledged monetary impact: Dollars spent on service programs (including the salaries of professional providers) are not available as cash income to the poor.
3. Impact on the community: Social service professionals become the authority figures in the neighborhood. Local citizens become impotent as problem solvers.
4. Impact on "clients": Human service programs in the aggregate create an overwhelming environment of deficiency, resulting in dependency and deviance and negating the potential for positive effects that singular programs may offer.

An emphasis on deficiencies, McKnight's first point, is evident in the shelterization response to homelessness. Homeless persons are regularly labeled as mentally ill, substance abusers, and otherwise generally incapable of, or unwilling to, live productive lives. This downplays and obscures homelessness as the simple lack of permanent housing. Social service providers then attempt to "fix" these deficient persons, rather than "fixing" the underlying causes of homelessness.

Doug A. Timmer's study of shelter ideology supports this conclusion. As he observed,

> The programs tend to treat their residents' homelessness as a matter of values, more specifically as a matter of culture of poverty values. Homeless persons tend to be regarded as the classic culture of poverty in action. They are often perceived as fatalistic, irresponsible, unable to sacrifice the moment and delay gratification (drinking instead of job hunting or buying cigarettes instead of saving their money), valuing education or training very little if at all, and suffering from a low achievement drive or lack of initiative and aspiration which is at once thought to be the cause of their homeless predicament and their inability to overcome it.

McKnight's second point, the unacknowledged monetary impact of social services, can also be seen in the shelterization response. Funds spent on shelter beds, food, and services are not available for federal and state cash assistance programs. Public investments for services would be more enabling as cash income. Putting this issue another way, McKnight's critique calls for a recognition of the trade-off between social services and housing. To give more to one set of activities—shelters and their programs—arguably means giving less to another—the construction and rehabilitation of low-income housing.

A Negative Effect on the Community

Shelterization also has a negative effect on the community and its willingness and ability to confront the problem of homelessness. Putting the homeless into shelters removes these persons from the streets and thus from public view. If the homeless are "hidden" in shelters, others do not have to see them or step around them. Homelessness thus disappears to an increasingly antagonistic public, which can assume that other people—paid professionals—will deal with these issues. As McKnight writes,

> Human service professionals with special expertise, technique, and technology push out the problem-solving knowledge and action of friend, neighbor, citizen, and association. As the power of profession and service system ascends, the legitimacy, authority, and capacity of citizens and community descend. The citizen retreats. The client advances. The power of community action weakens. The authority of the service system strengthens. And as human service tools prevail, the tools of citizenship, association, and community rust. Their uses are even forgotten. Many local people come to believe that the service tool is the only tool, and that their task as good citizens is to support taxes and charities for more services.

McKnight's fourth point, the negative impact on "clients" of an all-encompassing definition of deficiency, can be seen in the

shelter as an institutional setting. People there live wholly sur-
rounded by services and service providers. As McKnight argues,
this enveloping of the person creates a distinct environment—
one in which a circular process develops. The institutional environment causes persons in it to adapt, sometimes in deviant and
dependent ways, but the adaptive behavior itself is taken as
proof of the need for the services the institution provides.

Homeless Shelters Make the Problem Worse

[Media] accounts of those offering "help" to the homeless provide
pleasant glows, but they end up harming the poor. They lead
good-hearted citizens to offer medicine more likely to harm than
help. Those who wanted to help the homeless often worked hard,
sometimes as volunteers, to open new shelters, but as Gina
Kolata writes in a *New York Times* article,

> shelters only make the drug problem among the homeless
> worse. Although shelters are supposed to be drug free, drug
> use is often open and widespread. . . . Many shelter resi-
> dents actually have jobs, but they spend all their money on
> drugs. . . .

Addicts tend to use all available cash to feed their craving. Many
addicts who could afford apartments prefer shelters with free
room and board; such largess allows them to avoid wasting
money on low-priority items such as food. Of course, the choice
after a while is no longer available: addiction not only puts people on the street but keeps them there. Most addicts do not want
to go to work, and are physically unable to; they want to spend
every dollar on drugs.

Marvin Olasky, *The Tragedy of American Compassion*, 1992.

An example of this circular process is found in Timmer's
ethnographic account of a Chicago shelter for homeless mothers
and their children. There was conflict in the shelter between
women residents and the staff over the parenting of the women's
children. Corporal punishment was not allowed under any circumstances, even though this mode of discipline was the most
established and consistent method these mothers had in dealing
with their children's misbehavior. The parenting assistance of an
extended kin network, generally present prior to these women
coming to the shelter, was also missing. Living in the shelter, under the shelter's rules, these mothers were denied the ability to
parent in their accustomed way. They responded to their felt
lack of authority by generally ignoring their children's actions,
which resulted in the staff defining these mothers as incompe-

tent. To complete the circular process, these "incompetent mothers" were required to attend parenting classes as part of their shelter stay.

Self-Fulfilling Prophecy

The negative effect of shelters on their residents is not a new phenomenon. Charles Hoch and Robert A. Slayton's discussion in *New Homeless and Old* of the use of shelters during the Great Depression exemplifies the lengthy history of negative consequences for shelter residents:

> The effect on the men was predictable. They became despondent and often child-like, dominated by authority, going through the motions of life. One resident said that there should be no fear of communists' organizing the men in the shelters because "There's no life in these shelters. . . . They wouldn't fight nothin' in here."

The shelter's effect on its residents helps justify the professional and public emphasis on pathology and deviance. The homeless are seen as degenerate or sick, unable to make their own decisions and care for themselves.

Hoch and Slayton offer another approach from which to view the harmful effects of the shelterization response. They point out how in the mid-1980s social service providers succeeded in formulating the language of the homeless debate so as to emphasize the physical and social vulnerabilities of homeless persons rather than the right of all citizens to housing. Homelessness was thus defined as a social problem requiring professional caregivers and their skills. A population of "clients" whose "needs" warranted professional intervention was created. This ideological position portrayed and treated the homeless as passive, needy victims.

The Rejection of Shelters

The "politics of compassion" results in the provision of shelters and shelter services. But these "refuges" have been rejected by the homeless themselves, who resent the numerous rules and regulations common to the shelter experience. The overt control exerted over every aspect of life, including the scheduling of waking, sleeping, eating, and showering, restrictions on personal habits, and demands to be enrolled in required programs to continue to receive shelter, is compared by many shelter residents to that of correctional facilities. Perceiving shelters as places lacking in autonomy and privacy, most homeless persons avoid them. They use shelter facilities only when absolutely necessary, as when winter cold becomes life-threatening.

The rejection of the shelter must be placed in historical context. As Hoch and Slayton's work highlights, the economically marginal in America's cities have not always had such limited choices. Earlier in this century, a variety of housing options, from the SRO [single-room occupancy hotel], to the lodging house, to the working-class cage hotel, to the "flop" hotel, gave the poorest of the poor housing alternatives. Even though this housing may have been physically deteriorated, it provided residents what they most cherished: personal freedom and a lock on the door.

Suspicion and resentment of the shelter and its services are evident in reports of a growing "shelter rebellion" among homeless people. In New York, for example, homeless persons set up a tent city in Tompkins Square rather than enter the city's shelter system. Similar protests have occurred in Los Angeles, where a short-lived tent city was constructed in 1984, and Chicago, where homeless squatters broke into vacant Chicago Housing Authority units in 1988. This rejection of shelters is also evident in occupancy rates. In Chicago, for example, the average shelter occupancy rate in 1987 hovered around 84 percent, and the 4,250 available beds were filled to capacity less than half the time. These vacancies exist even as the City of Chicago Department of Human Services estimates the number of homeless at 40,000 to 49,000 over a year's time.

Those homeless persons who do enter shelters recognize them as dismal places of last resort, not welcomed "treatment centers." In the words of Kitty, a shelter resident in Tampa, "It's like a correctional institution and I'm not a criminal. . . . I haven't done anything wrong." Other first-person accounts quoted by Colette Russell speak of the hope of "escaping the shelters" and existing "on the verge of madness, so hungry for a little privacy and peace that I was afraid I'd start screaming in my sleep." "No one should have to live like that." Interviewing homeless persons in Chicago, researchers from the National Opinion Research Center found that most who had used shelters agreed that they offered a clean and decent place to sleep, but almost half complained about a lack of security and privacy and resented the restrictions on their personal freedom. Shelters are perceived by the homeless not only as demoralizing but also as dangerous. Fear, both of losing one's meager possessions and suffering personal injury, is often cited by those who have experienced shelter life. . . .

Shelters and shelter services are *not* the solution to homelessness. In addition, these responses detract both financially and politically from the *real* solution—the provision of sufficient low-income and affordable housing. Emergency food and shelter must continue to be available, but only as a *temporary* response in crisis situations. Shelterization must not persist as the primary institutional response to homelessness.

"Single-room occupancy units . . . are one of the last remaining forms of affordable living space available to the inner-city poor and transient."

More SROs Are Needed for the Homeless

Richard L. Cravatts

Single-room occupancy units (SROs)—small hotel rooms with shared bathrooms and kitchens—have often served as a source of housing of last resort for the poorest of the poor in the inner cities. During the urban renewal of the 1970s, hundreds of thousands of SROs across the country were razed, forcing many who lived in them onto the streets. In the following viewpoint, Richard L. Cravatts argues that modern building codes should be loosened so that more SROs can be built to replace those that were lost in the 1970s. If more SROs were constructed, he maintains, many of the homeless would be able to get off the street, and the homeless problem would be eased. Cravatts, the president of a publishing and advertising firm in Newton, Massachusetts, writes frequently about real estate investment.

As you read, consider the following questions:

1. How were single-room occupancy units perceived during the process of urban renewal, in the author's view?
2. What happened to existing SROs when a new SRO building was built in San Francisco, according to Cravatts?

Richard L. Cravatts, "Loosen Codes and House the Homeless," *Wall Street Journal*, February 6, 1992. Reprinted with permission of the *Wall Street Journal*, ©1992 Dow Jones & Company, Inc. All rights reserved.

Can the private sector be motivated to help build new housing for the nation's poor? If advocates of "entrepreneurial" government help modify regulations working against the creation of such housing, the answer may be yes. Consider, for instance Massachusetts Gov. William Weld's October 1991 refusal to continue penalizing—rather than giving incentives to—owners of low-income housing. [Weld vetoed a bill that would have extended a moratorium on the elimination of single-room occupancy units (SROs).]

Single-room occupancy units, typically found in rooming houses and residential hotels, are one of the last remaining forms of affordable living space available to the inner-city poor and transient. Unfortunately, their benefits were long unrecognized by social scientists and urban planners, who saw them as dangerous to tenants, undesirable to neighborhoods, and generally unwelcome in urban redevelopment plans. They were hastened out of existence nationwide by both federal and state policy beginning in the 1950s. Between 1974 and 1983 alone, some 896,000 housing units in the U.S. renting for less than $200 a month, many in SROs, were lost to demolition or conversion into co-ops.

Plummeting SRO Numbers

In New York City, for instance, one of the nation's most expensive housing markets, 98,400 people lived in SROs in 1965; by 1986 that number had plummeted to 18,720. Seattle had seen a similar decline when half the city's units (some 16,000) were destroyed for an urban redevelopment plan because they couldn't comply with a new fire code. A quarter of San Francisco's SRO units were lost (1,247) between 1976 and 1985.

Moreover, tightening fire and building codes had made the prospect of building new SROs impractical and unprofitable, particularly given the stringent requirements for minimum living-space square footage, parking, and cooking and toilet facilities commonly included in zoning and health bylaws.

In the 1980s, localities, belatedly realizing that SROs were needed for the single poor, instituted moratoriums on the elimination of these units. But these laws were coercive. In vetoing a bill that would have extended a moratorium on the elimination of single-room occupancy units, Gov. Weld was heeding a Supreme Court decision that determined that a similar New York City ban constituted an unlawful "taking" of private property. But this ruling need not be bad news for the poor. There are better ways to increase the number of SROs than forcing their owners to operate them.

One partial solution to the SRO problem was found in San Diego in 1984, and it may well appeal to Gov. Weld in Massachusetts as a model of how the "entrepreneurial government" he has advocated can meet a public-policy objective—in this case, the creation by the private sector of a vital type of affordable housing.

Hesitant to extend a moratorium on a small number of existing—but decaying and unsafe—SRO units, and squeezed by development pressure to change the face of older neighborhoods where SRO housing was located, San Diego policy makers were persuaded to let a private developer provide a model by which new SROs could be built. That model came to be known as the Baltic, an SRO named after the cheapest property on the Monopoly game board.

Build Single-Room Occupancy Hotels

My odd suggestion for social reform is "Bring Back the Flea Bag Hotels." The main goal is to get homeless people off the streets. . . .

The technical term here is "SROs," for single-room occupancy hotels. They sprang up in most downtowns during the early part of the century to house railroad workers and other transient laborers. Over time, many of them deteriorated into slum housing for drifters, drinkers, and the mentally ill. Then came developers, who, enticed by cheap land, razed the skid rows and replaced them with galleries and office towers. . . .

The hotels are slowly coming back, in an altered, flea-free form. The new models aren't run by slumlords but by nonprofit groups which keep social workers on hand to make sure schizophrenics take their medication and addicts avoid relapses.

Jason DeParle, *The Washington Monthly*, March 1994.

In a thorough case study written at Harvard's Kennedy School of Government, Andrew Jack and David Kennedy described the Baltic as "a four story, 207-room building with a density equivalent to more than 700 units an acre. The rooms were only 120 square feet each, but each contained, in addition to a bed and storage space, a microwave, a large sink with a garbage disposal, and a toilet (partitioned but not closed off from the rest of the room). Communal showers were on each hall."

Most significant, though, was the final per-room cost: "Construction costs—including land—were consequently very low, only $14,868 per unit. Even the Baltic's below-market rents in the $200 to $285 range would therefore be sufficient to cover costs and allow the developer a profit.

The developer, Chris Mortenson, was happy to pay for the new property himself, except for two concessions he eventually received from the city. One was a relaxation in the way the existing building codes would be interpreted and enforced. Tiny rooms with adjacent open toilets and partial kitchens might have been acceptable to SRO tenants, but they were expressly forbidden by existing California codes. Only after much negotiation did the developer and city come to terms with that problem: They designated and made legal a new type of dwelling unit—a "living unit"—which was something in between a hotel-sized room without a kitchen and a larger, residential-sized room with full kitchen and toilet facilities.

The only direct subsidy from the city was a low-interest second mortgage given to help complete the project's permanent financing. In return for that participation, 20% of the Baltic's units were set aside for poorer tenants at reduced rent levels—capped for the life of the loan.

The Baltic model illustrates how government can help ease—rather than constrict—development through cooperative entrepreneurialism. If Gov. Weld and other policy makers wish to help expedite the creation of affordable SRO housing, the time might be right for helping the private sector do the right thing.

A key factor in that equation is flexibility in interpreting zoning and building requirements. That means, for instance, that existing regulations defining acceptable density—number of units on a certain sized parcel of land—should be modified, given high land costs for the developer and the crying need for housing units for the very poor who might otherwise be homeless. City parking requirements that mandate that minimum numbers of parking spaces be provided for newly constructed residential buildings can also be re-evaluated, particularly since such rules drive up land acquisition costs, reduce the total quantity of residential units, and might be inappropriate for a target group of residents least likely to own automobiles.

An Unintended Benefit

The experience of the Baltic also indicated an unintended but significant side benefit: Existing San Diego SROs, many of them substandard, had to immediately improve amenities and upgrade overall conditions to successfully compete in a housing market where newer, more desirable units like the Baltic were being built. That model is favorable to one in which the housing market is regulated and an owner's right to use, convert, or renovate a property is legally restricted. And the lesson of the entrepreneurial marketplace has historically been that investors will more readily enter the market when government regulations enhance—rather than diminish—the prospect of profitability.

"[Most] adults crowding San Francisco's emergency shelters receive government benefits adequate to secure housing, yet they prefer to spend them on alcohol and drugs."

The Homeless Do Not Want to Live in SROs

Heather MacDonald

Homeless advocates have long claimed that a lack of affordable housing, such as single-room occupancy units (SROs), is one of the reasons for widespread homelessness, writes Heather Mac-Donald in the following viewpoint. Yet when San Francisco offered to house homeless people in SROs in exchange for a portion of their General Assistance welfare benefits, she maintains, suddenly the homeless and their advocates changed their rallying cry from "housing, housing and housing" to "choice." Providing affordable housing for the homeless will not solve the problem, she argues, if the homeless would rather spend their money on alcohol and drugs. MacDonald is a contributing editor of *City Journal*, the newsletter of the Manhattan Institute, a nonpartisan policy research organization.

As you read, consider the following questions:

1. According to MacDonald, how many of San Francisco's General Assistance recipients voluntarily took advantage of the city's offer of a discounted SRO room during the program's first five years?
2. How are the homeless and their advocates reacting to San Francisco's Proposition N, according to the author?

When Al Silbowitz came to Berkeley, California, from New York City in the 1960s, he and his fellow radicals rousted the liberal Democrats from the City Council. Now he spends his time rousting vagrants from the properties he manages and cleaning up their excrement. "God knows what diseases they've got," he fumes.

Mr. Silbowitz is part of a counterrevolution in the making. While Washington politicians are just starting to wheel out the big guns for welfare reform, hand-to-hand combat has already broken out in the nation's most progressive cities over welfare abuse and a declining quality of life. On Nov. 8, 1994, Mr. Silbowitz voted with a majority of Berkeley residents to severely restrict panhandling in the city and prohibit loitering by drug dealers. Across the bay in San Francisco, residents voted to require recipients of the city's generous welfare grant to use it for housing, rather than booze or drugs. These three initiatives represent a collective acknowledgement that the legal and social policies of the '60s have backfired.

Hard-Won Initiatives

The ballot victories in both cities were hard won. Activists for the homeless had plastered Berkeley with signs exhorting voters to "Say No! to the Poor Laws" and "Defy Unjust Laws." U.S. Rep. Ron Dellums, the godfather of Berkeley politics, opposed the initiatives, as did the poet Maya Angelou and South Africa's Archbishop Desmond Tutu. The ACLU [American Civil Liberties Union] trotted out the usual argument that the loitering law was irrelevant to the drug problem and would be enforced discriminatorily.

But in the end, common sense and sheer fatigue won out. According to Patrick Devany, a city planning commissioner, Berkeley is growing "impatient with the anachronisms of the 1960s." In passing the loitering ordinance, residents returned to the police a vital tool for crime prevention that the courts had earlier taken away. Lavell Spence, a black small-business owner who ran for the City Council, argued before the election that "people say the law will discriminate, but if you are a law-abiding citizen, a family person, you will not be hanging out on the corner at 2 or 3 a.m."

As for the panhandling ordinance, which prohibits begging at night and in front of businesses and ATMs, as well as sitting or lying in commercial districts, Berkeley's panhandlers have only themselves to blame. "People are tired of being threatened by people with a feeble grasp on reality," says Mr. Devany. Mr. Silbowitz has been punched in the face by a vagrant whom he had asked to move from the doorway of an apartment house; panhandlers have come after noncompliant pedestrians with knives.

Such behavior is leading residents to ask whether Berkeley's generous social programs, long a badge of honor, merely serve as a magnet for misbehavior. "For years, we put up a sign that proclaimed from coast to coast: 'Come here!'" laments Mr. Silbowitz.

If Berkeley's ordinances represent a watershed in the city's political culture, San Francisco's initiative requiring welfare recipients to rent housing was notable for the unusual response of its opponents: candor. In a desperate effort to scuttle the measure, advocates for the homeless began telling the truth about why people live on the streets.

San Francisco's Proposition N

For years, advocates blamed homelessness on the government's failure to provide housing for the poor. San Francisco's Proposition N puts that argument to the test. The city will offer a discounted room in a single-room-occupancy (SRO) hotel to recipients of General Assistance (GA), a welfare grant for able-bodied single adults, who cannot show proof of housing. The city will deduct rent from each monthly check. People who refuse the city's offer of housing will lose their benefits.

MISERY LOVES COMPANY

Sixty-five percent to 70 percent of the adults crowding San Francisco's emergency shelters receive government benefits adequate to secure housing, yet they prefer to spend them on alcohol and drugs. Indeed, San Francisco has offered its SRO-GA payment program on a voluntary basis for the past five years; of the city's 3,000 GA recipients who claim homelessness, only 770 have entered the program.

With the appearance of Proposition N, the usual argument for street living—that there is no housing available—suddenly lost its force. And just as suddenly, the advocates changed their tune. Randy Shaw, a housing advocate who operates the voluntary SRO-GA program, warned in the *San Francisco Chronicle* before the election that the new policy could backfire: "Forcing people into hotels doesn't mean they'll be good tenants. We have years of evidence. When people are put somewhere against their will, hotels get trashed and neighborhoods get trashed."

If Mr. Shaw and his colleagues had "years of evidence" that many of the homeless are too irresponsible to maintain tenancy, where, one wonders, were they hiding it during the 1980s, when all one heard was that homelessness was about "housing, housing and housing"?

No Longer Housing, but Choice

The advocates unwonted honesty is merely part of a new rhetorical strategy, however. The post–Prop. N rallying-cry among San Francisco's activists is no longer housing, but choice. The problem with the SRO-GA program, they say, is that it strips GA recipients of their autonomy. "Options is the key word," says Lydia Ely of the Coalition on Homelessness, the most powerful homeless advocacy group in San Francisco. "I'm opposed to the concept that because people are poor, we can tell them what to do."

Ms. Ely and other advocates charge that the rooms available through the SRO-GA program are in poor condition; therefore, they say, San Francisco has no right to force people to live in them. (The city counters that the SROs will be up to code and frequently inspected.) Ms. Ely offers a prediction: "If Joe Schmoe gets cut off of GA because he refused to take a room, what will he do? Will he go: 'I'll become an upstanding citizen and join the rest of productive society,' or will he do some pretty serious [expletive deleted] that will cost us in police money?"

Turning to Extortion

This thinly veiled threat represents the last gasp of the welfare rights revolution, In the name of freedom and empowerment, welfare recipients won the right to live as they wanted and spend their welfare checks as they wanted, unencumbered by traditional state oversight. At the same time, the cultural revolution of the '60s promoted the right of the individual to pursue his own concept of pleasure, freed from traditional social constraints.

This expansion of rights brought not utopia, but urban squalor and social decline. Faced with the growing demand to condition government largess on responsible behavior, the advocates of unconditional government-funded freedom are turning to extortion: Maintain the welfare status quo or expect to get mugged.

Such threats will not be availing, however. If the cities that brought us the People's Park and the Summer of Love have begun dismantling the legacy of their own "progressive" past, the rest of the country cannot be far behind. While Washington should pursue its own version of welfare reform, it must above all stand out of the way of local efforts at reform. Such efforts stand the best chance of encouraging responsible behavior and restoring order to public spaces.

---

*"Public takeovers of vacant buildings . . . provid[e]
immediate housing for people on the streets."*

The Homeless Should Take Over Vacant Buildings

Alex Vitale

Many cities have vacant buildings that could be used for housing. Some homeless people protest city housing policies and "warehousing" (the withdrawal of buildings from the housing market by landlords to force up rents and property values) by squatting: They move into, inhabit, and sometimes renovate abandoned buildings, even though such actions may be illegal. In the following viewpoint, Alex Vitale supports squatting in vacant buildings. He argues that taking over vacant buildings forces a shift in the focus of the homeless debate, from treating the symptoms of homelessness to addressing its root causes. Vitale is a former staff member of the San Francisco Coalition on Homelessness.

As you read, consider the following questions:

1. Which two of society's sacred beliefs are the homeless challenging when they take over abandoned buildings, in the author's opinion?
2. According to Vitale, what are the two types of properties targeted for housing takeovers by the homeless and activists?
3. What is the two-part strategy used by San Francisco's Homes Not Jails in their housing takeovers, and what does each stage accomplish, according to Vitale?

Excerpted from "Homes Not Jails: The Thanksgiving Day Housing Takeover" by Alex Vitale, *Z Magazine*, February 1993. Reprinted by permission.

Each Thanksgiving, people across the country are once again force-fed media images of the poor receiving charity and giving thanks. Homeless people are shown standing in line while middle class volunteers and political opportunists hand out oversized portions of good tidings and holiday cheer to people who eat a full meal like this only two or three times a year. Then come personal stories of thankfulness for "just being alive," culled from numerous Santa Claus–like inquiries of "and what are you thankful for this year?" In 1992, however, in San Francisco and several other cities, views of grateful charity were juxtaposed with the stark reality of homeless people and their supporters tearing the boards off abandoned buildings and taking them over and, in the process, challenging two of our society's most revered ideological beliefs: *private property is sacred,* and *people are poor/homeless because they want to be.*

In the last 10–15 years, public policy concerning homelessness in the United States has been based on personal competency, personal responsibility, and personal rehabilitation. Rising levels of unemployment, drug addiction, teenage pregnancy, and homelessness are all ascribed to a breakdown of "family values," while deindustrialization, the loss of low cost housing, and cuts to education and social services are either ignored or reported as an inevitable restructuring necessary for "American competitiveness."

Between 1978 and 1988, federal appropriations for subsidized housing dropped 80 percent. Over one million well paying industrial jobs have left the U.S. since 1980, and the real value of the minimum wage has declined relative to the overall cost of living. . . . The deep discouragement resulting from long term unemployment and racist and classist discrimination are more cogent explanations of family atomization and drug addiction than "loss of moral fiber." Government at all levels, the media, and private foundations continue to conceptualize poverty as a personal problem with personal solutions while ignoring the structural economic factors that have created widespread homelessness.

The Stewart B. McKinney Act

In 1987 Congress passed the Stewart B. McKinney Act, the first omnibus legislation dealing with homelessness. It provides for the creation of emergency shelter, food, and health care programs as well as transitional and permanent housing for homeless people. . . .

All of these [services] are based on the personal assistance model which relies on rehabilitation, temporary assistance, and the ever more pervasive and invasive case management programs. Case management assigns people who are in need of housing, employment, and support services a social worker, with almost no resources at his/her disposal, who tells "clients" how they should modify their behavior rather than advocating for the structural changes needed to end homelessness. Case management is increasingly a prerequisite to receiving the most basic emergency services. . . .

Trying to Survive on the Streets

You are homeless. All day you have looked for a place to sleep indoors for the night. Your search is urgent, for tonight will be bitterly cold. As the sun sets, the temperature falls into the single digits. Unfortunately, your city has no homeless shelters. As doors close, you head toward your hideaway, an abandoned apartment house with a side door that is usually unlocked. You do not go there every night—another homeless person might discover your secret and beat you to it on some freezing or snowy night. Instead, you save it for emergencies. Tonight you can either take shelter there or risk freezing to death. You enter the cold, empty building, cover yourself with newspapers and cardboard, and go to "bed." Although the abandoned building is not heated, at least you are not outside. The next morning you are awakened by a police officer, who promptly arrests you for trespassing.

Your story is based on a true one. A few years ago, in Long Beach, New York, Benjamin Franklin Pierce was arrested the morning after he had spent the night in an abandoned apartment building. Pierce, a forty-four-year-old man, had been homeless for seven years and lived in a community that had no homeless shelters. He had sought shelter when the wind-chill-adjusted temperature dropped to twenty-four degrees below zero.

David M. Smith, *Yale Law & Policy Review*, vol. 12, no. 2, 1994.

The Boston Foundation [a foundation that gives grants to non-profit community organizations in the Greater Boston area] recently released a report entitled *Giving to End Homelessness* which examines the funding patterns and public policy priorities of foundations. . . .

Many foundations (48 percent) cited "empowerment-oriented projects" as having the greatest impact on preventing homelessness. But, only one-third actually support organizing and advocacy projects. When asked to define empowerment, many described it as promoting individuals' ability to either successfully negotiate the social service system or to pass through it towards self sufficiency. Fortunately, some groups did mention collective action and organizing, and the Boston Foundation, in its listing of model organizations, described some that have engaged in housing takeovers (The Women's Institute for New Growth and

Support in Boston) and limited and sweat equity ownership programs (Dignity Housing in Philadelphia and Urban Home-
steading Assistance Board in New York).

Public takeovers of vacant buildings, more than almost any
other actions by homeless people, repudiate the personal rehabilitation discourse on homelessness while providing immediate
housing for people on the streets. Public takeovers emphasize
collective action aimed at structural inequalities while directly
challenging the underlying causes of homelessness (the elimination of affordable housing and decent paying jobs), by exposing
property owners who make money taking housing off the market in order to raise its and other properties' long-term value,
and by showing that homeless people have both the skills and
desire to change their situation.

Organized Squatting

In San Francisco, organized housing takeovers provide a hope-
fulness of changing one's personal situation through collective
action and the development of community. Members have
agreed to house rules that focus on group responsibility and a
clean and sober lifestyle. Individuals share responsibility for
cooking, cleaning, and security. Several members with previous
substance abuse problems have quit using. They say they feel
supported and have control over their lives in a way that the social service system doesn't allow.

On Thanksgiving day 1992 in San Francisco, San Jose, Oakland, and Boston, people took over boarded up buildings that
could be housing this country's 1–2 million homeless people. In
San Francisco there are over 8,000 homeless people and almost
the same number of abandoned or boarded up units, many of
them completely habitable, the rest requiring varying degrees of
rehabilitation. The situation is the same in almost all urban areas in the U.S.

In the mid 1980s New York City and Philadelphia were confronted by organized squatting. In response, these cities created
a program to turn over abandoned property in need of rehabilitation to poor people in return for an investment of labor into the
building: "Sweat Equity." Unfortunately, these programs rarely
funded rehabilitation and were short lived, often dying out due
to increased property values or declining organized squatting.

Sweat Equity has become one of the primary demands of
homeless people in San Francisco. The first unit occupied by
Homes Not Jails, a week before Thanksgiving, required some
immediate simple repairs and the reconnection of water and
electrical service. This was done by homeless people who have
experience in the building trades but who have been unable to
find or maintain employment in the depressed California econ-

omy where a million jobs have been lost since 1990. In subsequent media coverage, members consistently made the connection between unemployed skilled homeless people and the need to fix up this and many other buildings, and called on the city to develop a Sweat Equity program.

Highlighting Structural Causes

The other type of property targeted for takeovers is habitable buildings withheld from the market due to speculative interests. The building occupied on Thanksgiving day contained 40 units of rehabilitated Single Room Occupancy (SRO) housing in a low income neighborhood. The landlord was facing prosecution by the District Attorney's office for wrongful eviction and the building was vacant because of violation of the city's hotel conversion ordinance, which was passed in the mid 1980s to prohibit the conversion of low-cost housing into tourist hotels.

By taking over housing which is habitable but boarded up, activists highlight some of the structural causes of homelessness. During periods of economic uncertainty or in areas where gentrification is occurring, landlords will often evict tenants and leave a building empty or "warehoused" until it can be either rented to tenants with more money or sold to developers who are interested in building higher income generating properties such as high-rises or condominiums. This latter type of conversion has been the leading cause of the destruction of affordable housing. Opposing this process benefits both homeless people and low income tenants.

A new organization of homeless people in Atlanta is trying a different approach. Rather than taking control of abandoned housing, "Uprisings" is making arrangements with property owners to live in the buildings while fixing them up, then moving on to another building. While this provides shelter for those involved, it does nothing to insure that the buildings are added to the stock of affordable housing and no equity is gained. They are neither paid nor given control over the property. Rehabilitation increases the value of the property, contributing to gentrification, which is often the underlying cause of people's homelessness.

Organizers in San Francisco have been using a two part strategy of public and covert housing takeovers which serves several purposes: establishing immediate living spaces for homeless activists, organizing additional homeless people, pressuring the local government to make structural changes, and permanently acquiring housing for homeless people. This addresses many of the tensions that regularly occur when homeless people organize, by balancing the immediate personal needs of participants with the desire to struggle for systematic solutions.

Homes Not Jails began by occupying a building covertly,

which got people an immediate place to live so they were able to stabilize the organization and develop long-term plans. It also provided an ongoing sense of accomplishment for both current members and people interested in getting involved; potential new members see that something tangible has been accomplished. A stable location was also useful in working with the press, who did newspaper articles and live radio interviews inside the building. Homeless activists in Seattle, who were trying to get control of an abandoned hotel there, were given the use of a local union hall to sleep in for the same purpose.

The second stage is public takeovers. Unlike Philadelphia and New York in the 1980s, any attempt to publicly occupy buildings in San Francisco is met with an immediate eviction by the police. Homes Not Jails has used this to their advantage. Each time they publicly occupy a building they organize a march with media imagery foremost in their minds. The press love the visuals of people ripping off the boards, banners hanging out the windows and finally, the police moving in to evict people. The irony of homeless people being thrown out onto the streets is both visual and visceral. Public events and the accompanying press coverage also provides leverage for pressuring the city to respond in a public forum to the group's demands.

Articulating and negotiating demands, however, has been one of the weak points of Homes Not Jails. With support from the San Francisco Tenants Union and Food Not Bombs, they have developed some demands but haven't moved towards the negotiation stage. The group has asked that buildings that are empty be turned over to homeless people and that if the buildings need rehabilitation or minor repairs, homeless people be given the opportunity to do the work in return for control of the building. More concrete demands for laws turning over property automatically if left unoccupied or for financing for rehabilitation work haven't yet emerged. The group has discussed creating a nonprofit corporation, however, that could eventually take legal ownership of properties.

Organized squatting is not a new strategy for people unable to find adequate housing. It is, however, an especially provocative one at this time. With homelessness on the increase, . . . a new debate is emerging about how to address homelessness in America. There is the potential to move away from the personal rehabilitation model of homeless services to addressing the root causes and structural solutions necessary to solve it. Through public housing takeovers homeless people have an opportunity to send the message that they are homeless, not helpless.

*"Temporary and nearly permanent encampments
and shantytowns encumber public spaces . . .
and pose a health threat to the homeless,
sanitation workers, and the general public."*

The Homeless Should Not Be Allowed to Sleep in Public Places

Robert Teir

Dallas, Texas, enacted an ordinance prohibiting sleeping in public places to prevent homeless people from sleeping in city
parks. A police sweep of a homeless encampment under a
Dallas bridge led to a 1994 lawsuit against the city by the
American Civil Liberties Union (ACLU) on behalf of a homeless
man. The following viewpoint is an *amicus curiae* (friend of the
court) brief by Robert Teir supporting the Dallas law. Teir argues
that ordinances such as Dallas's ban on urban camping are necessary to keep cities safe places to live, work, shop, and relax.
Teir is the general counsel for the American Alliance for Rights
and Responsibility, an advocacy group that develops and defends policies on issues that affect the quality of urban life.

As you read, consider the following questions:

1. How does the ban on public sleeping help the homeless, in
   the author's opinion?
2. What would happen if the court granted the homeless the
   right to camp on public land, in Teir's view?

Excerpted from Robert Teir's *amicus curiae* brief in *Prince Johnson v. City of Dallas*, Fifth
Circuit, U.S. Court of Appeals, February 21, 1995.

The American Civil Liberties Union (ACLU) brought this law-suit on behalf of Prince Johnson and other homeless individuals residing in Dallas, Texas. The ACLU and the plaintiffs disagreed with the passage and enforcement of a variety of city ordinances addressing solicitation by coercion, removal of solid waste from trash cans, closing times at the City Hall–Public Library Plaza, public sleeping, as well as the Texas criminal trespass statute. As has become all too common in our litigious society, the plaintiffs expressed their disagreement with these laws by claiming that the measures violate their rights under the United States Constitution.

The constitutional challenge seemed primarily aimed at the City's plan to remove a shantytown that had emerged underneath an elevated freeway near the city's downtown and the revitalizing, integrated Deep Ellum neighborhood. The City Council, neighborhood residents (of all classes), small store owners, historic preservationists, and downtown businesses were concerned that the shantytown was not only a horrendous eyesore, but was also a health hazard, a sanctuary for drug dealers and prostitutes, and a launching ground for those who begged aggressively, walked the streets of Deep Ellum drunk, harassed pedestrians, and used nearby streets as their bathroom. City residents were also concerned that the shantytown enabled the homeless to avoid social services aimed at substance abuse and mental illness, and therefore facilitated a life on the street consisting of destruction and isolation. . . .

Quality of Urban Life

Years ago, urban flight was attributed to racial hostility and desegregation. Today, declining urban quality of life plays a leading role. The urban nuisances and sources of disorder that are growing include blockaded sidewalks, pedestrian harassment, unlicensed vendors, homeless encampments, excessive noise, public intoxication, litter, graffiti, and aggressive panhandling. Although crime and taxes also contribute to people avoiding urban centers, these problems have always been more common in cities than elsewhere. What is different today is a growing urban disorder, a sense that city streets and parks are out of control, that rule-setting and minimum standards of conduct are taboo.

Most people need and will seek places where relative calm, order, and civility prevail. If they can get these things in urban spaces, they will work, shop, eat, employ people, and live there. If they cannot, those with options will leave, leaving those left behind with a shell of what was once there.

These quality of life concerns are not just the afflictions of dilettantes, the hypersensitive, or the politically conservative. These measures, at risk in this litigation, defend accessible parks, which are many urbanites' backyard. Urban parks are places of integration and social interaction. However, these community-building advantages cannot work if lunch times are spent looking for a park bench that is not being used as a bed, or if parents have to fear their children's stepping on needles, used condoms, or human waste.

Urban nuisances do most harm to those without great means. While the wealthy may be able to retreat to country clubs and other private spaces, many urbanites do not have such options. They depend on the usability of public parks, and lose something irreplaceable when the parks become a no-man's land.

Reprinted by permission of *The Spectator*.

Nor is the choice confronted by cities one between lawlessness and a disregard for the suffering of others. Rather, the nation's most diverse, progressive, and caring cities are acting in this area because they have the most to lose. These cities, from Seattle to Atlanta, Miami to Berkeley, see little value in a right to slowly kill yourself abandoned on the streets, and recognize the harm of turning over the squares, parks, plazas, and sidewalks to those on the margin of society.

These new urban quality of life ordinances do not represent a return to the turn-of-the-century vagrancy or loitering laws. They differ in motivation, they differ in the scope of the people benefitting from them, and they differ in the amount of police discretion provided for. They have nothing to do with racial or class animus, and everything to do with preserving a useful, vibrant, safe urban lifestyle for all city residents. No one, Jew or Gentile, rich or poor, white or black, gay or heterosexual, benefits if parks are colonized, sidewalks are obstacle courses, and tax bases are decimated. . . .

Preserving Beauty and Safety

Temporary and nearly permanent encampments and shantytowns encumber public spaces. They deprive ordinary citizens of the use and enjoyment of the public streets and areas they occupy. They destroy the scenic beauty of areas. The occupants of these camps conduct bodily functions in public and leave litter, rotting food, used syringes, used condoms, and buckets of human waste in their wake. These encampments attract rats and other vermin, and pose a health threat to the homeless, sanitation workers, and the general public.

Such areas need more police attention and more sanitation facilities and, even so, remain largely unusable by large parts of the public that pay the taxes to maintain them. Moreover, the flight of people and businesses from such areas undermines a sense of order, and can precipitate a downward spiral of lawlessness and decay as more and more people abandon the area, opening it to the influx of more crime. Cities have a legitimate interest in preventing this scenario of decline.

Regulation Is Not "Compassion Fatigue"

Your *amici* [*amici curiae*, friends of the court] are well aware of the efforts by some to describe urban quality of life measures as cruel, heartless, or symptoms of "compassion fatigue." Attempts to avoid rational debate through name-calling are not new, after all. Here, such tactics are not only inappropriate, they are wrong.

Neither we nor the Court can or should avoid the fact that this case affects many homeless people, although the text of the Dallas ordinance and other urban quality of life measures are neutral and do not single out the homeless in any manner. By supporting the validity of these measures, the *amici* in no way intend to demean the plight of the homeless or to suggest that society should ignore their needs. Quite to the contrary, the *amici* believe that communities have a moral obligation to encourage and foster a range of programs to identify and correct the causes of homelessness and to provide food, shelter, medical assistance, and counseling for them.

Believing in compassion and assistance for the homeless does not mean distorting the Constitution to grant them special rights beyond the reach of the democratic system. It does not mean that courts, because of circumstances that naturally evoke our sympathy and distress, should deny local governments the ability to control and regulate behavior that threatens the health, safety, and other interests of the general public. It also does not mean that courts should seize control of local government budgets and require either more aid and beds for the homeless, or the allocation of public lands for their use.

Furthermore, it is hardly cruel or pitiless to be concerned with how public spaces are used, and to want to keep them accessible to all groups of people. Like any other property, public spaces require governance and rule-setting if they are going to be used for the purposes for which they were created. It is not cruel to propose a closing time at the National Zoo. Nor is it cruel to propose a closing time at Dallas's City Hall Plaza.

Finally, it strains credibility (and is insulting) to argue that the city officials and residents of the cities that have taken the lead in this area—San Francisco, Seattle, Baltimore, Atlanta, etc.—are mean-spirited, racist, or heartless. Indeed, it is these cities that are internationally known for their tolerance, diversity, compassion, and attempts to build a vibrant, integrated urban community. What these cities have set out to do is to show that a tolerance for diversity does not have to mean an abandonment of standards of public conduct.

Urban camping, for the affected community, represents a loss of its urban meeting places, its common, a loss of the vibrancy and utility of its sidewalks, a deterioration of its central core and neighborhood commercial centers, and continuation of the abandonment of urban centers. No one wins when this occurs, while so many lose. To stem this tide, communities should be allowed to end the enabling, encourage street people to seek help for their underlying problems that lead to homelessness, and ask that the parks and sidewalks be places free of harassment, open to all for the purpose for which they were built. . . .

No Constitutional Right

If the plaintiffs' constitutional theories were to be followed, cities across the country would be left with a brutal choice: they would have to refrain from enforcing, at least against the homeless, laws prohibiting camping (no matter how neutrally enforced with respect to natives and migrants), or they would have to provide whatever levels of public assistance the courts will decide is appropriate to afford the homeless their necessary life-sustaining functions.

The effect of such decisions is to either grant free shelter at the expense of other government programs (or taxpayer assets), or to create an entitlement to camp on any of the community's public facilities. Wherever the number of homeless exceeds the number of shelter beds, the homeless will be able to appropriate the balance from the public itself.

The implication of this argument is that local communities, as a matter of federal constitutional law, must, as the price for enforcing facially neutral laws aimed at preserving public property for the public, provide free property for all who cannot afford it. While government may provide support and shelter for the less fortunate of its citizens, it is simply not the province of the judiciary to impose such support obligations on communities. Such decisions involve dividing today's increasingly strained public resources, and are most appropriately left to the democratic process. . . .

The assertion of a constitutional right to take public property for one's own needs is not only without basis in precedent, it would be unworkable. Most cities simply cannot afford to provide land and support for all who may wish to reside there. Ironically, communities that make the most charitable efforts to help the homeless will find themselves most penalized by the doctrine advocated by the plaintiffs. Such communities will likely attract larger numbers of the homeless and others, and will find their efforts swamped unless they are able to impose, neutrally, limitations on the use of their public property. The inevitable result is a further and regrettable hardening of attitudes against the homeless, a result that can and should be avoided by allowing communities to decide for themselves what level of support they can afford.

Periodical Bibliography

The following articles have been selected to supplement the diverse views presented in this chapter.

Kevin Clarke — "Are We Winning the Fight Against Homelessness? *Salt of the Earth*, January/February 1995. Available from 205 W. Monroe St., Chicago, IL 60606.

Connie Driscoll — "Chicago's House of Hope," *Policy Review*, Summer 1993.

Financial World — "Homelessness: St. Louis; Beyond the Crisis," March 2, 1993.

Malcolm Gladwell — "The Road to Homelessness, Paved with Good Intentions," *Washington Post National Weekly Edition*, May 2–8, 1994. Available from 1150 15th St. NW, Washington, DC 20071.

Lynette Holloway — "Airport Homeless: A Long, Pleasant Layover," *New York Times National Edition*, February 23, 1995.

David L. Kirp — "A Sedan Is Not a Home," *Commonweal*, February 12, 1993.

Abigail McCarthy — "Gimme Shelter: A House Can Be a Home," *Commonweal*, April 9, 1993.

Lucia Mouat — "Home-Sharing Programs Target Shelter Gap," *Christian Science Monitor*, February 17, 1993.

Louis M. Nanni — "Not by Bread Alone," *American Enterprise*, January/February 1995.

Elena Neuman — "A New Lease on Life Beyond the Inner City," *Insight*, March 14, 1994. Available from PO Box 91022, Washington, DC 20090-1022.

Neal Peirce — "Dynamited Public Housing: What's Next?" *Liberal Opinion Week*, May 29, 1995. Available form PO Box 468, Vinton, IA 52349-0468.

Louisa R. Stark — "The Shelter as 'Total Institution,'" *American Behavioral Scientist*, February 1994. Available from Sage Publications, 2455 Teller Rd., Thousand Oaks, CA 91320.

Richard J. White Jr. — "The System Subsidizes Failure," *Insight*, June 6, 1994.

How Can Society Help the Homeless?

THE HOMELESS

Chapter Preface

During the late 1980s the term "compassion fatigue" began to crop up in news stories about the homeless. Journalists reported that many Americans, frustrated by the lack of progress in solving the homeless problem, had become tired of caring about a situation that appeared to have no solution. They said that Americans were tired of confronting outstretched palms on every block, tired of stepping over bodies sleeping in doorways, and tired of looking for a park bench that was not already occupied by a homeless person. Americans had grown weary, the media reported, of spending time, money, and energy to help the homeless, only to see the problem get worse, not better.

Perhaps in response to such sentiments, in the early 1990s many cities began criminalizing behavior associated with homelessness. New York and many other cities banned panhandling and aggressive begging. Seattle prohibited sitting or lying on public sidewalks. The California cities of Fullerton, Long Beach, Orange, Santa Ana, and Santa Barbara all passed ordinances banning public camping. Even Santa Monica, California, which most residents once considered a homeless refuge, made it illegal for service organizations to provide meals for the homeless at outdoor sites. Robert Teir, general counsel for the American Alliance for Rights and Responsibilities (an advocacy group that promotes plans to improve the quality of life in cities) defends these policies. He maintains that unless cities take strict measures to control the activities of the homeless, the homeless will threaten "the preservation of the safety, civility and attractiveness of . . . public spaces."

Yet other cities continued to accommodate the homeless. In 1992, Miami provided a safe haven under a local freeway underpass where the homeless could sleep, bathe, and cook without fear of arrest. In 1994, Nashville, Tennessee, rejected an anti-panhandling ordinance and Dade County, Florida, placed a 1-percent tax on restaurant meals in order to fund facilities and services for the homeless people. Robert M. Myers, who in 1992 was fired from his job as Santa Monica's city attorney for refusing to enforce antihomeless legislation, maintains that "it doesn't do anyone any good to simply keep the homeless on the move. . . . How can we expect people to participate in society and adhere to the rules of society when you're telling them they're not wanted?"

Whether society can or should help the homeless and what steps it should take to help them are some of the issues discussed in the following chapter.

"There are many direct reciprocal benefits from assisting the homeless and reclaiming them as social insiders."

The Homeless Should Be Helped

Robert C. Coates

There are many reasons to help the homeless, writes Robert C. Coates in the following viewpoint, including humanitarian and practical concerns, the need to set a good example for children, and self-interest. But perhaps the most important purposes of all, he maintains, are ethical ones. Religious and philosophical ethics require that society help the less fortunate, he contends, so society must help the homeless. Coates is a municipal court judge for San Diego, California, and the founder of the San Diego Mayor's Task Force on the Homeless.

As you read, consider the following questions:

1. What are some of the reasons to help the homeless involving self-interest, in the author's opinion?
2. What two elements are necessary in any ethics philosophy, in the author's view?

From Robert C. Coates, *A Street Is Not a Home* (Buffalo: Prometheus Books). Copyright 1990 by Robert C. Coates. Reprinted by permission of the publisher.

"Why help the homeless?" can be answered with, "Why *not* help the homeless?" This is especially true because there are so many reasons to do so, ranging from the humanitarian to the purely practical, such as the state of public health, the functioning of streets and parks, good business conditions, and aesthetic values. Most convincingly to me, we need to set an example to our children. As an educational opportunity for us, America's homeless afford the chance to reveal to our children that they belong to a responsible, capable—and, most importantly, *competent*—species. . . .

Reasons of Self-Interest

Why help the homeless? The most obvious reasons involve self-interest. Perhaps it is part of one's job to provide benefits, to create or sponsor social programs, to solve problems relating to homelessness. One might be motivated by concern over the public health problems that will inevitably result from growing populations of sick, homeless people packed into areas of already high density. One might be motivated by concern for the health of one's city's downtown business climate. Other concerns might include the potential harm to citizens of the community or to one's family at the hands of someone driven to desperation, the loss of easy use of parks and other public areas because they have been "taken over" by homeless people, the loss to society of the economic contribution that could be made by the homeless, and the general psychological damage done by a decline in the quality of the social environment. One might be motivated by genuine and deep feelings of compassion and charity ("It feels good to help"). Some might be seeking the appearance of charity for promotional purposes or to impress others.

What is it that causes some individuals and groups to feel a greater obligation to their fellow human beings and to the world as a whole? Since human beings have begun reflecting upon their own behavior and that of their social institutions, there have been many attempts to explain why people act altruistically, apparently counter to immediate self-interest, and also to explain the basis for the proliferation of moral codes that are so ingrained in human cultures. This is the study called ethics. . . .

The traditional religions, of course, provide ethical codes. Each school of philosophy develops its own ethical approach. Political party platforms have ethical underpinnings. The learned professions regulate themselves with ethical codes. Some businesses develop "corporate cultures" that include elements of ethical philosophy. There is also the plethora of service organizations, volunteer groups, youth groups, and clubs. Finally, there are grassroots sources of ethical attitudes, such as folk wisdom and street etiquette. Some of these ethical sources conflict or contradict one another, or simply represent alternative approaches and points of view. Some are internally inconsistent. Some are proud of their inconsistency. . . .

Biological Origins of Ethics

Biologists have identified two forms of altruistic behavior in nonhuman species that are readily recognizable as rudimentary possible bases for much of human ethical thought. The first is kinship altruism. Many species of animals act in ways apparently counter to self-interest, in order to protect or advance members of the family or group. Social animals have an inherent need for cooperative behavior patterns, and one way of achieving cooperation has been through developing a capacity to recognize and be concerned with the welfare of the closest genetic relatives. The closer the relationship, genetically, the greater the concern. The more refined the animal's apparatus of intuition and communication, the more forceful are these demands. . . .

Reciprocity is the other identified form of nonhuman altruistic behavior known to biologists. There are many examples of animals who act selflessly, in exchange for similar treatment. Monkeys take turns grooming each other. This behavior also arises out of the need for cooperation, and notions that cheating at a bargain is morally wrong would seem to have their origins in the development of reciprocal forms of altruistic behavior. The roots of this are, of course, deep in "the wiring," the nervous system.

Although many today may see the homeless as completely devoid of resources, and thus hardly candidates for mutually beneficial relationships with them, there are many direct reciprocal benefits from assisting the homeless and reclaiming them as social insiders. The abilities of all human beings to contribute to social and economic achievement are in fact incalculable. . . .

Ethics from Religions

Charitable acts are considered part of a good life in Jewish ethical and moral philosophy and tradition. In the Talmud, the section on the teachings of the rabbis begins with a passage called, simply, "Benevolence." Charity is viewed as a species of benevolence, but inherently inferior because it can only be practiced toward the poor, and the poor are deprived of practicing it themselves, whereas "benevolence" can be shown toward all people (true reciprocity?). . . .

Central to all of Christianity is the belief in the divinity of Jesus of Nazareth, and his role both as savior and teacher. Some of the most profound and broadly sweeping ethical propositions ever to have been set into language are found in Jesus' teachings, as contained in the New Testament. . . .

Charity is the supreme ethical imperative of Christianity. Christians are urged, without haughty judgments, to serve individual people and humanity selflessly, as symbolized by Jesus' washing the feet of his disciples, and by the parable of the Good Samaritan. Jimmy Carter once declared that, "We should live our lives as though Christ was coming this afternoon." How is it that people calling themselves Christians can sleep in houses with empty rooms while their fellow human beings, their *neighbors*, are sleeping on streets or in dumpsters? Christian charity insists on personal involvement.

Being a Neighbor to Street People

Jesus tells the parable of the man who was robbed and left by the side of the road. He was ignored by pious clergy and prominent laypeople who passed by on the other side of the street and was finally saved by a Samaritan, a member of a despised minority. The Samaritan picked up the wounded man, bandaged his wounds, took him to an inn and paid his bill until he recovered.

If this parable teaches us how to be a neighbor to those in need, aren't we flatly contradicting Christ's teaching when we walk by a street person? Aren't we being hypocrites if we claim to be Christians and yet fail to follow the example of the Good Samaritan? Either we are Good Samaritans or we aren't.

Of course, we might argue, we can't possibly help all the street people we pass. During an average half-hour walk in midtown Manhattan, it is not unusual to see a dozen street people all needing help of some kind. If we stopped to help every one of them, we would end up being full-time social workers.

In saying this, are we constructing an easy way out for ourselves? In the past year, I heard two sermons preached at the Episcopal Cathedral of St. John the Divine which claimed that we cannot simply pass by those who are suffering on the streets. One sermon even went so far as to say that we shouldn't just give the poor we encounter 50 cents or a dollar; we should "enter into dialogue" with the beleaguered souls. We should let them know of our concern, and like the Good Samaritan, help them on their way to a happier and more fruitful life.

J. Douglas Ousley, *The Christian Century*, January 3–10, 1990.

The central figure of Islam, the prophet Mohammed, was born in Mecca around the year 570. About 610 he had a vision of a being, later identified as the angel Gabriel, and he heard a voice saying to him, "You are the messenger of God." Thereafter, until his death, Mohammed received frequent revelations, which he and his followers believed came directly from God. He never heard a voice during the revelations, but rather found a message in his "heart." It is the collection of these messages that make up the Koran, the sacred writings of Islam. At the time of Mohammed Mecca was a rich trading city, and wealth was for the most part in the hands of a few merchants. Traditional tribal order was breaking down, and these merchants were viewed by Mohammed as ignoring their responsibilities to the less fortunate. These duties have traditionally been viewed as tribal obligations, but under Mohammed's new preaching such duties became divine edicts. . . .

Caring for Each Other

To be effective motivators we have to care genuinely about the people we are attempting to influence. It was said of Theodore Roosevelt that the more different someone was from him, the more interested in that person he became. Leaders must care with a deep passion to learn about the people around them, about their inevitably fascinating cultural backgrounds, social positions and perspectives, political views, and aesthetic tastes. To be an effective leader one must learn, responsibly, to touch people at their deepest moral cores, perhaps deeper than they (or we) have ever before had occasion to delve. No one gets to that point without presenting themselves openly, honestly, with love.

A simple ethic is that people ought to have a continuous state of truthfulness between each other (a condition without which paleolithic tribal members could not long survive, occupied as they were with the high teamwork of the Great Hunt and pitted against the surrounding elements). The second "at bottom" element I believe we owe each other is *acknowledgment* of each other. It helps if this is in a context of acknowledging our common humanity, our relatedness. I believe that there can be no ethics without these.

Ethical considerations are important because ethical ideas have power. The would-be recruiters to causes aiding the homeless must *live* a powerfully compelling ethic, or they court failure. Even so, life is inexorable and coercive. It rushes at us, demanding correct action before we have figured it all out. Humans are a familial and tribal species and as the veil lifts, slowly, from the mysteries of our ancient origins and our biology, what is being discovered on all sides is what we already know: we are one. What is being discovered is that we humans care, utterly. And we are also all capable of laziness and of elegantly lying about the fact of our caring.

"In the second decade of widespread and obvious homelessness, people are experiencing a kind of compassion fatigue."

Society Is Tired of Helping the Homeless

Isabel Wilkerson

After opening their hearts and wallets to the homeless since the 1980s, Americans see little change in the homeless situation, writes Isabel Wilkerson in the following viewpoint. She relates how Americans have become hardened to the plight of the homeless because it seems nothing has made a difference in their predicament. Wilkerson examines how cities, businesses, and individuals have begun to fight back against what they perceive as an intrusion by homeless people by banning panhandling and sleeping in public places and by lobbying to close homeless shelters. Nothing will change for the homeless, she concludes, until something is done about the root causes of homelessness—poverty, lack of affordable housing, and an economy that continues to eliminate well-paying jobs. Wilkerson won a Pulitzer prize in 1994 for feature writing. She is the bureau chief for the *New York Times* in Chicago, Illinois.

As you read, consider the following questions:

1. According to the author, what is so striking about Washington, D.C.'s decision to close shelters and reduce the number of beds in the remaining shelters?
2. What reasons are given for more closely regulating the homeless, according to Wilkerson?

Ten years after the wan face of homelessness first captured the nation's attention, empathy is turning to intolerance as cities impose harsher restrictions on homeless people to reduce their visibility or force them to go out on their own.

New York City, Santa Barbara, California, and a number of other cities are acting out of both frustration and desperation, pressed by hard times and by a public that has grown increasingly impatient with a problem that has worsened despite the programs aimed at relieving it and previous shows of good will.

"People want to help, but they don't want to feel that they're just being suckers," said Mayor Loni Hancock of Berkeley, California. "The cities that try to help get overrun and then comes the backlash. There comes a time when people want to step back and insulate themselves."

Cities Fight Back

Atlanta, preparing for the 1996 Olympic Games, passed a law in July 1991, authorizing the arrest of anyone loitering in abandoned buildings or engaging in "aggressive panhandling."

New York's transit authority has banned panhandling in the subway system and imposes a $50 fine on anyone caught doing so.

In Miami, where officials briefly considered shuffling several hundred homeless people off to a city-owned baseball stadium, panhandlers who approach motorists at intersections to wash car windows face a fine of as much as $500 and a jail sentence of as many as 60 days.

In August 1991, the District of Columbia closed two emergency shelters and announced plans to eliminate half the beds in its shelters. It also plans to severely restrict the number of nights that homeless people can stay in them. The city's tough new stance comes with strong public backing. A 1984 law required the city to shelter all in need; in the fall of 1990 the voters repealed it.

And in 1990 Santa Barbara banned homeless people from sleeping on public streets, beaches or sidewalks and in parking lots; the measure leaves them to sleep on a public lot filled with eucalyptus trees where they are out of sight of downtown boutiques.

Attitudes Are Hardening

Advocates for the homeless and city officials alike see these as signs that attitudes are hardening toward what became a badge of social responsibility in the 1980's when people could better afford to be magnanimous.

"People are a bit weary," said Mary Brosnahan, executive director of the Coalition for the Homeless, a New York advocacy group. "They have heard all the solutions for the last 10 years, but it doesn't seem to make a dent in the problem."

The world is a very different place than it was when homeless people were swept from Madison Square Garden in New York on the eve of the Democratic National Convention in 1980 in an incident that gave birth to a nationwide advocacy movement. That was before crises like AIDS and crack that competed for the nation's compassion even had names and before two recessions made life tougher for everybody.

In the early, naïve days of the homeless crisis, people pinned their hopes on the legions of soup kitchens and armories-turned-shelters to reduce the number of people sleeping in doorways and soliciting money on street corners. But the numbers only grew.

Compassion's Stores Are Empty

Now, in the second decade of widespread and obvious homelessness, people are experiencing a kind of compassion fatigue, as Mayor Hancock of Berkeley, calls it.

In that city, where tolerance is a religion, officials have taken steps to keep the homeless from abusing the public's generosity. In July, the city arranged for residents to buy vouchers from local merchants that they can give to homeless people instead of cash, which can all too easily be used for drugs or liquor. The vouchers are redeemed for things like food or laundry service.

No city officials contacted would say publicly that they were seeking to push the homeless aside. But all said they were feeling the public's impatience.

"In a sense, the fad is over with," said Paul Relman, acting president of Central Atlanta Progress, a business group that pushed the city to regulate the homeless. "I don't know if it's tolerance or it's, 'Let's just not see it anymore.'"

Statements like those especially disturb advocates. Such sentiments are taken as evidence that the public may be becoming inured to the sight of disheveled people pushing their life's possessions in a shopping cart or washing themselves on the sidewalk.

It is in this new and unforgiving climate that merchants and others are speaking out in ways that would have been considered blasphemous not long ago. At the urging of merchants in Santa Barbara, for example, one downtown plaza is being rebuilt to remove the seats, which they say invite the homeless.

"They Can Move On"

"Our goal is to make things as uncomfortable for them as we can so they can move on," said Pete Gherini, president of the Santa Barbara Chamber of Commerce. "When you look at these characters sitting out in the middle of the day when everybody else is working just to survive, you don't get a lot of sympathy."

Part of the problem, advocates say, is that career panhandlers have capitalized on sympathy for the homeless, confusing the two issues, and the careerists are now hard to distinguish from the downtrodden.

Whether on hustlers or the homeless, the city of Atlanta is bearing down and has made it a crime to solicit money in a way that causes a "reasonable person to fear bodily harm" or to panhandle "in close proximity" to a person who has said no.

"As long as you do it in a respectful way, where you're not threatening folk, it's O.K.," said Thomas Cuffie, an Atlanta City Council member who sponsored the measure.

"But once you go beyond that, badgering folk and making them feel you're going to do something to them if they do not give up some money to you, then that's when the person would have a right to bring a charge against you."

Reprinted by permission of Mike Luckovich and Creators Syndicate.

On the tiled sidewalks of downtown Santa Barbara, homeless people with shopping carts and backpacks walk briskly past the palms and bougainvillea, and they tend not to linger in front of the adobe-style storefronts. Many have been arrested for panhandling, public drinking or sleeping on public grounds. They move from one out-of-the-way lot to another at night fearing arrest and they say they feel the tide has turned against them.

"They're trying to run us out of here," said Paul Stellwag, one of the city's homeless. "It's getting worse and worse and worse. I can feel the animosity."

Mr. Stellwag says he believes that the hard time he and others are getting is because of the city's concern for tourism. And he resents it. "I don't give a flying hoot about the damn tourists," he said. "If they tried to help us, we wouldn't be here."

But there is widespread agreement that private generosity would not solve the problem. The main flaw in public policy, advocates say, is that emergency shelters and soup kitchens do nothing about the root causes of homelessness—poverty, lack of affordable housing and a changing economy that has eliminated entire classes of well-paying, low-skilled jobs. While these larger problems have intensified the plight of the disadvantaged, cities have tried to keep the patient comfortable, to the dissatisfaction of merchants, residents and advocates. . . .

Turnabout in Washington

There has been perhaps no greater turnabout than in Washington, where Mitch Snyder, a radical advocate for the homeless, helped to give homelessness national prominence as an issue. But a year after Mr. Snyder's death in 1990, and under the pressure of city budget deficits and a public change of heart, there appeared to be little room for sympathy.

Robert Moon says his compassion has turned to bitterness over the homeless shelter in his northwest neighborhood.

"There's gotten to be just too many of them in one area," said Mr. Moon, a military officer. "And after awhile, it's hard to feel sorry for them. It's made our neighborhood unlivable."

He and others lobbied the city to shut down the shelter. It was one of the two that was closed in August 1991.

"If persons meeting the criteria for involuntary detention . . . refuse to accept help, clinicians have no alternative but to pursue involuntary treatment."

Some of the Homeless Mentally Ill Should Be Treated Involuntarily

H. Richard Lamb

H. Richard Lamb argues in the following viewpoint that the mental health profession has a special obligation to help the homeless mentally ill. Lamb maintains that psychiatrists, social workers, and other mental health professionals can help erase the stigma of mental illness by providing housing alternatives and comprehensive treatment—involuntary treatment, if necessary—for the homeless mentally ill. He concludes it is better for the homeless mentally ill to receive less-than-ideal care and services than none at all. Lamb is a professor of psychiatry at the University of Southern California in Los Angeles.

As you read, consider the following questions:

1. What two important problems facing the homeless mentally ill are described by the author?
2. What reason does Lamb give for urging mental health professionals to accept less-than-ideal care and services for their homeless mentally ill patients?
3. What point of view should mental health professionals avoid taking, according to Lamb?

H. Richard Lamb, "Perspectives on Effective Advocacy for Homeless Mentally Ill Persons," *Hospital and Community Psychiatry*, vol. 43, no. 12 (December 1992). Copyright ©1992, the American Psychiatric Association. Reprinted by permission.

Alec Guinness, in his memorable role as a British Army colonel in *Bridge on the River Kwai*, exclaims at the end of the film when he finally realizes he has been working to help the enemy, "What have I done?" As a vocal advocate and spokesman for deinstitutionalization and community treatment of severely mentally ill patients for well over two decades, I often find myself asking that same question. Such concerns are raised constantly as I see evidence of the flawed way in which deinstitutionalization has been carried out and the ensuing monumental problems of homeless mentally ill persons and mentally ill persons in jail.

Some writers claim that the effects of deinstitutionalization on homelessness among mentally ill persons is minimal; they may be defining deinstitutionalization too narrowly by equating it solely with state hospital depopulation of long-term residents, thus leaving out the diversion of admissions to hospitals of a whole new generation of mentally ill persons. It is largely from this generation that members of the homeless mentally ill population are drawn.

Other observers have suggested that psychiatrists and other mental health professionals surely share responsibility for some aspects of homelessness among the chronically and severely mentally ill population. I agree that mental health professionals do bear a heavy responsibility for this situation. We therefore need to look at the unintended adverse consequences of our policies toward this population, just as we often find ourselves defending these policies in light of arguments to return to the practice of long-term hospitalization for all chronically and severely mentally ill persons.

At this time, however, there needs to be a pause in which everyone involved with the chronically and severely mentally ill population in general and homeless mentally ill persons in particular steps back, puts preconceived ideology aside, and tries to assess the current state of affairs, to understand how we got to where we are, and to decide what to do next. The kind of dialogue begun by such an assessment can be nothing but positive if mental health professionals and nonprofessionals step down from hardened and fortified positions and rethink the issues.

A Special Obligation

A number of issues need to be clarified. It is extremely important not to confuse the overall homeless population with the portion of the homeless population who are mentally ill—persons who are both homeless and have a major mental illness such as schizophrenia, schizoaffective disorder, bipolar disorder, or major depression. As citizens, we are, or should be, concerned about the homeless population generally. And as citizens, we have a responsibility for their welfare. But as psychiatrists and mental health professionals, we have expertise about mental illness that ordinary citizens do not have. Thus, we have a special obligation to do something about the plight of mentally ill persons who are homeless.

Further, homeless mentally ill persons constitute a subpopulation of the overall homeless population with special problems and special needs. Differentiating between the two groups is not just a semantic exercise. If we do not make this differentiation, we may confuse the issues and make inappropriate public policy recommendations. Different solutions must be targeted to different homeless subpopulations.

Surprisingly, an even more basic point—that mental illness does exist—still needs to be made to many who are involved with the homeless mentally ill population. A growing avalanche of evidence from modern psychiatric research has shown that the major mental illnesses are biologically based brain diseases. Those findings do not exclude a role for environmental stresses in precipitating acute exacerbations of illness, but they should put an end to denying the existence of mental illness and rationalizing it away as simply the result of the problems of our society.

Effective Advocacy

Are the homeless mentally ill affected by the pervasive reluctance in our society to grapple with social problems and the lack of resources of all kinds, including decent, affordable housing and universal access to health care? Of course they are. Persons who are least able to provide for themselves are the most vulnerable to the effects of any reduction in supports and programs. Compounding these problems is a grossly inadequate mental health system and, in the view of many, an undue concern for civil rights that has contributed to the erosion of needed protection and support for severely mentally ill persons.

Chronically and severely mentally ill people who suffer from cognitive and social deficits as a result of their illnesses and who are left to fend for themselves in the community are likely to be more profoundly affected by the overall problems of society and more in need of protection and services than other citizens. That does not mean, however, that we cannot effect meaningful change for chronically and severely mentally ill persons. By focusing on their specific needs for such services as supervised and supportive housing, case management, and sheltered employment, it may be possible to improve their level of functioning and improve their quality of life. Is this a realistic goal?

We have the example of the success of advocates for developmentally disabled persons. Mental illness and developmental disability have similarities and differences, as do advocacy efforts on behalf of those who suffer from the two kinds of conditions. Nevertheless, advocates for developmentally disabled persons recognize that they are dealing with a biologically based disability that makes those persons members of a special population with special needs. Although many advocates for developmentally disabled persons might wish to change society, in fact they usually focus their actions where they can be most effective—on influencing society to meet the specific needs of the population they represent.

Involuntary Treatment for Those Who Need It

As another possible step toward alleviating the problem of mentally ill homeless persons, involuntary or mandatory outpatient treatment has been recommended for those who meet the following criteria: high use of inpatient services, failure of status as a voluntary patient, acute need for treatment, available treatment modalities with a high likelihood of effectiveness, and expectation of further deterioration without treatment. These criteria would be added to the usual requirements of dangerousness and grave disability, but presumably these would be less intense than would be required for direct, involuntary commitment to a mental hospital. All plans assume that if the patient is uncooperative or violates the rules of the treatment program, he or she would be referred to the mental hospital without further due process. Statutory provisions for involuntary outpatient treatment now exist in about 20 states.

Milton Greenblatt in *Homelessness: A National Perspective*, edited by Marjorie J. Robertson and Milton Greenblatt, 1992.

The result? Regardless of the political party in power, the state of the economy, or the general attitude toward social programs, developmentally disabled persons are very well served in most jurisdictions. Their advocates are aggressive, knowledgeable about the disability, and relentless in their efforts. They have made a point of understanding the system and how to make it work to meet the specific needs of developmentally disabled persons. Why cannot the same be done for chronically and severely mentally ill persons in general and homeless mentally ill persons in particular if mental health professionals, together with the families of mentally ill persons, take a similar stance?

Ineffective Advocacy

Let us take an example of ineffective advocacy. In 1984, the American Psychiatric Association's first Task Force on the Homeless Mentally Ill made a series of recommendations for addressing the crisis of homelessness among chronically mentally ill persons. I believe these recommendations are as timely and applicable today as they were when they were written. Had they been implemented, they probably would have greatly reduced the prevalence of homelessness among persons who are severely and chronically disabled by major mental illnesses. However, today too little has been done to substantively address the problems of the great majority of homeless mentally ill persons.

Had a similar task force made recommendations to alleviate a major problem for the developmentally disabled population, their advocates surely would have worked tirelessly and effectively to have them implemented. Although these actions would help resolve only one of the multitude of problems facing our society, nevertheless something important and definitive would have been accomplished.

The 1984 task force regarded homelessness as but one symptom of the many problems besetting chronically mentally ill persons throughout the United States, and it called for a comprehensive and integrated system of mental health care that would address the underlying problems precipitating homelessness among mentally ill persons. Such a system of care would include high-quality psychiatric and medical services; an adequate number and range of supervised, supportive housing settings; a well-functioning system of clinically oriented case management; adequate, comprehensive, and accessible crisis intervention services, both in the community and in hospitals; less restrictive laws governing involuntary treatment; ongoing rehabilitative services; and consultation to community agencies and organizations that provide other essential services to homeless mentally ill populations. Moreover, such a system of care would have provided individually prescribed treatments and interventions designed to meet patients where they are, not where the mental health system would like them to be.

No Appreciable Improvement

In fact, some impressive efforts have been made. For instance, assertive outreach programs to homeless mentally ill persons in Washington, D.C., Chicago, and New York have combined effective clinical case management with, when necessary, involuntary hospitalization and treatment. Many other excellent programs could also be mentioned. Generally, however, the numbers served have been small compared with the total homeless mentally ill population, and the plight of this population as a whole is not appreciably better.

Nor has there been a concerted, large-scale, aggressive effort to place pressure on legislators, mental health administrators, and other influential citizens to address the specific needs of homeless mentally ill persons. Failure to implement the recommendations of the first task force on the homeless mentally ill led to the American Psychiatric Association's creating a second task force, which issued its report, *Treating the Homeless Mentally Ill*, in 1992. That report endorsed the first task force's recommendations and called for immediate interim action to alleviate the desperate situation of homeless mentally ill persons. These recommendations are discussed below.

Two Crucial Issues

The homeless mentally ill population has many problems, but two of the most important are the degree to which they have been stigmatized and the fact that they have been the focus of a polarized controversy in which hospital-based treatment has been pitted against community-based treatment.

Certainly we want to root out stigmatization of mentally ill persons, which has long been an ugly reality for those persons and their families. However, there is now an additional source of stigma, for what is more stigmatizing than the everyday sight of blatantly mentally ill homeless persons in torn filthy clothing using pathetic shopping bags and shopping carts to carry their meager possessions, eating out of garbage cans, and subject to other degradations that are part of life on the streets? Unfortunately, such sights have come to characterize mental illness in the minds of ordinary citizens. Surely, one of the most powerful actions we could take to fight stigma would be to help homeless mentally ill persons not to have to live on the streets.

Involuntary Treatment May Be Necessary

The issue of taking homeless, severely mentally ill persons to hospitals, voluntarily if possible, involuntarily if need be, also needs to be clarified. The second APA task force and others do not advocate long-term hospitalization as the general treatment for homeless mentally ill persons, although some of those persons may need such interventions. The criteria for emergency involuntary detention and observation in a psychiatric hospital vary in different states. In California, for example, the criteria are danger to self, danger to others, or grave disability (due to mental illness and an inability to provide for one's basic needs of food, clothing, and shelter). If a homeless person meets such criteria and is taken to a psychiatric hospital, how does that differ from what happens as almost a routine matter to any person who meets such criteria in psychiatric emergency rooms across the nation? That issue is hardly controversial.

Clinicians, family members, and policymakers would like all patients to be treated voluntarily. But if persons meeting the criteria for involuntary detention present themselves at a hospital or are brought to a hospital by family members, police, or a mobile psychiatric emergency team and then refuse to accept help, clinicians have no alternative but to pursue involuntary treatment. What better place to evaluate and stabilize a person who meets criteria for involuntary detention than an acute psychiatric hospital? After the person's condition is stabilized, the person and society are in a better position to decide what is needed next.

Less-Than-Ideal Services Are Better Than None

Facing up to the realities of solving the problems of the homeless mentally ill population has not been easy for mental health professionals. Not only do we feel uncomfortable with the idea (although usually not the practice) of involuntary treatment, we are also often unwilling to entertain the idea of providing services that are less than ideal—even if the ideal is clearly unattainable in the foreseeable future.

For instance, appropriate community-based living arrangements with on-site treatment capabilities must be made available to severely mentally ill patients who are discharged after inpatient treatment. Further, residential and treatment services for homeless mentally ill individuals should meet the same high standards of care as services needed for severely mentally ill individuals in general. However, how can we in good conscience condone leaving homeless mentally ill individuals to live a dangerous, chaotic, and deprived life on the streets while we wait for such standards to be developed and for the needed resources to be gathered? In the short run, we shall probably be compelled to settle for facilities and services that are acceptable, if less than ideal, even as we advocate for additional and better resources.

Homeless mentally ill persons who need the degree of care that only highly structured 24-hour facilities can provide should also receive the highest quality of care, and our hospitals and intermediate care facilities must be upgraded toward that end. Once again, however, we cannot wait until sufficient funds are available to provide ideal care. It is more humane to place persons in facilities whose charts and even staffing fall somewhat short of the highest accreditation standards than it is to leave these neglected human beings living on the streets.

The great majority of chronically and severely mentally ill persons are able to live in the community. While they are entitled to live in safe, high-quality residences such as the St. Francis Residence in New York City, it is apparent that the resources to provide such places to live do not currently exist for a substantial proportion of the homeless population. Although they are far less desirable, interim community living arrangements that are less than ideal will continue to provide the only residences for many of these persons. If such residences provide safe, decent physical surroundings and a caring professional staff, they are far preferable to living on the streets or in most temporary shelters. In the meantime, while working to provide services using resources that are currently available, we can and should mount an aggressive and focused campaign to mobilize support for increased funding to meet the needs of chronically and severely mentally ill persons in general and homeless mentally ill persons in particular.

Potential Pitfalls

Neglect of chronically and severely mentally ill persons has long been a characteristic of our society. Unfortunately, this neglect can be easily rationalized. Their plight can be attributed to social problems that affect all parts of society, and our task can be formulated as attempting to solve these basic problems of society. If mental health professionals accept this point of view, we will be attempting a task that is beyond our power and scope. Moreover, we will fail to concentrate our efforts, as advocates for developmentally disabled persons have done, and we will miss an opportunity to do something definitive to meet the special needs of chronically and severely mentally ill persons.

If we misunderstand the causes of stigma and do not realize that our failure to help homeless mentally ill persons has further stigmatized mentally ill persons in general, then the problem of stigma can only worsen. If we do not see mental illnesses as biologically based brain diseases that need special approaches, including biological, psychological, and social interventions, then we will fail to resolve the problems of the homeless mentally ill population.

Neglect of severely mentally ill persons can easily result from the actions and advocacy of well-intended persons. The time has come to put preconceived ideology aside. We must let what we learn from clinical experience determine our ideology and our actions rather than let preconceived ideology determine what we do with our patients. If we fail to to this, we will not be able to take a humane approach to helping homeless mentally ill persons.

"Protecting liberty and property from those who disrespect or destroy them ought to be the task of judges, juries, and prison guards, not psychiatrists."

The Homeless Mentally Ill Should Not Be Treated Involuntarily

Thomas Szasz

Thomas Szasz has been a leading critic of the psychiatric profession since the 1960s. In the following viewpoint, he argues that psychiatry is an illegitimate profession and that psychiatrists routinely coerce their patients into receiving unwanted and unnecessary treatments. He maintains that involuntary hospitalization violates the rights of the homeless mentally ill. Only those who break laws should be incarcerated, Szasz contends, and they should be dealt with by the criminal justice system, not the medical community. Szasz is the author of numerous books, including *The Myth of Mental Illness*, *Insanity: The Idea and Its Consequences*, and *Cruel Compassion*, from which this viewpoint is excerpted.

As you read, consider the following questions:

1. What justifications are used by the psychiatric profession to incarcerate and decarcerate mental patients, according to Szasz?
2. What characterizes the history of psychiatry, in the author's opinion?
3. According to Szasz, what personal and social needs are fulfilled by the mental health system?

Ever since individuals deemed to be insane were first incarcerated in madhouses, each new method of coercing them—from replacing chains with commitment laws, or exchanging camisoles for chemicals—has been romanticized as a reform and defined as a "patient liberation." Indeed, one of the most ironic features of psychiatric history is that the greatest oppressors of the mental patient—Philippe Pinel, Eugen Bleuler, Karl Menninger—are officially venerated as their most compassionate champions. In their zeal to diagnose and doctor madness, psychiatrists have tried everything except eschewing coercion and treating the patient as a responsible person. . . .

The justifications for incarcerating and decarcerating mental patients are mirror images of one another. The rationale for institutionalization is that the patient is so seriously ill he requires hospital treatment; his objection to hospitalization proves how sick he is and justifies confining him against his will. The rationale for deinstitutionalization is that protracted residence in the state mental hospital is so deleterious to the patient's welfare he must be released to the community; his objection to being discharged proves how sick he is and justifies drugging him against his will outside the hospital.

It is not possible to understand the ugliness of the policy of drugging and deinstitutionalization unless we recognize that, once more in the history of psychiatry, it is something psychiatrists have done to involuntary mental patients. In the past, psychiatrists used their power to imprison individuals in mental hospitals for life. Now they use their power to drug patients for life. . . .

The Cure Is Coercion

While the media celebrates the discovery of the chemical causes and cures of mental illnesses, psychiatrists and their allies are preoccupied with the politics of housing the chronic mental patient. On the face of it, housing people does not seem to be a medical procedure. Nor would it be accepted as a treatment unless it were tacitly understood that, in a psychiatric context, housing means incarceration. An October 26, 1989, editorial in the *New York Times*, titled "How to House the Mentally Ill," explains:

> Across the nation, the mentally ill living on the streets number in the hundreds of thousands. Many of them fear the public shelters now available but are too dysfunctional to take advantage of new cheap housing on their own. Mental health workers know how to get them off the street. . . . New York City now operates an outreach program empowered to hospitalize the homeless mentally ill, *even against their will*. [Emphasis added.]

Disenchantment with deinstitutionalization has prompted psychiatrists to renew their attack on their old foe, freedom. After criticizing my views, Paul Applebaum, an authority on legal psychiatry, states: "That freedom *per se* will not cure mental illness is evident from the abject condition of so many of the deinstitutionalized." Applebaum's assertion that freedom does not cure mental illness illustrates the cynicism with which he treats psychiatry's cardinal claim that mental illness is an illness. Freedom does not cure cancer or heart disease. Why, then, should we expect it to cure mental illness? Because if freedom does not cure mental illness, then we can use that fact to justify coercive psychiatric drugging and deinstitutionalization. Declares Applebaum:

> [We need] greater authority for the state to detain and treat the severely mentally ill for their own benefit, even if they pose no immediate threat to their lives or those of others. . . . Our intervention, though depriving them of the right to autonomy in the short term, may enhance that quality in the long run. In such circumstances, benevolence and autonomy are no longer antagonistic principles.

H. Richard Lamb, a prominent advocate for the coercive psychiatric treatment of the homeless, takes this argument a step further. He maintains that certain mental patients have a right to be deprived of their rights:

> Many homeless mentally ill persons will not accept services even with assertive outreach case management. . . . If homeless persons with major mental illnesses are incompetent to make decisions with regard to accepting treatment . . . then outreach teams including psychiatrists should bring all of these patients to hospitals, involuntarily if need be. . . . These persons have *a right to involuntary treatment.* . . . A very important right that I believe needs to be recognized. [Emphasis added.]

Along with psychiatrists, conservative and liberal social observers alike have also rediscovered the charms of the old psychiatric plantations. James Q. Wilson declares: "Take back the streets. Begin by reinstitutionalizing the mentally ill." Charles Krauthammer agrees: "Getting the homeless mentally ill off the streets is an exercise in morality, not aesthetics. . . . Most of the homeless mentally ill . . . are grateful for a safe and warm hospital bed." But if they are grateful, why do they have to be coerced? Remarking on the plight of the "solitary homeless persons who live on the streets," George Will opines: "Most are mentally ill." How does he know? He knows, because "many were in institutions.". . .

A Cyclical Pattern

The history of psychiatry, unlike the history of medicine, exhibits a distinctive pattern of cycles of patient abuse and institutional reform. Each cycle is characterized by the psychiatrist's staunch claim that he is a genuine medical healer, that his involuntary subjects are sick patients, that the buildings in which the subjects are imprisoned are hospitals, and that the inmates' detention and subjection constitute medical treatments.

The cycles begin with the confinement of the insane in private madhouses. Soon, their proprietors are accused of incarcerating sane persons. The abuse is attributed to the profit motive. The solution is the public madhouse system, managed by physicians on the public payroll, supervised by authorities accountable to the public.

Once established, the public mental hospital system turns out to be a method for warehousing society's undesirables. Its managers and staff are even more corrupt and sadistic than the keepers of private madhouses had been. The problem is attributed to insufficient funding and inadequate doctors. The solution is spending more money on psychiatry and more time on training psychiatrists.

Psychiatry's True Purpose

The institution of psychiatry—epitomized by the practice of incarcerating persons innocent of crimes in buildings deceptively called 'hospitals'—has always been dangerous to the welfare of its inmates. It has never been the purpose of psychiatry to help the inmates rendered powerless by psychiatric imprisonment. Psychiatry's aim has always been, and still is, to help a relatively more powerful person—primarily the denominated patient's parent, spouse, or other relative—by disqualifying his less powerful kin whose behavior troubles him as 'troubled,' which is to say mad, and by incarcerating the victim defined as a 'patient' in a madhouse.

Thomas Szasz in *Madness, Heresy and the Rumor of Angels*, by Seth Farber, 1993.

Meanwhile, mental hospitals multiply and flourish. Psychiatrists claim therapeutic success for one new intervention after another. Mental patients are subjected to bleeding, cupping, tranquilizing chairs, ice-cold showers, threats of drowning, and other sadistic measures. After a few decades, the treatments are rejected as useless or harmful.

Toward the end of the nineteenth century, genetic explanations of diseases become fashionable. Psychiatrists declare that earlier therapeutic enthusiasms were naive and misplaced. Insanity is an incurable, hereditary disease. Once a person is insane, he is destined to remain so for the rest of his life. The prominent psychiatrists of this era, exemplified by Emil Kraepelin, do not pretend to cure their patients. Instead, they model themselves after the pioneering pathologists who studied cadavers and classified diseases. In short, the great state hospital psychiatrists were nosologists [those who study diseases]. They studied living corpses, called chronic mental patients, and classified their alleged diseases, creating mythological entities such as dementia praecox, manic-depressive illness, paranoia, and schizophrenia. Almost a century ago, psychiatry's most celebrated madman, Judge Paul Schreber, faulted his psychiatrist, the famous German psychiatrist Paul Flechsig, for focusing on diseases rather than persons. In his *Memoirs* Schreber wrote: "[Flechsig] *did not understand the living human being* and had no need to understand him, because . . . he dealt only with corpses."

Psychiatry Expands Its Reach

During the nineteenth century, society opened a second front in its war against mental illness. Psychiatrists and jurists joined forces and expanded the hitherto limited scope of civil commitment and the insanity defense. Coerced psychiatric examinations and psychological testing were introduced into every nook and cranny of the social fabric, from schools to divorce courts. The closer the alliance of psychiatry with the law and with education grew, the more indispensable coerced psychiatric interventions seemed to become.

After World War I, medical scientists made rapid advances in controlling infectious and metabolic diseases, notably the contagious diseases of childhood and diabetes. Psychiatrists imitated these discoveries by introducing into the practice of psychiatry so-called somatic treatments, such as insulin coma, convulsions caused by metrazol and electricity, and lobotomy.

And so we arrive at the present scene, drugs and deinstitutionalization. Once again, politicians and psychiatrists clamor for mental health reforms. Now they claim that the patients are sicker than we thought they were; that mental illness makes them refuse to take the medications that make their maladies manageable; that the drugs previously hailed as having revolutionized the treatment of chronic mental illness are, in the words of Alan Breier, "ineffective or inadequate for as many as 60 to 80 percent of the patients"; that it was a mistake to give mental patients freedom, which they only abuse by not taking the drugs that keep them sane and law abiding. The reforms proposed are predictable: More money for mental health programs and for research on new psychiatric drugs; more legal and medical control of mental patients; more mental health education to teach the truth about mental illness. . . .

A Constant Theme

Nevertheless, psychiatry and the media continue to bedazzle a public eager to believe in the impersonal nature and miraculous cures of mental illness. For more than two hundred years, the scenario conveying this theme has remained constant, with appropriate modernizations of the actors' lines. It is a story of the imprisoned patient's coerced validation of himself as a mentally ill patient, of those who imprison him as physicians, and of his prison as a hospital. In the past, the patient had to play his part by submitting to insulin shock, electroshock, and lobotomy. Today, he must play it by ingesting toxic chemicals called "antipsychotic drug treatment," participating in periodic meetings called "group therapy," or going through the hoops of some other performance scripted by the psychiatrists. The observer sees people called "patients" ingesting antipsychotic drugs and participating in group therapy, and is misled into believing that he is witnessing the cure of the sick. In fact, he is witnessing a medical-social ritual, the providers of homes for the homeless disguising the banality of their enterprise as proof of the powers of psychiatry. . . .

Reform Versus Abolition

The so-called mentally ill homeless person illustrates the problem the chronic mental patient poses in and to American society today. The issue is epitomized by the case of the legendary New York City bag lady, Joyce Brown, a.k.a. Billie Boggs, who had camped in front of an upper East Side ice cream shop, urinated and defecated on the street, and thus injured nearby business proprietors and passersby in their property rights. Commenting on the Brown case, Carl Horowitz, a scholar at the Heritage Foundation, begins by writing eloquently about the need to restore respect for property rights in contemporary American society. Blind to psychiatry's hostility to those very rights, he thus actually seeks the better protection of our besieged property rights through greater reliance on the use of psychiatric sanctions. Horowitz emphasizes that Brown's behavior was deliberately disruptive, describes how the city's mental health bureaucracy "removed her from the street and placed her into a hospital for her own safety," castigates the New York Civil Liberties Union and the judge who heard her protest against psychiatric imprisonment for freeing her, and then concludes: "The legal system granted more rights to a demented derelict than to property-holding entrepreneurs harmed by her." This is wrong and wrong-headed. Joyce Brown was not demented; she knew what she was doing and, as a reward for her exploits, was invited to lecture at Harvard Law School. Also, Horowitz knows, or ought to know, that Brown was not committed "for her own safety," but for the benefit of the community; and he is mistaken in stating that Brown was "granted rights." Our legal system does not grant adults a right to liberty, because they already possess that right; it only revokes the right to liberty (for certain offenses) or restores it (if the deprivation did not conform to due process).

I cite the Brown case because it illustrates our collective enthusiasm for avoiding the use of the criminal justice system as a means of controlling a large class of lawbreakers, many of whom commit crimes against both property and persons. In view of this, it is especially ironic that Horowitz ends his comments on the Brown case with this reminder: "As Ludwig von Mises recognized, where civil behavior cannot be defined or enforced, liberty and property are easily destroyed." Precisely. But protecting liberty and property from those who disrespect or destroy them ought to be the task of judges, juries, and prison guards, not psychiatrists, psychologists, and social workers. And the means of enforcing such protection should be the criminal justice system, not the mental health system. . . .

Coercive psychiatry cannot be reformed. Moreover, hardly anyone now wants to abolish it. People are so accustomed to subjecting others, and also themselves being subjected, to coercive psychiatric interventions that they cannot contemplate living without such meddling. Abandoning the illusory safety net of psychiatric sanctions would, indeed, require difficult personal and social readjustments.

The mental hospital system endures because it fulfills important personal and social needs. It segregates and supports adult dependents—who embarrass, burden, and disturb their families and the community. It incarcerates and incapacitates troublesome lawbreakers—who embarrass, burden, and disturb the judicial and penal systems. And, most importantly, it performs these functions by means of civil law sanctions—in a manner that pleases and pacifies the consciences of politicians, professionals, and the majority of the people. Hence, not only is there no popular interest in abolishing involuntary psychiatric interventions, but, on the contrary, there is intense pressure—especially from the parents of mental patients, the judiciary, and the media—to reinforce the institution of psychiatry.

"Mentally ill tenants who do not receive treatment are at great risk of getting evicted from their apartments or simply walking away from them and becoming homeless once again."

The Homeless Mentally Ill Should Receive Community Treatment

Sally Satel

The Interagency Council on the Homeless released a report in March 1994 detailing the Clinton administration's official policy on homelessness. In the following viewpoint, Sally Satel examines the report's response to the homeless mentally ill. Although the report recognizes the seriousness of homelessness among the mentally ill, she maintains, its recommendations focus on housing, not treatment. But without treatment, she contends, the mentally ill are likely to be evicted from or simply leave their homes. Satel is an assistant professor of psychiatry at Yale University School of Medicine in New Haven, Connecticut, and was a 1993–94 Robert Wood Johnson Health Policy Fellow.

As you read, consider the following questions:

1. Why does the administration's plan to reduce homelessness focus so little on treatment for the homeless mentally ill, in the author's opinion?
2. What treatment options are available to the mentally ill, according to the author?

On a November night in 1993 a 43-year-old mentally ill homeless woman named Yetta Adams died on a bench across the street from the Department of Housing and Urban Development in Washington, D.C. Earlier that day administration officials had been hunkered down in the HUD building, writing Bill Clinton's policy on homelessness. Although the tragic coincidence did not go unnoticed, its lessons did. The government's proposal, *Priority Home!—The Federal Plan to Break the Cycle of Homelessness*, still leaves many homeless people out in the cold.

The problem with the 126-page plan is that it doubles the HUD housing budget, from $823 million to $1.7 billion per year, but doesn't increase the $50 million the Department of Health and Human Services [HHS] devotes to treatment services for the mentally ill homeless, such as psychiatric care, intensive case management and on-site supervision. While housing is key to getting people off the street, mentally ill tenants who do not receive treatment are at great risk of getting evicted from their apartments or simply walking away from them and becoming homeless once again.

Why So Little Treatment?

The administration recognizes the seriousness of this issue. According to government estimates, 200,000 homeless people—about one-third of a nightly homeless count—are mentally ill; about half of them use drugs or alcohol. The administration also talks of forging "linkages" between housing and mental health services. So why does *Priority Home!* offer so little treatment? Perhaps because the group that wrote the plan, the Interagency Council on the Homeless—a coordinating body for federal agencies—is dominated by HUD. It is financed by HUD, its chairman is the HUD secretary and its office is located in the HUD building. No wonder *Priority Home!* is fixated on housing.

Also, the council assumed that universal coverage would be enacted through the president's Health Security Act and that the mentally ill homeless would get the same Health Security Cards as the rest of us. Of course, no such coverage is likely to pass Congress anytime soon. Even if it did, it wouldn't help the homeless negotiate the red tape involved in obtaining the cards. Moreover, the act's benefit package would not cover long-term psychiatric care until the year 2001.

While waiting for the millennium, the plan would have the mentally ill homeless receive care from mainstream public mental health and substance abuse programs. But not only are these treatment sources inadequate for this special population, they are overflowing. According to the Center for Mental Health Services, thirty states have acknowledged that they can serve only 40 percent of their severely mentally ill residents in community mental health centers. Without greater financing, they couldn't possibly absorb all the mentally ill homeless.

"Bundling" Treatment with Services

Most homeless people with severe mental illnesses can be treated effectively in the community on an outpatient basis. However, because severe mental disorders tend to be long-lasting or recurrent, people with these disorders need ongoing treatment to lessen the symptoms, impairments, and disruptions they produce. For a variety of reasons—including active avoidance of traditional treatments by some individuals as well as resistance by some caregivers to dealing with certain difficult clients—the treatment needs of the homeless mentally ill population are largely unmet. In addition, unlike shelter, food, and other fundamental necessities, treatment of mental illness often is not high on their list of priorities. Thus, it has been suggested that treatment of mental illnesses be "bundled" with (but not a prerequisite for) other basic services that address immediate needs for daily living.

Federal Task Force on Homelessness and Severe Mental Illness, *USA Today*, March 1994.

This mismatch between what *Priority Home!* says and what it does also may reflect a larger confusion about the relationship between mental illness and homelessness. In the early 1980s psychosis and severe depression were said to be responses to the stress of street life. While this notion has lost popular support, some still subscribe to it, believing the logical remedy is housing—not services. Today, it is generally accepted that mental illnesses such as schizophrenia or manic depression are not caused by homelessness. And while mentally ill people can become homeless because of poverty and alienation, mental instability makes it even more likely. This is why treatment must accompany housing.

What kind of treatment? That depends on one's condition. The hard-core mentally ill homeless, who make up an estimated 5 percent of the total homeless population, cannot be treated in the community; they need to be institutionalized. An example is Larry Hogue, New York City's "Wild Man of Ninety-Sixth Street." For years 50-year-old Hogue smoked crack and terrorized residents of the Upper West Side. After many trips to the emergency room and jail, he was finally sent, against his will, to a state mental hospital. Homeless people who are threats to themselves, such as Yetta Adams, also require forcible treatment. A schizophrenic substance abuser, Adams was "gravely disabled"—unable even to secure food, clothing and medical care. Why was nothing done? Washington, D.C., does not permit forced institutionalization of the gravely disabled.

For the rest of the mentally ill homeless, one approach is placement in a hotel-like building with small private rooms. Some psychiatric professionals believe this option, Single Room Occupancy, is viable, as long as mentally ill occupants visit their local mental health clinic regularly. The administration seems to agree. *Priority Home!* worries about our inability to accommodate the mentally ill homeless in the community and calls for more "low-demand, non-threatening housing alternatives"—i.e., more SROs.

Yet others believe SROs are too unstructured. They prefer an intensive community-based approach known as Assertive Community Treatment. This strategy begins with outreach workers combing cities to persuade the mentally ill homeless to accept a brief psychiatric hospitalization designed to stabilize, detoxify and diagnose them. Next comes placement in housing staffed by mental health professionals. Residents are assigned case managers, who assess clinical needs, work with a psychiatrist in the community, instill abstinence and teach patients how to manage on their own. Medication is given in a long-lasting injectable form, so noncompliance is less of a problem.

Community Treatment

Community treatment has been perfected since 1979 by clinicians who treat schizophrenic patients. It has been tested in Baltimore, New York, St. Louis and other major cities, where it reduced the number of days individuals stay in jail, on the street and in the hospital. Despite the programs' success, however, less than half of HHS's treatment program for the mentally ill homeless goes for case management services. Admittedly, the process is expensive: the cost of coordinated mental health treatment is $8,000 or more per person annually. Yet the administration plans to spend only one-tenth of that on treatment. Even with contributions from state and local governments and not-for-profit groups, more federal resources are needed—at the very least, a proportionate increase in treatment services to match the expansion in housing. . . .

While HUD reauthorization bills allow states to spend part of their financing for treatment, they aren't obligated to—and that's too bad. All the housing in Washington wouldn't have helped Yetta Adams. She needed intensive psychiatric care. On the night she died, a home was not a priority for her.

"Before the 'right to shelter' was litigated in New York, there was little public debate about homelessness."

The Legal System Can Help the Homeless

Gary Blasi and James Preis

In the following viewpoint, Gary Blasi and James Preis examine the role of litigation in easing the plight of the homeless. Legal challenges have established homelessness as a status, not a crime, they write; and litigation has made it easier for the homeless to get shelter in some major cities. Blasi and Preis maintain that while lawyers must advocate for systemic changes to help the homeless, they must also advocate for homeless individuals. Blasi is a law professor with Loyola Law School in Los Angeles, California. Preis is the executive director of Mental Health Advocacy Services in Los Angeles.

As you read, consider the following questions:

1. What is the common-law defense of necessity, and how does it apply to the homeless, according to the authors?
2. What is the importance of the *Callahan v. Carey* case, in the opinion of Blasi and Preis?
3. What are the limits and dangers of using litigation to address the needs of the homeless, in the authors' views?

Excerpted from Gary Blasi and James Preis, "Litigation on Behalf of the Homeless," in *Homelessness: A National Perspective*, edited by Marjorie J. Robertson and Milton Greenblatt, ©1992 by Plenum Press. Reprinted by permission of Plenum Press and the authors.

According to the Department of Housing and Urban Development, Los Angeles has more homeless people than any other community in America. Between 1983 and 1987, largely in response to litigation against the Los Angeles County government, the number of shelter beds available to the homeless was expanded significantly in both the public and the private sectors. Yet in the winter of 1987, the city government confronted the fact that thousands of people were still sleeping on the streets and that many were dying there. After a spate of unfavorable publicity, the city quickly opened 1,000 shelter beds in the heart of Los Angeles. As the cold weather subsided, however, these beds were eliminated and were replaced by self-help shelters, shantytowns, and "cardboard condos" erected on city sidewalks.

Yielding to pressure from the business association in the area, the city moved to demolish these shantytowns. The demolitions were slowed for a time by court actions, but eventually the decision was made to use the police to solve the problems. The homeless would be arrested if they did not move from the streets. Again, following an outburst of publicity and further legal action, the city created the "urban campground," known by its residents as "New Soweto," "Camp Dirt," or just "the camp." Now the police could offer an alternative to the homeless: Go to jail or go to the camp. The camp filled quickly and people were turned away.

Even though the policy failures evident in the camp are balanced in Los Angeles by some truly exemplary shelters and transitional housing projects, the camp serves as a reminder of the limits of advocacy and litigation on behalf of the homeless. Our purpose here is to inform a larger discussion about homelessness in America with some insights from the perspective of lawyers and advocates, gleaned by hard experience in Los Angeles and elsewhere. For whatever its limits, the legal system has occupied a peculiarly central place in public debate and decision making about homelessness. It is no accident that New York City has the dual distinction of being the first site of homelessness litigation and the city with the largest emergency shelter system in the United States. Indeed, one could argue that before the "right to shelter" was litigated in New York, there was little public debate about homelessness at all. In cities across America, the homeless and their advocates have turned to the courts for redress, with varying degrees of success.

The Law and the Homeless

In order to understand fully the role of the law in dealing with homelessness, one must understand the role of our laws in American society as a whole. First and foremost, the law is a mechanism of social control, a method of controlling behavior regarded as deviant. Thus the experience of many individual shelterless people with the law has come in the form of police action enforcing some local ordinance. For example, laws against "vagrancy" have existed for hundreds of years. Such laws typically make destitution a penal offense.

Not until 1962 did the United States Supreme Court declare that such crimes of status could not be applied constitutionally. The Court held that the states and localities could not criminalize the status of being ill or poor. In place of vague vagrancy statutes came ordinances that criminalized not the status of poverty or homelessness itself but the inevitable manifestations of poverty and homelessness. For example, although it is not a crime in Los Angeles to be homeless, it is a crime to sleep on a sidewalk or in any other public place, to have one's possessions on the street, to sleep in a car, or to sleep at a bus stop.

As a result, a great deal of legal effort has been made merely to prevent the incarceration of people whose primary offense is lack of funds for housing. In Los Angeles, criminal prosecutions for sleeping in a vehicle and for trespass have been defended successfully with the common-law defense of necessity. This defense has roots deep in ancient common law; it codifies the commonsense notion that people sometimes may break the law in order to avoid a greater harm. Thus one who breaks into a building to put out a fire is not guilty of breaking and entering. As applied to homeless persons, the necessity defense means that it is not a crime to sleep in a vehicle or on another person's land if there are no reasonable alternatives. In recognition of this fact, Los Angeles officials constructed the urban camp described earlier in order to continue police raids on homeless people's encampments because the camp was the legal alternative that deprived the homeless of the necessity defense.

Even where homelessness has not been criminalized, public officials have sought to treat homeless persons as less than full citizens. For example, the homeless often have been denied the right to vote. Here litigation has been successful in restoring the franchise to the homeless poor.

The Right to Shelter

Much of the legal activity on behalf of homeless persons has been categorized as "right-to-shelter" litigation. Such litigation has been based on state or local laws, primarily because the United States Supreme Court held in 1974 that there was no federal right to housing and by implication no right even to emergency shelter. Indeed, there is a very long tradition in American law that "rights" consist mainly of the right to be free of government interference. The notion that a person also might have a right to survive is alien to most American law, even though the United States is signatory to several international treaties and accords that recognize such rights.

In the context of specific statutes, however, the situation may be different. In New York, homeless persons may be said to have "right to shelter" by virtue of the decree in the *Callahan v. Carey* case. In fact, the order in the *Callahan* case was notable not so much because of the right it created for homeless persons but because of the obligations it imposed on the City of New York. Those obligations consisted of the duty not to turn away any homeless person from the city's long-standing municipal shelters and of the duty to maintain those shelters in accord with certain minimal conditions. . . .

Litigation in Los Angeles

Litigation challenging the failure of safety net programs to provide food and shelter to homeless persons has focused predominantly on two issues: access and adequacy. A series of cases brought in Los Angeles County by the Homeless Litigation Team [a group of lawyers and legal workers from eight public-interest law firms] demonstrates how these issues were attacked in Los Angeles's general assistance program, referred to as General Relief.

As part of the General Relief program, the County of Los Angeles provided an emergency shelter system, which ostensibly issued hotel vouchers to any homeless applicant who needed assistance. While thousands of homeless people lived on the street, hundreds of voucher hotel rooms went unoccupied. Investigation of this phenomenon pinpointed two practices by the county that had the effect of keeping homeless people out of the emergency shelter system and therefore out of the General Relief system itself.

First, in order to receive an emergency shelter voucher, an applicant was required to provide a certified birth certificate or a driver's license. Yet because of the high rate of victimization and the transient nature of homelessness, such identification often was lost or stolen. As a result, individuals in immediate need of shelter were left on the street. The identification requirements also were used to fine-tune the emergency shelter caseload. In winter, when demand for shelter was high, the identification requirements were enforced strictly; in summer, when demand slackened, lesser forms of identification were accepted.

In addition to the identification requirements, the county controlled the number of persons who received emergency shelter vouchers by establishing daily quotas for the number of persons they would assist with General Relief. If a homeless person sought assistance after the quota was reached, he or she was told to return on another day. In the first case brought by the

Homeless Litigation Team, the court found both practices to be inconsistent with the county's statutory obligation to "relieve and support" the indigent and the disabled.

Other Barriers

Other bureaucratic barriers often are created to control approved caseloads and ultimately to protect the amount of funds spent by counties on general assistance programs. Perhaps the most absurd is the requirement that one have an address before he or she can qualify for assistance. Thus homeless people are denied assistance because they have no address; yet it is impossible to pay rent and to establish an address without assistance. Courts at times have struck down address requirements and at other times have upheld them as necessary to control fraud. In Los Angeles County no litigation was necessary in this area because no address was required for participation in the emergency shelter program; in turn, the shelter provided an address for receiving the General Relief grant.

Litigation was pursued, however, challenging as a barrier to General Relief the extremely complex, convoluted application and intake process itself. In that case the judge approved a county plan that provided for special assistance to individuals identified as mentally or developmentally disabled. The county promised to provide individual help to such disabled applicants in maneuvering through the myriad forms and the countless outside appointments required in order to obtain General Relief. The complex nature of the application process presented mentally disabled homeless persons with as insurmountable an obstacle as does a stairway to paraplegics. Because Los Angeles County received federal funds in its welfare system, such a barrier was in violation of Section 504 of the Federal Rehabilitation Act of 1973 and similar state laws prohibiting discrimination on the basis of handicap.

Even for individuals in Los Angeles who are able to surmount the numerous obstacles and eventually to qualify for General Relief, a final barrier to assistance has been created in the form of a "60-day penalty," which prohibits persons who have been terminated from General Relief from reapplying for assistance within 2 months of termination. This penalty is imposed on individuals for being late to their work projects, failing to turn in a form on time, or failing to document the required 20 job searches per month. Approximately 2,500 people per month are terminated and are given a 60-day penalty. This penalty was challenged by the Homeless Litigation Team on both procedural and substantive law grounds. The procedural challenge resulted in new regulations requiring that violations of General Relief rules be "willful" before the county can impose sanctions. . . .

In addition to focusing on process requirements that restrict the number of persons allowed on general assistance, it also was necessary to challenge the adequacy of the program for those receiving benefits. Inadequate benefits and uninhabitable voucher hotels are as much a deterrent to general assistance as are access barriers. Indigent individuals may prefer to remain on the street rather than giving up their privacy in a county-sponsored poorhouse. For homeless individuals a shelter that does not meet minimal standards of cleanliness, warmth, space, and rudimentary conveniences is no shelter at all.

Four Categories of Litigation

When case law on the rights of the homeless is examined in some detail, Linda S. Dakin finds that the litigation and pending litigation surrounding particular cases could be separated into four categories:

> litigation that attempts to draw attention to the plight of the homeless through public protest; litigation that attempts to obtain rights to short-term emergency shelter for the homeless; litigation that attempts to prevent specific placement of shelters and other facilities for the homeless; and litigation aimed at requiring states and the federal government to eliminate structural causes of homelessness.

The point is that no single legal strategy can adequately begin to reach all the subpopulation groups of homeless people and the multiple levels of homelessness causation. With this in mind, litigation strategies have employed a series of actions in both state and federal courts; some attempting to meet the short-term needs of the homeless and some attempting to make long-term changes that would prevent homelessness in the first place.

Gregg Barak, *Gimme Shelter*, 1991.

In Los Angeles, clients felt that the voucher hotels were more dangerous and more unsanitary than the streets, parks, and alleyways in which they slept. Litigation challenging the conditions in these hotels has led to a requirement that heat be provided in all voucher hotels in the winter and to an agreement that specific hotels be brought into compliance with all applicable housing, building, fire, health, and safety codes. Even for those willing to live in skid row hotels, the total amount of their General Relief grant would not cover an entire month's rent. Consequently, individuals who had to spend some of their grant on food would find themselves unable to pay the rent toward the end of the month. Thus many people lived on the street at least part of every month. Litigation of these issues led to a settlement increasing the General Relief housing allowance over a 2-year period. . . .

Individual Advocacy and Systemic Change

The role of lawyers is to represent clients. Sometimes that role consists of the relationship between two people: the client and the lawyer. Often the lawyer is called upon to represent a group of clients, although he or she may have contact with only a few of the group members. Most of the publicized work of lawyers on behalf of the homeless, however, has been of the latter type: class actions and other legal efforts to cause systemic change beneficial to people who are homeless. Yet throughout the United States, individual attorneys and legal services work daily to resolve the specific problems of individual homeless clients without attempting to change the system in which those clients find themselves. In the vernacular, these are known as "service" cases. Although this work seldom is recognized in the media, it is absolutely essential for two reasons.

First, without individual advocacy, many homeless people might die while waiting for the systemic change. People interacting with the bureaucracies ostensibly established to aid the poor already have considerable rights—on paper. Yet without advocates who know the often Byzantine regulations that govern such programs and who can deal socially and politically with the bureaucrats who implement such rules, the poor in general and the homeless in particular frequently are deprived in practice of those rights granted to them on paper. Indeed, this fact makes individual advocacy essential for a second reason: Without it, the results achieved in court and on paper regarding such systems are likely to be purely theoretical and abstract. It is not what happens in court that determines whether the poor and the homeless win in litigation; it is what happens in the streets and the welfare office waiting rooms.

Approaches to Systemic Advocacy

In any careful approach to whether and how the suffering of homeless people may be alleviated through legal action, one must begin with an understanding of the place of the legal system in our political structure. Whatever we are taught in civics classes, it is not some abstract notion of justice that is dispensed in our courtrooms. Conservative rhetoric to the contrary, virtually every judge in America sees himself or herself as an interpreter of rules made by the political departments of the government, not as a maker of rules. Only within the framework of those accepted juridical principles may significant differences exist between judges of different backgrounds or social perspectives.

186

Moreover, to the extent that what advocates seek is complex or requires intervention or supervision over time, all judges are reluctant to become involved. Judges do not want to operate the welfare system. By contrast, if the judge can achieve a significant result merely by ordering the government to cease doing something, a favorable result is much more likely. In general, then, it is not enough to demonstrate to a judge that something is wrong; lawyers also must demonstrate that the judge can do something practical about it, something supported by the laws enacted by the political departments of government.

Homeless Litigation

Some examples may illustrate these principles. The first piece of "homeless litigation," *Callahan v. Carey,* often is called a "right to shelter" suit. In fact, however, the court in Carey ordered the City of New York to cease turning people away from the men's shelters that had long existed in New York. A later settlement presented in great detail the conditions of the shelters and other points. It is very important to note that both by law and in practice, New York already had a shelter system of sorts; the city, however, was turning people away from the shelters, and the shelters were such miserable places that many people preferred to risk sleeping on the streets. Similarly, in *Eisenheim v. Board of Supervisors,* the first "homeless litigation" in Los Angeles, the situation that was challenged was not the lack of any shelter system for homeless people but the mechanisms that kept people out of that shelter system.

In communities where a public shelter system is nonexistent, advocates face a much tougher challenge. As noted earlier, it is much easier to persuade a judge to order local officials to cease turning people away from shelter than to persuade a judge to order the creation of an entirely new system. In such a case, significant concrete results may be obtained by the way of settlement and political pressures that flow from a lawsuit. In St. Louis, for example, a suit was brought on an ancient statute requiring the county to care for the poor. Such statutes exist in most American jurisdictions, although local government may observe them primarily in the breach. If such a case proceeds to trial or appeals, the most that is likely to be achieved in court in such a case is an order requiring some abstract recognition that the homeless should be sheltered by someone. As occurred in St. Louis, however, the case can serve as a framework for achieving an enforceable settlement.

In any event, obtaining recognition of the abstract right of the poor to be cared for by someone in particular may be an important first step, particularly toward creating a shelter system where one has not existed before. The nature and the scope of such a shelter system can be the focus of later advocacy activities. As noted earlier, even mandatory, sweeping orders issued from the courthouse may have no effect at all on the streets and in the alleys of the community unless the advocacy community is prepared to reach out to homeless people and to advocate for their individual rights. . . .

Limits and Dangers of Litigation

There are many approaches to litigation and advocacy on behalf of the homeless. No one experience is translated easily to another community, but attorneys and advocates hope that they have learned both from their mistakes and from their successes.

On another level, it is important to recognize the limits and dangers of litigation as well as the possibilities. One such danger is the bringing of lawsuits that are not well thought out or adequately prepared; the results are likely to be legal defeats from which it is hard to recover. Furthermore, all litigation carries the risk that energies that could be put to use more effectively in political or other settings may be diverted to a legal system that can offer no ultimate solutions. It is always important to remember that the courtroom is most often a place of last resort, the place to which the disenfranchised turn when they have been turned away by every other institution in society.

The end to homelessness in America will not come ultimately from judges or from legal opinions. Homelessness will end only when sufficient numbers of people are organized with sufficient cohesion to demand the necessary resources. In the meantime, attorneys and other advocates can try to ameliorate the suffering of the homeless poor and they can work with many others to keep the awful truth of homelessness in America before the public and in the halls of power.

Periodical Bibliography

The following articles have been selected to supplement the diverse views presented in this chapter.

Richard Cohen	"Mentally Ill Homeless Should Be Institutionalized," *Liberal Opinion Week*, December 20, 1993. Available from PO Box 468, Vinton, IA 52349-0468.
Maurice de Ford	"Lawyering for the Homeless," *America*, June 20, 1992.
Joelle Fishman	"Organizing the Homeless in Connecticut," *Political Affairs*, August 1993.
Robert L. Gaskin	"Taking Back the Streets," *National Review*, September 12, 1994.
Katherine Gordy	"Criminalizing Homelessness," *In These Times*, April 4, 1994. Available form 2040 N. Milwaukee Ave., Chicago, IL 60647.
Dianne Hales	"What Americans Say About the Homeless," *Parade*, January 9, 1994.
June B. Kress	"Homeless Fatigue Syndrome: The Backlash Against the Crime of Homelessness in the 1990s," *Social Justice*, Fall 1994. Available from PO Box 40601, San Francisco, CA 94140.
John Leo	"Distorting the Homeless Debate," *U.S. News & World Report*, November 8, 1993.
Colman McCarthy	"Destitute Kicked from Main Street to Mean Street," *Liberal Opinion Week*, December 26, 1994.
Bill Mesler	"The Homeless Learn to Hit Back," *Third Force*, May/June 1995. Available from 1218 E. 21st St., Oakland, CA 94606.
Elena Neuman	"Cities Get Tough with the Homeless," *Insight*, February 14, 1994. Available from PO Box 91022, Washington, DC 20090-1022.
Christian Parenti	"Sidewalk Mercenaries vs. Homeless," *Z Magazine*, November 1994.
Ellen Perlman	"Getting Tough on the Down and Out," *Governing*, April 1994.

How Can Government Help the Homeless?

THE HOMELESS

Chapter Preface

When the Stewart B. McKinney Homeless Assistance Act was passed in 1987, it specified that the first priority for the future use of closed military bases would be to provide housing for the homeless. Many communities affected by the 1992 base closures, in which 103 bases were selected for closure, were unhappy that the bases—with their medical clinics, airfields, seaports, warehouses, and machine shops—would not be used to create civilian jobs to replace those lost by the base closings. Pete Wilson, governor of California—the state hardest hit by the base closings—argued that the act was written in such a way that it ignored the communities' needs in favor of the needs of the homeless, who might not even live in the affected community.

An amendment to the McKinney Act, passed in the fall of 1994, gave the local communities priority in determining how the closed bases would be used, as long as a plan for housing the homeless was submitted to the U.S. Department of Housing and Urban Development. Laurel Weir of the National Law Center on Homelessness and Poverty maintains that the change in the act benefits both the community and the homeless: "The community has to look for a way to develop the base to sustain itself, and homeless needs are not incompatible with that." Alameda, California, illustrates how the seemingly contrary needs of the homeless and of the community can come together for the benefit of both. The future-use plan for Alameda's naval air station, which is scheduled to close in 1999, will include housing and job-training facilities for homeless people. An employee pool of homeless persons will be established, and future employers on the base will have the option of hiring from this pool. Preliminary feedback from homeless advocates and government officials is positive: The amendment gives both parties greater latitude in searching for creative solutions to homelessness and for uses for the closed bases. They believe that the plan will ensure that the homeless will receive housing and job training, while benefiting the community through the base conversion and the addition of productive workers.

The McKinney Act and its amendment serve as an example of one way that the government can help the homeless. Policymakers and homeless advocates do not always agree, however, on how government programs can best approach the problem of homelessness. The authors in the following chapter debate the ways in which the government can help the homeless.

"Homelessness may be largely prevented by intelligent and humane public policies."

Homelessness Can Be Prevented

Rob Rosenthal

The fact that the extent of homelessness varies in different countries suggests that homelessness can be prevented by public policies, argues Rob Rosenthal in the following viewpoint. He contends that by reforming U.S. housing, welfare, mental health, and employment policies, the government can eradicate homelessness. Furthermore, Rosenthal maintains, these policies should be aimed at specific problems (such as lack of affordable housing) rather than at lifestyle groupings (such as bag ladies or Latino families). Rosenthal was involved in the Homeless People's Project in Santa Barbara, California, and is the author of *Homeless in Paradise: A Map of the Terrain*, from which this viewpoint is taken.

As you read, consider the following questions:

1. What is the key to preventing homelessness, in Rosenthal's view?
2. According to the author, why is reform of welfare and social services needed?
3. What characteristics should all homeless programs share, in Rosenthal's opinion?

Excerpted from *Homeless in Paradise* by Rob Rosenthal, ©1992 by Temple University. Reprinted by permission of Temple University Press.

"Is homelessness the result of our capitalist system?" Marjorie Hope and James Young ask. "Of course it is," they answer. But, as they further argue, the great variation in the extent of homelessness in different countries suggests that even within a capitalist framework, homelessness may be largely prevented by intelligent and humane public policies. . . . Here I outline some of the more important measures that might be taken.

Policies can best be envisioned by looking separately at prevention, escape, and amelioration (that is, cushioning the lives of homeless people while they remain homeless), though, of course, there will be considerable overlap. I begin with two basic assumptions: Homeless people, by and large, are neither slackers nor crushed disaffiliates, and therefore will respond to programs that remove the structural barriers they face; and the aim is to prevent and eradicate homelessness rather than merely contain it.

Housing Is the Key

Creating enough affordable housing to meet actual (not market) need is the key to preventing homelessness. The 1949 Housing Act set as a goal "a decent home and a suitable living environment" for all Americans; the 1968 Kaiser Commission recommended a ten-year national housing goal of building or rehabilitating 26 million units, including 6 million low- and moderate-income units. We have fallen far short of the latter goal, to say nothing of the former one. What would it take to house our nation? . . .

The size of the problem, the limits on local resources, and local fears of becoming a magnet for low-income people all point to the importance of a substantial federal role. The very first steps should be to reauthorize all housing programs that create additional units or preserve existing affordable housing at funding levels equal in current dollars to 1980 funding levels, to rescind all restrictive regulations passed since 1980 (such as the requirement that assisted tenants spend 30 percent rather than 25 percent of household income), and to require state enactment of tenant protections as a condition for receiving federal housing funds.

In the immediate short run, it may be desirable to pursue policies that reward private investment in building and maintaining affordable housing. Employer-assisted housing programs could be supported through liberalized corporate tax treatments of such benefits. A variety of local programs have provided below-market loans and outright grants to producers of affordable housing, or combined one-time subsidies with government-owned land, zoning density bonuses, or other inducements. The provision of the 1986 Tax Reform Act that used tax credits to encourage corporate funding of low-income housing has been very

193

successful. These carrots should be balanced by a large stick: strict regulation of lenders to guarantee a supply of credit for builders and buyers of affordable housing.

In the long run, however, eradicating homelessness—or at least its housing component—will require reexamining both our ideological and our programmatic approaches to housing. On an ideological level, Jonathan Kozol says we need "a clarification of the status housing holds within our national imagination. Is it 'a gift'—a kindliness, a favor—or is it more properly perceived as an inalienable right?" Clearly I see it as an inalienable right, a form of security a civilized nation should guarantee to all residents. Perhaps the best analogy is to education. We believe that universal free education is necessary both for the good of the individual and for the good of the society. Housing should be seen similarly. As with education, this view does not preclude private housing for those who desire and can afford better facilities than the norm, but it guarantees everyone a decent standard. . . .

Welfare and Social Services

Homelessness can be prevented through the provision of housing, but many of those vulnerable to homelessness have other serious problems that must be addressed if they are to live productive lives. Reform of our welfare and social service systems is badly needed.

As with housing, a humane public assistance system can be achieved only after a national consensus is reached on its goals. And, as with housing, the defense of a true safety net rests on the twin assumptions that such a goal is good for the individual and ultimately beneficial for the society as a whole. Poverty appears to depend on macro-economic trends, but the history of this country and others makes it clear that economic growth in itself will not eliminate poverty, though it may decrease it. The creation of a welfare system that lifts all residents above the poverty line, of course, runs against the contention of conservatives and business ideologists that generous welfare benefits sap people of initiative and hurt productivity. In fact, many Western European countries and Japan have more complete welfare systems than our own while achieving higher productivity.

Welfare programs are currently funded at cynical levels—cynical because policy-makers are well aware that only a fraction of the eligible population is making use of those programs. Welfare reform should insure universal coverage instead of restricting each program to an arbitrarily chosen subgroup of the needy while emphasizing cost containment and the winnowing out of "cheats," a tiny minority in all welfare programs.

But it is not enough to make public assistance *available*; as our examination of public assistance in Santa Barbara made clear, availability must be combined with *active outreach* by caseworkers. Waiting for people who are impoverished, in some cases confused, and in many cases ignorant or terrified of service agencies to approach those agencies and ask for help is absurd. Welfare policies should be proactive, emphasizing early intervention. Targeting "at risk" individuals and families is, of course, far more difficult than responding to stated need when someone applies for welfare, yet an active outreach effort would help such targeting immensely. . . .

Examples of Prevention Cost Savings

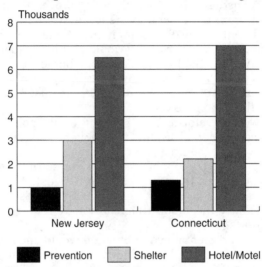

The chart reflects the comparative cost advantage of prevention versus housing homeless households in hotels or shelters for two selected programs. While it cannot be definitively argued that all households assisted by prevention programs would have ended up in shelters, all programs had minimum eligibility requirements which targeted "at-risk" households.

Source: National Housing Institute, and American Affordable Housing Institute, *Preventing Homelessness: A Study of State and Local Homelessness Prevention Programs,* 1991.

Two additional principles need to be embodied in all welfare reform. First, "family" integrity must be supported, in contrast, for example, with the policy in many states of denying AFDC [Aid to Families with Dependent Children] to two-parent households. Second, welfare policies should encourage transition to employment by providing real financial incentives and a practical support system for those seeking work. Most fundamentally, jobs must be available for those who complete training, whether they are encouraged in the private sector through local and federal tax incentives for employers or created by the federal government itself. . . .

Mental Health Reform

Public policies concerning mental health and homelessness are analogous to those concerning public assistance: The key issues are coordination and organization, levels of aid, availability of services, and outreach. Deinstitutionalization has led to a vacuum of responsibility in which there is no overall direction or coordination from the federal to the local level, although it was clearly the intent of the 1963 Community Mental Health Centers Act that the federal government would assume leadership and responsibility. Thus the first step, and one immediately possible, is to clarify levels and areas of responsibility within localities, between local, state, and national governments, and between agencies at the national level. . . .

As with welfare reform, sound mental health policy requires active outreach. Mental health practitioners must venture into the field, investing the time and care required to build a trusting relationship with people who have good reason (as well as behavioral tendencies in some cases) to distrust "the system." Even the pretreatment stage of gaining public assistance to stabilize a mentally ill person financially may require extensive outreach efforts.

Finally, a sound mental health program would encourage independence for those capable of independent living and provide appropriate confinement for those who are not. The legal restrictions surrounding involuntary confinement were a reasonable reaction to the arbitrary abridgement of the rights of mentally ill people in the past. Yet sometimes confinement is as necessary for the individual as it is for the society at large. More restrictive laws, however, must also establish the right to decent and humane conditions for those confined, including the ability to challenge confinement orders, and the right to local care, including outpatient commitment. For those who are gravely disabled, confinement must not become a form of warehousing that robs the patient of initiative or control. As a volunteer in a shelter told Hope and Young, "Nothing is worse on the human spirit than having nothing to do.". . .

Employment

Many theorists (including homeless advocates) stress the importance of education and training in fighting unemployment.

Yet this emphasis masks a more fundamental problem, the occupational structure of the nation. As long as the number of jobs, and the number of jobs with decent wages, remains the same, education is of little importance on the macro level. It may change the players, but not the number who cannot find a job that pays decent wages. While literacy and other skills are clearly essential for employment, poverty and unemployment cannot be solved through education alone. An employment strategy that will effectively prevent homelessness must ensure job placement as well, through government-created jobs, hiring incentives, or other inducements to the private sector. This is, of course, much easier when the economy is expanding than when it is stagnating or shrinking.

Further, structural supports are needed to ensure that people can take these jobs, chief among them the provision of high-quality, affordable day care and an adequate transportation system. Even if jobs and support are available, wages must be high enough to lift workers out of poverty. Finally, care must be taken that tax policies do not penalize the working poor to such an extent that unemployment is a better option than employment. . . .

Addressing Specific Issues

The specifics of the detailed suggestions in this viewpoint are less important than the general principle underlying all of them: Programs to fight homelessness must be designed with specific *problems, not lifestyle groupings*, in mind. Doing so will not only focus programs but will help eliminate needless duplication of efforts. Of course, lifestyle groupings will still matter: There may be instances in which mixing groups is ill-advised because of mutual animosity or differences in what sorts of approaches can work. But programs must consciously address a particular level of the problem (prevention, amelioration, or escape) and specific issues within that level. A program aimed at helping "bag ladies," or even "Latino Families," for instance, will be less successful than one aimed at preventing homelessness through first/last/deposit loans to displaced households, or one facilitating escape through outreach to homeless people by entitlement program workers. This is not to say that creating a slew of uncoordinated programs is the way to attack homelessness. Coordination is essential, but planners must understand that each component of a coordinated overall plan must tackle a defined problem within a defined stage of homelessness.

Some programs will affect all or nearly all subgroups among the homeless and potentially homeless population. Most obviously, prevention would be greatly aided by a governmental and societal commitment to building affordable housing. Many subgroups would be helped by such prevention strategies as guaranteeing full employment and indexing entitlement levels to the cost of living; by such amelioration strategies as health care outreach and increased funding of shelters; and by such escape strategies as centralization of entitlement programs. Other approaches will be aimed at problems that affect parts of the homeless population, such as low-cost, high visibility, substance abuse programs.

Program Characteristics

All programs should share certain characteristics. The first is easy entry and minimal screening at entry levels. Excessive regimentation drives away those who cherish their freedom, such as Wingnuts [mentally ill homeless persons], Kids, and Street People. Excessive means tests scare away those who cherish their housed image, such as Skidders [women who skidded into homelessness via divorce or separation] and Latino Families. High visibility and easy geographic access encourage homeless people of all subgroups to enter a program.

Second, services should be centralized. Time is precious to many homeless people, particularly those who are employed or have children. Programs that require people to travel all over town will not be used.

Third, shelter and food needs must be met before escape strategies are launched. Both materially and psychologically, emergency, transitional, and then permanent housing is essential for fighting homelessness.

Fourth, programs must convey a sense of stability; only if they are likely to be there tomorrow can they coax people into making that first, difficult step of using a service today. When the first Church shelter was opened in Santa Barbara, its availability was tied to weather conditions. Weeks later, virtually no one had used the shelter. Few were willing to walk fifteen blocks from the downtown area to find out whether the church had deemed it cold or rainy enough that night to warrant opening; nor were they willing to move belongings from their sleeping places to the church since good weather on the following night would mean having to move everything back again. When the church abandoned the weather test and merely announced that it would be open for a month (and then replaced by another church), the shelter filled immediately.

Fifth, programs that seek to encourage independence and renewed (or greater) affiliation must encourage a sense of efficacy. The desire to resume a mainstream life is strong among most of the homeless population, and it should be used and encouraged.

Finally, there must be coordination between programs, both to avert duplication and to insure that eligible people are being reached. A single directing agency with ultimate responsibility for overseeing the various programs can ensure that programs mesh well with each other and the researched needs of homeless and potentially homeless people.

Shelter and service agency personnel find it challenging to provide help beyond the basic necessities to individuals and subgroups with extremely disparate characteristics and needs. Many providers argue that unattached children, families, those with mental illnesses, and so forth, ought to be separated. Yet how can such separation be reconciled with the importance of centralization and easy entry stressed here?

The National Coalition for the Homeless has advocated a three-tiered approach to the problem: a first stage of emergency shelters, open to anyone who needs help; a second stage of "transitional" housing, segregated by groups' differing needs, with auxiliary linkages to work, entitlement, counseling, and housing programs; and a third stage of "long-term" nonprofit homes, including appropriate in-house services for special populations such as those with chronic mental or physical disabilities. Such a plan incorporates the desirable characteristics mentioned above: easy entry, centralization, meeting of basic needs, stability, and coordination. . . .

The Role of Government

For a number of reasons, real progress in eradicating homelessness depends on leadership from the federal government. To begin with, despite the paucity of evidence in its favor, the magnet theory remains a potent obstacle to progress at the local level. Unless services are mandated and funded at the national level, each community is hampered in its own progressive efforts by the fear that generosity will bring ruin.

Similarly, however cost estimates turn out, it is clear that local communities will not be willing or able to spend the lump sums needed to eradicate homelessness, even if convinced of an eventual financial payoff. Social service agencies dealing with every social problem have argued over the years: "Give us money now to prevent this problem and you will spend less in the future on the effects." But such initial outlays are invariably more than even the most receptive local government can afford. Homelessness is clearly a national problem with national causes. It is unreasonable and unrealistic to expect local communities to pick up the tab for a national problem. If we expected local communities to build Army bases with their own funds, Army bases would never be built. There is simply no substitute for federal funding.

Additionally, if the safety net of social services and mental health care is to be restructured in the ways I have outlined above, the initiative must come from the federal government. As the highest and wealthiest level of government, it is the only

199

one that can structure compliance among lower levels. . . .

Further, the federal government has great power to frame the terms of the public discussion about homelessness. Homeless advocates in Santa Barbara noted a marked change in the political atmosphere after the City and County committed themselves to social solutions through the creation of an activist Task Force on Homelessness, not because of any specific actions taken by the Task Force but because of the aura of legitimacy it conferred on their efforts. Public opinion polls examining social (as opposed to "blaming the victim") approaches to homelessness suggest that support for progressive solutions is available but "soft." A simple declaration by the federal government of the right of all people to housing would have profound effects on public discourse that would extend far beyond the obvious legal advantages.

Finally, the federal government should take the lead in combating homelessness because in many ways it *created* homelessness. The withdrawal of commitment to public and affordable housing and a national mental health system, the cutbacks in social services, and the rise in entitlement eligibility reviews helped trigger the explosion of homelessness in the United States. Some of these trends were already in motion when Ronald Reagan took office, but that administration greatly exacerbated them. The Bush administration neither restored the Reagan cuts nor demonstrated a clear intention to return the federal government to the role of leading provider of affordable housing.

An Increasing Split

The growth of homelessness is the most visible sign of the increasing split in the country between the haves and the have-nots, a manifestation of the deterioration of the American Dream. We pride ourselves on being a middle-class nation that takes care of our poorer citizens; now our middle class is embattled and declining, while those living in poverty face a bleaker future every day. Faced with our personal difficulties, we can fall back on comforting notions of homeless people as different, separate, adrift "out there" in a world other than that of housed people. But this is an illusion: Homeless people are tied to the rest of us in the ways they live, the goals they seek, and the reasons they are homeless.

Homelessness is a political question. Studies continue to be useful, but programs will come only when the political forces supporting homeless people are strong enough to back up their studies with political muscle. This, in turn, requires coalitions with the many groups who are also adversely affected by current policies concerning housing, health, employment, welfare, and social services. The problem now is not primarily a lack of information. It is a lack of political will and political power.

"It makes little sense to attempt small-scale, let alone large-scale, prevention, because prevention has failed."

Homelessness Cannot Be Prevented

Jerzy Kosinski, Benedict Giamo, and Jeffrey Grunberg

Jerzy Kosinski, who died in May 1991, was an acclaimed novelist and writer who survived World War II as a child in Nazi-occupied eastern Europe. Benedict Giamo is an assistant professor of American studies at the University of Notre Dame in Indiana. Jeffrey Grunberg is an associate professor of clinical psychology at Columbia University, New York. The following viewpoint, which is excerpted from Giamo and Grunberg's book *Beyond Homelessness: Frames of Reference*, is a dialog in which Kosinski, Giamo, and Grunberg discuss homelessness in the United States and Kosinski's unusual idea to ease the suffering of the homeless. During their conversation, they assert that life is chancy, and that homelessness is a part of the American system and, as such, cannot be prevented.

As you read, consider the following questions:

1. What does Kosinski say about a society that allows the state of homelessness to continue?
2. How does homelessness fit in with the free enterprise system, according to Kosinski?
3. What does Kosinski think is the reason he has been unable to convince his wealthy friends to help the homeless?

Benedict Giamo: Since so much of a society's approach to homelessness depends upon the eye through which it sees the problem, I was hoping that you could elaborate on your own particular perspective that you bring to the social situation. Consider this a preface to the interview.

Jerzy Kosinski: Well, then, let me first qualify the optics, the lenses that I will use to view homelessness. One lens is going to be very wide angle and that stems from my background in Eastern Europe, being uprooted together with everybody else in 1939. Homelessness is, therefore, a state imposed from outside when societies are in a state of war. War, of course, is homelessness. It presupposes destruction, the breaking up of the family. One could say that a state of war is a state of homelessness. A soldier is homeless. At best, war is a temporary shelter.

Homelessness also means less-than-home. It presupposes somehow that one ought to have a home and that, therefore, a homeless person is somehow deprived of something that some other people may take for granted. Here I'm referring to the second aspect of the wide-angle lens, the collective state where homes belong to the state, which means you are already less-than-home. Now, if you ask me, "Do you own this home?" I would say, "No, I rent. Why do I rent? I don't want to own. I want to be, to a degree, homeless." Let me further narrow this point of view. Consider being homeless in a country in which having a home is taken as a status. In fact, it is something one works toward as a kind of tenure (comparable to the tenure system in academia). Well, to someone from Eastern Europe who was uprooted and who could have faced destruction, not having a home is a rather minor dramatic predicament in life. I would take it far more for granted that I could be expelled from my domain tomorrow morning by forces other than the landlord's. Perhaps my American counterpart would say, "What? What do you mean they treat you like this? What right do they have?" And I would say, "Well, you know they could have killed me." We have to start with that premise.

Shelter Versus a Sense of Self

I should add that I came from a Communist state that fraudulently assured a shelter, while taking away the notion of self. The state provided minimum services for the body, while taking maximum means away from the mind. In fact, it very openly conducted this transaction by saying, "I'm giving you a home. I'm giving your kid a breakfast and a luncheon and a resemblance of dinner; and I'm giving you education and medical services. True, I'm taking care of your physical being. However, I parenthetically add that there will be nothing parenthetical about this condition. There will be no parenthesis in which you will be able to conduct your own affairs in any way you want. You will be mercifully treated, but at the mercy that can be merciless." Now that condition is given.

Narrowing further to the more or less average point of view, or the regular sociological lens, leads to a focus on two subjects: the nineteenth century in Europe, which was the century of the homeless (where the middle class was just developing and all the various Marxist parties came into being), and the American family. These were my two specialties. In a way, these two broad areas summarize a basic dialectic of the nineteenth century: establishing the middle-class ethos or destroying it. The former can be seen in American society, which has the most predictable middle-class fortress, and where the notion of "home" is essential; the latter can be evidenced in the Communist movement that emerged during this time in European societies.

A Home on Wheels

Therefore, narrowing it even further, I look at the homeless not from the society's point of view, but from the point of view of the homeless person himself or herself. And I can tell you exactly what my focus is and about my concern, my preoccupation. Right now I'm looking at a specific design of a home on wheels. It's a cart that you see in this neighborhood. Actually, it's a version of a cart; call it a "vehicle" if you want to be very American about it. It's a four-wheel vehicle, a sort of shopping cart, that most of the homeless in this neighborhood would steal to have. The concept I'm working on is just this type of shopping cart that would collapse into a portable home in which one can carry one's belongings, open it at night, lock oneself in it, take the wheels off,—put the wheels inside, close oneself off from the outside—and be safe from heat, from frost (far more importantly), and from being hit over the head when asleep by someone else in the neighborhood. Not even a police club can break it. There is also a window made of fiberglass.

Giamo: You even put a picture window into that device.

Kosinski: Yes, indeed, so you can see who else is out there. You can look at other people's homes. . . .

It's self-propelled—Self with a capital *S*—since in this case I have great respect for the homeless individual, whom I refuse to see as a victim of society and I refuse to see as a victim of his or her own self. I see the homeless person as a chance being at the mercy of forces that he or she was not able to figure out or may not be able to figure out. And if he or she cannot figure out the state of homelessness, why should he or she when the state cannot figure it out either?

Narrowing it further, if this community (one of the most affluent neighborhoods of New York City) isn't smart enough to resolve the fact that there are people who have no place to sleep, why should the homeless be smart enough to resolve their own predicaments? Are the avenues to "home" as simple as that? Clearly they are not.

Prevention Programs Do Not Help the Homeless

After a full decade of concern for the homeless, the American public seems to be giving up on those who are already homeless. It is as though people have redefined the "few who are beyond help" to include the entire homeless population. Some new prevention programs exploit the issue of homelessness to accomplish what many in the public housing arena, including tenant organizations, have wanted for many years—training programs, health clinics, day-care, anti-drug and anti-gang activities, and building improvement projects. Other prevention programs, like the $14 million New Jersey Homelessness Prevention Program, target the "'working poor' who have temporary setbacks that make them unable to meet their housing expenses." These may be good and necessary programs, but they are not programs to help the homeless.

Alice S. Baum and Donald W. Burnes, *A Nation in Denial*, 1993.

Jeffrey Grunberg: Is the community not smart enough or is there something intentional about its desire to watch some people suffer? Is racism a part of the social problem?

Kosinski: I prefer to see it (I say "prefer" because maybe it is a way of wishful thinking or of wishful seeing) as a community not being smart enough, not being intelligent enough, pragmatic enough to realize the dimensions of the problem. The homeless have very little to lose and very little vested interest in the notion of order, home, and the philosophy of having in a society which is based on free enterprise. So I'd like to think that a society that allows the state of homelessness to continue (providing that the homeless person wants to have a home) is a society not smart enough to resolve the problem.

Homelessness and Free Enterprise

Giamo: What does homelessness reveal then about American society? Or let's say the American dream?

Kosinski: Homeless people in my neighborhoods, whether in New Haven, where there are a great number of homeless people right outside the fortress of Yale, or here in New York, cause one to establish a new parameter. One should accept that these are a category of people who cannot afford a standard mobile home, since there is right above them a category of people who can. Homelessness then, according to this view, is a perfectly valid category of the free enterprise system. For whatever reason, this person who is homeless finds himself or herself in a mini-enterprise. This mini-enterprise is reduced to asking for help, for money, from passersby. Now had this homeless person been a foundation, this would have been considered a tax-deductible operation. If one were to make this condition tax-deductible, as with the Jewish Presence Foundation of which I am president, then this person—and the needs of this person—would and should be tax-deductible. Hence the mini-van home would serve such a purpose.

Grunberg: You're going to upset a lot of people if your idea takes off.

Kosinski: I don't know whether the mini-van home should upset people or the sight of someone who is frostbitten in the morning.

Grunberg: Which would bother people more?

The Pursuit of Happiness

Kosinski: Simply put, it is just a condition that is very prevalent today on the streets. It is a condition to be acknowledged, regardless of whether it is bothersome or not. It is certainly bothersome to the person who is frostbitten. It can also be bothersome to some individuals who pass this person by, and to assume that everyone is indifferent to someone else's misery may simply not be true. It could be safely assumed that people with homes, which in the winter are very warm, can take far less enjoyment from their well-deserved homes by seeing a homeless person sleeping at the entrance to their homes. Hence the myth of the pursuit of happiness—or the reality of it—can be infringed upon by the sight of someone who simply doesn't participate as fully in this society.

Grunberg: We can rest comfortably knowing that the homeless are not freezing?

Kosinski: Precisely. This means that some sleeplessness of my own could be reduced by the fact that the homeless are no longer frostbitten, but sleep in mini-van homes of their own which protect them from frost, attacks by dogs, drunkards, and drug addicts—or attacks by those who simply want to experience the power of their own hands or feet on someone else's flesh.

Therefore, I don't want to enter into an argument with myself or with anyone else relative to what is right or what is wrong. I'm too pragmatic for that and too philosophical. What interests me is the degree to which one can accept the state of homelessness as being a given, an inherited given perhaps, and as being unavoidable (I haven't seen it resolved, at least not in American society). And I have not been able to convince those who are in charge of wealth that they should help those who can no longer help themselves, because the notion that people should be able to help themselves is a very firm Protestant notion. . . .

A Fact of Life

Giamo: Basically, what you're saying is that it makes little sense to attempt small-scale, let alone large-scale, prevention, because prevention has failed and American ideology will not accept the prevention that might be needed in the cooperative ventures of both public and private sectors to resolve the social problem.

Kosinski: Yes, prevention has failed. But we do accept business cycles and recession and unemployment as facts of life. We do accept ruin by bad investments. We do accept crime and being shot at, and we do accept chance. Are we absolutely so deterministically minded that we no longer acknowledge that life is chancy? After all, we do take chances. Therefore, now we live in an ethos in which a homeless person should find far more understanding than in a welfare state. In other words, a person who is right now homeless in front of my home carries within himself or herself all basic American ingredients.

Giamo: And, whether it's valid or not, some of the homeless do tend to blame themselves for their predicaments.

Kosinski: Just as a businessperson might who has invested wrongly. Now if one were to be positive about it, as one should be, and pragmatic, one could improve this condition. Homelessness is very much a part of our American system and, basically, there should be nothing wrong with this condition as long as the individual is not sentenced to unnecessary suffering and punishment—since the system makes all provisions for that condition three miles away downtown in Wall Street.

Grunberg: Often, people seem to vacillate between feeling sorry for the homeless or being angry at them. Also, there's a great deal of energy expended in trying to determine who to blame. Is it the homeless individual's fault? Or is it society's fault?

Kosinski: These concerns represent non-American values injected into the American character from the outside. They came as the residue of the nineteenth century in its idealized state. And I think one can very easily turn it around. In fact, I think turning it around and improving the lot of a great number of people who now occupy the parking lots at night, and other lots to which they are not entitled, would be far easier than to act against the basic grain of American character.

Grunberg: So the millions of dollars, the hundreds of millions of dollars that cities are spending in their attempt to rehabilitate, rehouse, feed. . .

Kosinski: Work to a degree but, basically, one can also assume that persons who have been homeless carry within them (and we accept it in many other areas of life) a certain philosophy of life or certain experience which makes them, to say the least, apprehensive about ownership. I mean, here's Jerzy Kosinski who is relatively stable (with which most of my literary critics would disagree, judging by my fiction) and who doesn't want to own. Now if I don't want to own a home but prefer to rent one because of my experience of World War II (consider this an experience of homelessness, I repeat that), then why not make a provision for a certain number of people who simply may not be comfortable, or not psychologically or pragmatically equipped anymore, to deal with the state of being rehabilitated, when in fact they may prefer to remain mobile but safe?

> "Until the federal government gets back into the housing business, we're not going to see a solution."

A National Housing Policy Can Reduce Homelessness

Gregg Barak

The homeless crisis that began in the 1980s will not be remedied in the future unless public policies securing housing for America's poor are expanded, writes Gregg Barak in the following viewpoint. Although many state and local governments are working hard to find solutions to the affordable-housing crisis, he maintains, without federal help their efforts will do little to alleviate the problem. Barak is the chair of the Department of Sociology, Anthropology and Criminology at Eastern Michigan University in Ypsilanti. He has written several books on criminal justice and is the author of *Gimme Shelter: A Social History of Homelessness in Contemporary America*, from which this viewpoint is taken.

As you read, consider the following questions:

1. What are some of the negative effects Americans will experience if an expanded housing policy is not adopted, according to David C. Schwartz, Richard C. Ferlauto, and Daniel N. Hoffman, as quoted by the author?
2. What three measures do Schwartz, Ferlauto, and Hoffman advocate as a way of preventing, treating, and curing homelessness in the United States, according to Barak?

The decade of the 1980s has sufficiently demonstrated that without a federal mandate to alleviate homelessness in the United States, the significant efforts of volunteerism and privatization acting in concert with each other are not enough to conquer this societal problem. The decade of the 1990s will determine whether or not the U.S. government is sincere about fulfilling its commitment (obligation) to provide secure and decent housing for all Americans. Such a pledge was first articulated nearly a half century ago in the 1949 Housing Act. Social problems such as homelessness do not just occur in some kind of vacuum. Ultimately they are the products of public policy and can never fully be separated from their social, political, cultural, economic, and legal context. . . .

Funding War, but Not Housing

The poverty of political will that characterizes both the Republican and Democratic parties is rationalized by the budget deficit paralysis, a statistical fiction if there ever was one. Not that the deficits are not real. But the statistical reality is that despite the deficits, money in this wealthiest of all nations can be found when Congress and the president have the will to do so. There have been funds enough for Operation Desert Shield and for the Contras, death squads, defense forces, anticommunist and antidrug crusades. There have been trillions spent on murderous weapons and the military-industrial complexes. In 1989 there was enough money for Congress to recommend itself a 50 percent pay raise. There is going to be between $500 billion and $1 trillion to bail out the savings and loan institutions. But when it comes to the welfare and the health of ordinary citizens, and when it comes to the needs of the homeless or the poor, including some 30–40 million children, then we hear all about the need to balance budgets. As an editorial in *The Nation* puts it, the refrain is always the same, it makes no difference nowadays which of the two great American parties is singing:

> Money for housing? The word is No. National health plan? Uh-uh. Social investment, public enterprise, child care, support for the elderly, research and development, progressive taxation, antitrust enforcement, environmental action, job security, reindustrialization, economic justice—a thousand times No.

The decade of the 1980s, if public policies do not change, has revealed what the future will look like. What first emerged with the Reagan revolution and has continued unabated into the early 1990s does not forecast a bright future. The immediate and not so immediate consequences of failing to achieve a new housing policy for the United States has been described by David C. Schwartz, Richard C. Ferlauto, and Daniel N. Hoffman:

> If our national government is unable to adopt a new, more ex-

pansive housing policy soon, profoundly negative consequences are likely to be visited upon millions of American families, on the American economy, and on many American communities. Acceptance of lowered homeownership levels, inattention to the needs of the frail elderly, continued failure to prevent homelessness, malign neglect of both urban and rural housing requirements, cuts in needed housing construction programs for the poor, weak anti-discrimination laws weakly enforced—these characteristics of our present policies just don't hurt individuals and families. They hurt our economy; they truncate our middle class; they reduce equality of opportunity; they sap the vibrancy of our efforts to revitalize cities or to restore farm communities; they create new ghettos (mostly for the aged) while reinforcing a culture of poverty in the too many older ghettos and slums. A national governmental decision to continue these policies, or a non-decision (which has the same effect), will accelerate these hurtful trends and diminish the quality of life, the moral stature, and perhaps the social peace of the nation.

When it comes to the policies that address housing and homelessness, there are certainly more than a few good ideas. One such idea is the growing number of "linkage" laws that require developers to fund public works, including anything from improved streets and sewage facilities to affordable housing or job training and employment. It comes as little or no surprise that linkage works best in those communities where land is scarce and valuable. Boston, San Francisco, and Portland, Oregon, are three prominent cities that have adopted linkage programs. In these cities developers have lined up despite the fact that they are being forced to contribute some of their enormous profits to various civic projects. But even supposing that all of the deteriorated cities across the United States were ripe for the kinds of redevelopment that has been occurring in such geographical places as Chicago, Miami, and Santa Monica, it should be clearly understood that linkage money will not come close to providing enough of the necessary finances for public housing and other infrastructure projects. Such projects must be initiated and underwritten by governmental enterprise and social investment. As one of linkage's strongest proponents, Lawrence Dwyer, chairman of Boston's Neighborhood Housing Trust, has admitted: "Until the federal government gets back into the housing business, we're not going to see a solution."

Government and the Housing Market

Historically, most developed countries have recognized the responsibility of government to provide housing to its citizens. How and to what extent governments should intervene in the housing markets, however, has been a matter of considerable debate. Arne Karyd has characterized, even exaggerated, the two extreme (or pure) positions of this debate. Respectively, he identified the free market "believers" and the free market "opposers" as follows:

> Almost every kind of services and goods are available on a market which means that there are sellers as well as buyers. There are markets for single-dwelling houses, condominiums and multi-dwelling houses. . . . The need for housing will be satisfied by the forces of the market—demand and supply. Compared to these real forces, the power of government is small. Because of its limited power and because the market is the best way to distribute housing, the role of government should be confined to lubricate and facilitate activities on the markets. If extremely high rents or sales profits are observed, this is not an indication of insufficient government control but a sign of improper market function. The reasons are often to be found in vainful attempts from the government to offset the market, e.g. by constraints on construction and supply.

> Adequate housing is a basic human right, not a merchandise. The influence of markets over such an essential sector of human life should be removed or at least rendered harmless. Government should exercise control over physical planning, construction of new housing, rent levels and price levels. Although private-owned single- and multi-family dwellings may be tolerated, realized capital gains occurring at sale should be heavily taxed. For multi-family dwellings, prospective buyers should be subject to approval by the local tenant organization. The forming of condominiums should not be encouraged. In general, housing should be subsidized to prevent people from choosing inferior housing conditions in order to use money for other kinds of consumption.

My own position is that the eradication of homelessness in the United States will realistically require a vision that incorporates a mixture to these two ideological positions. In other words, the emergence and development of global capitalism can be adapted to meet simultaneously the housing needs of both privatization and socialization. Hence, if minimal levels of housing are to prevail for all people, residing both inside and outside this country, then some integrated and comprehensive approach must emerge to replace the privately based and inadequately supported present policy configuration. . . .

A New Housing Policy

Schwartz et al. have helped draft and enact state legislation. Their ideas and legislation on housing have been recognized nationally and internationally. Their New Jersey legislation in particular has provided models for other states. Referring to their landmark New Jersey legislation, Senator Bill Bradley (D-NJ) said it "has helped to expand homeownership opportunities, provide affordable rental apartments, and prevent homelessness for tens of thousands of New Jerseyans." Nevertheless, Schwartz et al. argue that without federal involvement, leadership, and partnership local and state efforts, such as the ones that they have been involved with, are only drops in the bucket that cannot possibly offer a viable solution to the crisis in low- and moderate-income housing in America. Consequently, they advocate a national housing program that includes, among other things, a federal down payment program, an employer-assisted home-ownership plan, mortgage interest rate buy down fund, shared equity mortgages, a National Housing Investment Corporation, and a Federal Housing Trust Fund for the construction of needed rental units. If such programs were put into operation during the 1990s, Schwartz et al. estimate that about 11 million new jobs would be created as a result.

Solutions Through Leadership

The private market alone can not provide affordable housing for all citizens—especially the disabled, elderly, and poor. The conservative, free-enterprise approach mostly has been a disaster. On the other hand, reliance on the traditional liberal strategy of providing massive tax breaks and subsidies for builders and landlords is too costly and inefficient. New and bold measures must be implemented.

The housing crisis can be solved, but only through the leadership of the President. He can turn the nightmare of homelessness into the American dream of good and decent homes for everyone.

John I. Gilderbloom, *USA Today*, November 1991.

These authors of *A New Housing Policy for America: Recapturing the American Dream* are convinced that the successful political adoption of these policies is dependent on the ability to link the aspirations of the middle class, particularly young families, with the needs of the poor and the homeless. Moreover, as Senator Bradley asserts in the foreword to their book:

We must all be concerned when a majority of America's 30 million tenants now live in dwelling units that our federal government acknowledges to be inadequate or overcrowded or cost-burdened. New policies must focus on the 10 million American families who are consigned to overcrowded or dilapidated homes and the 14 million more who pay much more of their incomes than they can afford for shelter.

More specifically, when it comes to stopping homelessness at its source and to preventing, treating, and curing the homeless in America, Schwartz et al. have advocated a threefold plan.

First, the authors call for a series of measures designed to avert the eviction of families on the verge of destitution. They argue that such a policy would not only stop the suffering from becoming homeless, but that there would be the added benefits of avoiding the social and financial expenses of emergency assistance. For examples, they point to state statutes in Maryland, New Jersey, and Pennsylvania that have addressed homelessness at the front end—before it happens. New Jersey's Homelessness Prevention Program provides temporary assistance as a last resort for those who have inadequate funds beyond their control and face imminent homelessness. For those who have a mortgage, loans are provided; for those whose rents exceed more than 50 percent of their income, grants are provided.

Second, there are the homelessness efforts such as the 1987 Urgent Relief for the Homeless Act. In addition to this act's provision of emergency shelters, transitional housing, and the rehabilitation of rental property, Schwartz et al. call for the establishment of group homes, halfway houses, congregate care centers, and multigenerational shared living arrangements. They also want to see that specialized medical and mental health services become integrated components of housing complexes. Such policy developments would facilitate the coordination of prevention and treatment for the homeless.

Third, as a backdrop to the specific programs above, these three housing analysts and activists call for a reversal in the social and domestic spending trends of the 1980s. Specifically, they want to see a restoration of federal cuts in income assistance to poor people, in disability payments to handicapped people, in Medicaid funds for sick people, in food stamps for hungry people, and in rental assistance to homeless-vulnerable people. Last and certainly not least, Schwartz et al. want the restoration of the once expansive construction subsidy program for low-income housing in America.

The policies called for by these three comprehensive approaches to the U.S. crisis in low-income housing and homelessness have been well thought out. And the United States is quite capable of fully engaging this alternative and progressive plan for confronting its problem of homelessness. The only question that remains is: do the federally elected members of the House and Senate have the political will to "do the right thing" for a group of people whose interests are perhaps the most politically vulnerable of any in this society? . . .

The Results of Reaganism

The United States has its share of homeless people, young and old, living in alleyways and beneath the city streets in sewers and subways. What is unusual, however, is the magnitude of

213

the homelessness problem for a postindustrial nation. The only other postindustrial society in the world today that is experiencing both a rise in the number and in the rate of homelessness is Great Britain. Of course, it does not take a mental giant to see how the policies of Reaganism and Thatcherism have had similar negative social consequences. I also suspect that other traditional liberal democratic countries of Western Europe, in response to the competitive markets of global capitalism, will soon follow with their own repressive versions of austerity capitalism, complete with the emergence and development of their own new homeless classes. Jurgen Friedrichs writes that with respect to the United States, in any event, it seems that the basic "law of homelessness" for an advanced capitalist society applies: "If a society cannot provide affordable housing, for instance by subsidizing rents, the number of homelessness [sic] will increase." By the end of 1990 such was already the case in the newly capitalizing countries of Eastern Europe, for example, where previously subsidized and state-owned housing has been transferred to the private sector of free enterprise.

It seems to this author that if the United States can employ a myriad of every technique imaginable to subsidize the wealth of this society, then it ought to be able to afford the subsidies necessary for satisfying the fundamental human needs of its poor. And if because of the inhumane, irrational, and destructive domestic U.S. policies, there must be poverty in the first place, then the very least that this society could do would be to eliminate homelessness within its borders. Given this nation's material wealth, it is the only socially just course of action to take. In other words, give America's new homeless and near homeless the security and the well being of permanent housing. GIVE IT TO THEM NOW!

> "Local government policies on land use, along with rent control, may explain half of contemporary homelessness."

Local Housing Policies Can Reduce Homelessness

Richard W. White Jr.

Most advocates for housing reform suggest that a national housing policy is needed to make housing more affordable and reduce homelessness. Richard W. White Jr. contends in the following viewpoint that efforts to promote such a national policy are misguided. He argues that local and state governments restrict housing developments and growth through zoning, rent control, and growth restrictions. It is these restrictions, not the lack of a federal housing policy, that lead to high rent rates and homelessness, White maintains. He believes housing activists should direct their energies toward changing local and state housing policies. White is a research scholar at the Institute for Contemporary Studies, a public policy research group in San Francisco, and the author of *Rude Awakenings: What the Homeless Crisis Tells Us*, from which this viewpoint is excerpted.

As you read, consider the following questions:

1. What three forms of federal housing assistance have been available to most Americans over the years, according to White?
2. Why do direct government construction subsidies not work as a policy for producing low- and moderate-income housing, in the author's opinion?

Reprinted by permission of ICS Press, San Francisco, from *Rude Awakenings: What the Homeless Crisis Tells Us* by Richard W. White Jr., 1992.

The variety of existing and proposed policies and programs aimed at increasing the availability of housing to low-income families is truly bewildering. Over the years federal housing assistance has assumed three forms: direct dollar assistance through grants or loans either to suppliers of housing or to those wishing to rent or purchase it; interventions in financial markets such as mortgage insurance and related programs; and tax incentives, especially the mortgage interest deduction. Until recently federal housing policy has been spectacularly successful for most Americans. They have been able to buy and live in their own homes. In the 1970s and 1980s, however, housing prices rose dramatically in many areas and skyrocketed in booming cities, pricing middle-class families, particularly would-be first time home buyers, out of the market. In response, increasing numbers of middle- and upper-income families have begun purchasing houses in low-income neighborhoods. This "gentrification" reverses the filtering-down process that historically provided housing on the private market for low-income families. At the bottom of the scale, some families and individuals, usually otherwise troubled, lose their housing and cannot find another place to live. . . .

Recommendations for More Affordable Housing

Recognizing that the mainstream American housing system has serious problems, leaders in the housing industry—public and private—formed the National Housing Task Force (NHTF), with James M. Rouse, arguably America's most renowned housing developer, as chairman. It set forth findings and recommendations in "A Decent Place to Live," the final task force report. NHTF proposed "a new federal delivery system" that it called the Housing Opportunities Program, along with $3 billion for grants to states and local governments in the first year. . . . The report also called for federal leadership in creating new sources of capital for low- and moderate-income housing, increased emphasis on preserving and improving the existing stock of low- and moderate-income housing, "a complete modernization" of existing public housing, tax policies that stimulate development of new low- and moderate-income housing, rental assistance tied to federal housing quality standards, improved access to federal mortgage insurance (easier down payments, for example), continued support for the current housing finance system, renewed and extended efforts to combat discrimination in housing, and special emphasis on rural housing.

The mainstream theory is that housing for low-income families and individuals will never be profitable in an unregulated free market but that such housing can be produced successfully both publicly and privately with the proper mixture of subsidies and other palliatives. . . .

The NHTF comprises a broad spectrum of leaders from the U.S. housing industry. They know how to produce housing. But the task force has given short shrift to the most critical element in the problem—local government practices. Despite any programs it may add to those already in effect, then, little progress will be made. . . .

Subsidies Do Not Work

Like many other proposals, those of the NHTF include recommendations for direct government construction subsidies. These, however, do not work as a policy for producing low- and moderate-income housing, although sometimes they appear to. Such subsidies may produce several hundred housing units here and there, but hundreds of thousands are needed each year—and only the private market has the potential to produce such volume. Chester Hartman, a leading socialist, inadvertently makes this point:

> In the forty-five years since we began subsidizing housing for poor people . . . all of those programs together, rural and urban, have provided roughly 4.5 million subsidized housing units. That is what the private building industry provided in two good years, back-to-back.

Nonprofit housing corporations should be encouraged for their good work. Whether federal cash subsidies should support the nonprofit corporations is a separate question; William Tucker believes not, and I agree with him. What such entities can accomplish is minuscule compared with the need, and they distract the public's attention from solutions that might work. . . .

The Role of Local Government

William Tucker has analyzed the mushrooming of housing costs between the early 1970s and early 1990s and demonstrated that the problem lies primarily in local government actions that hinder production—a libertarian approach to the homelessness problem. Because all housing in the United States is produced locally, local government permission is needed to build. Michael Carliner, a respected housing expert, adds credence to Tucker's view of the role of local government:

> The local role in regulating land use, construction, and the operation of private housing markets has probably, on balance, been inimical rather than conducive to the production and retention of low-income housing. Exclusionary zoning (such as requirements that lots be larger than necessary) and other controls tend to raise the cost of housing and direct new construction toward the high end of the market. Overly strict building codes have inhibited the construction and rehabilitation of low-cost housing. Housing codes have encouraged

abandonment. While these codes ostensibly protect poor people, they effectively rank homelessness as preferable to substandard housing.

Tucker goes further, demonstrating that local government has been not merely "on balance, inimical" to low-income housing, but profoundly so to those of low income and to newcomers in general. Exclusionary zoning and growth controls present the major problems. As a result, housing is not built because there is nowhere to build it. Tucker believes that local government policies on land use, along with rent control, may explain half of contemporary homelessness.

Tucker has explained the way local governments respond to pressure from constituents who stand to gain much and lose nothing by resisting further development of housing. He attributes housing scarcity to free-lunch "rent-seeking" by present property-owners:

> Residents of any community can improve the value of their homes and turn their community into an exclusive enclave by practicing exclusionary zoning. . . . It is this use of the political system to gain unearned advantages that is at the heart of the housing problem.

If Tucker is correct in this analysis, and I believe he is, there is surprisingly little understanding of the problem either among housing specialists around the country or among advocates for the poor. The NHTF report mentions exclusionary zoning and growth controls only in the details of its discussion and never mentions rent control. Much of the housing literature vastly underrates or ignores completely the role of local government in the housing problem. Perhaps Rouse and the NHTF deserve some credit in the matter, since the casual mention they make gives the local government problem more ink than it usually gets. . . .

A Local Industry

Advocates at the national level assume the solution requires major federal action. They give little or no attention to how policies and practices of either state and local government or the construction industry affect the problem and might be changed without recourse to massive federal intervention. They seem to be unaware that housing construction is one of the most localized industries in America, totally unlike the centralization of automaking. These advocates have come to set the terms of discussion for their counterparts across the country, just as civil rights first and then antipoverty politics have been focused since the early 1960s on getting the federal government to pass laws and create programs.

A recent experience I had in San Francisco illustrates how little attention national advocates pay to local government actions or to practices that local housing developers can easily change. The Center on Budget and Policy Priorities (CBPP) was touring the United States to promote a series of reports that publicized the shortage of affordable housing "in all regions" of the United States and called for "major action on the part of the federal, state, and local governments, as well as the private sector." It held a press conference in San Francisco in April 1990, after which I joined local agency representatives for a briefing on the study findings.

Local Government Can Make Housing Affordable

America's housing crisis is solvable, beginning at the local level. It is particularly so if HUD [the U.S. Department of Housing and Urban Development] should bestir itself to immediate actions. The great myth about American homelessness is that it is not solvable. The great myth about our housing crisis is that funding for the housing that is needed cannot be found. However, for a half century, America had a federal low-income housing program that worked: this program built houses. The near-elimination of that program beginning in 1981 has been a major cause of homelessness, and the resumption of some federal support would greatly help us now. Federal help for new, low-income housing is not, however, on the immediate horizon, but even if the federal government should begin to contribute some funding, we will have to look to local areas for the working mechanisms, the real solutions. . . .

Local codes should be revised to accommodate affordable housing. Strict state building codes and local ordinances are a major problem. These aim at worthy goals—saving energy, upholding civilized light and air standards, caring for the handicapped, and keeping things fire-safe—but collectively they cost a lot of money. Relaxing these codes has been a consistent demand of the builders and operators of new lowest- and low-income housing, including those of homeless shelters. Examples of standards that could be relaxed include requirements for off-street parking (many people who pay $200 to $300 a month for SRO [single-room occupancy hotel] housing don't have cars, nor do they attract many driving visitors), landscape standards (extra set-backs, more trees, more lawns) that cost more to maintain, and micro-design standards such as requirements for, say, red tile roofs.

Robert C. Coates, *A Street Is Not a Home*, 1990.

The CBPP study gave no attention whatsoever to differences in the structure of the problem among regions of the country, no look at how local economies work, and no glance at how the problem results from interference with the private market. The only entries about local government in the report were a few words of praise for local promotion of low-income housing. Neither did Edward Lazere, author of the report, mention local government in his oral presentation. CBPP appears to see the state and local government role as that of adding dollars or other support to programs initiated by the federal government. It does not refer to local government prevention of housing development or to ways state and local governments might play primary roles in encouraging housing.

Until I did, no one in the audience had raised any of these issues. The local attendees readily accepted CBPP's national mindset about public policy, but I felt like an alien. When I asked if there was some reason why the report makes no mention of the effect of local government policies and practices on the housing supply, Lazere's answer was that CBPP is not equipped to deal with local issues because it has a national perspective. No one raised a protest. Lazere's response suggests the need for federations of local institutions that believe in private markets to come into the open, attend these conferences, develop a public position, and focus attention on what is needed to let markets operate.

Federal Housing Programs

Tucker has rejected most of the past and present federal grant programs that subsidize construction or rehabilitation of low-income housing as being too expensive. With all the added costs under government regulation, a unit of low-income housing costs as much or more to build than a private-market unit of middle-class housing, but its quality is not as good. Administrative capacity and funding limit the potential to build housing this way. Consequently, such programs serve only a small minority of those who need housing. Moreover, it is means tested and therefore stigmatizes. Housing produced by federal grant programs is a form of welfare that adversely affects the people living there (for example, they cannot move without losing the subsidy). Such housing provides too many opportunities for corruption. . . .

Low-income housing is not profitable without government subsidy. All housing in this country is subsidized in one way or another, if only through a tax deduction for mortgage interest. Most middle-class homeowners also benefit from government-subsidized mortgage insurance. Although draconian attempts to increase efficiency might result in the elimination of many federal housing programs and activities, many would either be continued or housing, and not just low-income housing, would find itself in much bigger trouble than it is. Mortgage insurance and tax deductions in support of home ownership and of rental housing construction are relatively simple, administratively inexpensive, and effective. These federal programs do not discourage personal responsibility. Perhaps such programs should be extended to those further down the economic scale. . . .

Programs That Will Not Work

Federal assistance, in the form of mortgage insurance and loan guarantee programs, generates millions of housing units, either by helping buyers in financing a home or the industry in constructing one. The main problem now is that these programs do not extend down the economic scale far enough to reach low-income families, because housing prices are too high and because the incomes of many families, even with two full-time workers, are too low.

To the extent that any program uses tax money inefficiently—that is, produces the desired result at high unit costs—it retards national growth by taking capital away from more productive uses. Direct construction of federal housing surely has this effect, as does most directly subsidized private construction. Mortgage insurance and other loan guarantees can be carried out efficiently and be used to leverage multiples of the amount directly allocated. Because these policies produce amounts of goods and services comparable to those one might expect if the funds were left in the free market rather than collected as taxes and disbursed as mortgage insurance and loan guarantees, the effect of these programs on national growth should be neutral. The redistributive effect can be positive if these programs are directed to low- and moderate-income families.

Because mortgage insurance and loan guarantees give responsible choices to individuals and families about where to live, such programs need not create ghettos of stigmatized families. Direct housing subsidies and public housing do create such ghettos, weakening a culture of responsible self-governance.

Mainstream programs will continue to fail to provide adequate amounts of low-income housing in growing cities until the local government practices Tucker has described are changed. Building new housing in communities where exclusionary zoning and growth control are predominant has become so difficult and expensive, cautions Stuart Butler, that any increases in federal housing appropriations (such as those recommended by the NHTF) will likely force up prices of existing units instead of creating new ones. . . .

Programs That Will Work

Examples of [successful low-income housing] programs and policies are quite varied, but they have some important things in common: first, they are focused locally, recognizing that the housing industry in America is local; second, they treat the market as a tool rather than as a problem to be circumvented; third, they recognize the importance of the policies and practices of local government in housing. These three elements are necessary ingredients in any low-income housing policy for it to succeed in producing large numbers of suitable and affordable housing units where they are needed.

The largest underutilized potential for progress in housing currently resides in state government, and advocates would do well to campaign at the state capitols. The reason for this is that states set the rules under which local governments must operate, not that states have money to spend on housing. Most, as a matter of fact, do not have money to spend, but this should be no impediment to action. The principal need from the state level is for leadership in governing, not for programs and money.

Where there is money to deliver, as the voters through initiative ballots have instructed California to do, this money should be incorporated into a strategy to change local practices so that the market can function more effectively, not as a substitute for local leadership or the market. Only the market has the potential to solve the low-income housing problem. Intelligently designed and managed policies at all three levels of government are necessary to provide an environment in which the market can work.

Periodical Bibliography

The following articles have been selected to supplement the diverse views presented in this chapter.

Les Bayless	"Public Housing Tenants Say: Cuts Will Make Us Homeless," *People's Weekly World*, May 27, 1995. Available from 235 W. 23rd St., New York, NY 10011.
Alexander Cockburn	"Cut Out His Heart in San Francisco," *The Nation*, July 4, 1994.
Stuart Creque	"Brrr!" *National Review*, October 10, 1994.
Jason DeParle	"Despising Welfare, Pitying Its Young," *New York Times*, December 18, 1994.
John I. Gilderbloom	"Rent Control: The Second Best Way to Create Affordable Housing," *Governing*, July 1993.
Malcolm Gladwell	"Enough Already!" *Washington Post National Weekly Edition*, January 30–February 5, 1995. Available from 1150 15th St. NW, Washington, DC 20071.
Maria-Luisa Gonzalez	"School + Home = A Program for Educating Homeless Students," *Phi Delta Kappan*, June 1990.
Patricia M. Hanrahan	"No Home? No Vote," *Human Rights*, Winter 1994. Available from 750 N. Lake Shore Dr., Chicago, IL 60611.
Howard Husock	"The Folly of Public Housing," *Wall Street Journal*, September 28, 1993.
Ann Mariano	"The Rent's Due and the Cupboard Is Bare," *Washington Post National Weekly Edition*, May 8–14, 1995.
Mary Rose McGeady	"Welfare Reform: The View from Covenant House," *America*, September 24, 1994.
Newsweek	"A Burning Question," October 17, 1994.
New Yorker	"Homelessness Revisited," February 28, 1994.
Neal Peirce	"Housing Vouchers May Be the Best Idea," *Liberal Opinion Week*, June 5, 1995. Available from PO Box 468, Vinton, IA 52349-0468.
Task Force on Homelessness and Severe Mental Illness	"Outcasts on Main Street: Homelessness and the Mentally Ill," *USA Today*, March 1994.

For Further Discussion

Chapter 1

1. Robert Rosenheck and Jon Katz cite widely varying statistics on the numbers of homeless people in the United States. Both authors explain why their numbers are correct and why other numbers are wrong. Which viewpoint do you believe is the strongest? Support your answer with references to the viewpoints.

2. Robert J. Samuelson and William Raspberry both argue that homelessness is here to stay, despite any attempts the government, society, or churches make to eliminate the problem. Henry G. Cisneros, secretary of the U.S. Department of Housing and Urban Development, maintains that efforts to help the homeless are succeeding across the country. Based on the viewpoints of Samuelson, Raspberry, and Cisneros, do you think spending more money on homeless programs such as the D.C. Initiative will help alleviate the homeless situation? Why or why not?

Chapter 2

1. Elliot Liebow argues that the primary need of homeless people is housing. Alice S. Baum and Donald W. Burnes contend that the homeless are unable to retain housing unless they are first treated for their mental illnesses and addictions. Whose argument do you find more convincing? Support your answer using examples from the viewpoints.

2. Carl F. Horowitz is a policy analyst at a conservative think tank. Susan Yeich is a homeless advocate and a former member of the Homeless People's Union. Are the backgrounds of these two authors evident in their viewpoints about the government's role in the homeless problem, and if so, how? Does knowing their backgrounds influence your assessment of their arguments? Explain your answer.

3. L. Christopher Awalt writes of his personal experience with the homeless when he contends that many homeless people choose to be homeless. David A. Snow, Leon Anderson, and David Wagner argue that they found very few people in their studies of homeless people in Texas and New England who admitted to being homeless by choice. Whose argument do you think is stronger, and why? Describe a situation in which you feel living on the streets would be preferable than the alternative.

Chapter 3

1. Doug A. Timmer, D. Stanley Eitzen, and Kathryn D. Talley express concerns about the negative effects of emergency shelters on homeless people. How does Ralph Nunez respond to some of these concerns?

2. Heather MacDonald argues that most homeless adults in San Francisco would rather spend their general assistance check on drugs or alcohol than on housing. Do you agree with MacDonald's characterization of the homeless? Why or why not?

3. Alex Vitale argues that homeless people should take over vacant buildings in order to secure housing and to protest the "warehousing" of rental buildings. Robert Teir contends that communities should not allow the homeless to squat on public property. Which of these viewpoints is more convincing, and why? Support your answer with examples from the viewpoints.

Chapter 4

1. Isabel Wilkerson describes "compassion fatigue" and says people are tired of being confronted by homeless people and are frustrated by a lack of progress in solving the homeless problem. Have you ever come in contact with any homeless people? What was your response to their presence or request for help? Would you respond differently today after reading the viewpoints in this book? Explain your answer.

2. Both H. Richard Lamb and Thomas Szasz are psychiatrists, yet they have radically different views concerning the homeless mentally ill and their treatment. Which viewpoint do you support, and why?

Chapter 5

1. Rob Rosenthal studied the homeless in Santa Barbara, California, for 4½ years. Jerzy Kosinski lived through World War II as a homeless young boy. Their viewpoints on preventing homelessness are diametrically opposed. How do the authors' views reflect their experiences? Do you think homelessness can be prevented? Support your answer using examples from the viewpoints in this book.

2. Gregg Barak believes that the federal government should subsidize housing for the homeless. Richard W. White Jr. believes that it is up to the local governments to make housing more affordable for the poor and homeless. Which viewpoint is more convincing, and why?

Organizations to Contact

The editors have compiled the following list of organizations concerned with the issues debated in this book. The descriptions are derived from materials provided by the organizations themselves. All have publications or information available for interested readers. The list was compiled on the date of publication of the present volume; names, addresses, and phone numbers may change. Be aware that many organizations take several weeks or longer to respond to inquiries, so allow as much time as possible.

American Alliance for Rights and Responsibilities (AARR)
1146 19th St. NW, Suite 250
Washington, DC 20036-3703
(202) 785-7844

The AARR works on issues that directly affect the safety and quality of life in communities. It identifies, promotes, and defends new ideas on crime, public safety, drug and alcohol abuse, and national and community service that make citizens a part of the solution. Its newsletter *Re: Rights & Responsibilities* frequently covers the issue of homelessness.

Better Homes Fund
181 Wells Ave.
Newton Center, MA 02159
(617) 964-3834
fax: (617) 244-1758

The fund strives to help homeless families attain the support and skills they need to return to mainstream life. Founded in 1988 by *Better Homes and Gardens* magazine, the Better Homes Fund gives grants to local homeless support programs, develops training materials, and evaluates programs. It publishes the quarterly newsletter *Helping Homeless Families* and the report *Community Care for Homeless Families*.

Cato Institute
1000 Massachusetts Ave. NW
Washington, DC 20001
(202) 8428-0200

The institute is a libertarian public policy research foundation. It opposes rent control, restrictive zoning laws, and other regulations on the housing market, and it advocates vouchers to solve the problems of homelessness. Its publications include the book *Zoning, Rent Control and Affordable Housing* and the monthlies *Policy Report* and *Cato Journal*.

Co-operative Housing Association of Ontario (CHAO)
2 Berkeley St., Suite 207
Toronto, Ontario M5A 2W3
CANADA
(800) 268-2537
(416) 366-1711
fax: (416) 366-3876

CHAO is a provincial housing advocacy group that primarily works with other housing and homeless organizations throughout Ontario in education and political campaigns. It maintains a housing research library and resource materials on housing issues in Ontario, in Canada, and around the world. CHAO commissions and publishes studies on a variety of housing issues. Its publications include the monthlies *Dispatches* and *Co-op Memo*, the biweekly *Resource Group Memo*, the quarterly newsletter *Co-Op Bulletin*, and the semiannual *Cross Sections*.

Downtown Eastside Residents' Association (DERA)
9 E. Hastings St.
Vancouver, British Columbia V6A 1M9
CANADA
(604) 682-0931

DERA works to make decent and affordable housing available in the Downtown Eastside area of Vancouver. It established the Portland Hotel in 1991, a "transitional" hotel for residents with mental illness, alcohol or drug dependencies, and other debilities. It publishes a monthly newsletter and pamphlets concerning homelessness.

Empty the Shelters (ETS)
25 14th St.
San Francisco, CA 94103
(415) 703-0229
fax: (415) 703-0276
e-mail: ets@igc.apc.org

Empty the Shelters is a national organization of young people attempting to end poverty through social change. It sponsors programs in different cities to fight poverty, homelessness, racism, and sexism, and it cosponsors the "Break the Blackout" campaign against the lack of media coverage about the oppression of poor people. ETS publishes several brochures on social action and the criminalization of poverty and homelessness.

Foundation for Economic Education (FEE)
30 S. Broadway
Irvington-on-Hudson, NY 10533
(914) 591-7230

This libertarian organization advocates free markets and limited government. It believes governmental controls of the housing market such as rent control and restrictive zoning practices are responsible for the homeless problem. FEE's monthly publication the *Freeman* has often covered the issue of homelessness.

The Heritage Foundation
214 Massachusetts Ave. NE
Washington, DC 20002
(202) 546-4400

The foundation is a conservative think tank that conducts research on public policy. It advocates free enterprise with limited government involvement and believes the free market can best meet the housing needs of the homeless. Its periodic publications *Backgrounder* and *Issues Bulletin* have dealt with homelessness and related issues.

Homes for the Homeless (HFH)
36 Cooper Square, 6th Fl.
New York, NY 10003
(212) 529-5252

HFH strives to reduce homelessness by providing families with the education and training they need to build independent lives. Participating families are housed in one of four residential educational training centers throughout New York City, where they learn job, literacy, and parenting skills. Participants are also counseled on substance abuse and domestic violence. HFH publishes the reports *Homelessness: The Foster Care Connection*, *The New Poverty: A Generation of Homeless Families*, *An American Family Myth: Every Child at Risk*, and *Job Readiness: Crossing the Threshold from Homelessness to Employment*.

Housing Assistance Council (HAC)
1025 Vermont Ave. NW, Suite 606
Washington, DC 20005
(202) 842-8600
fax: (202) 347-3441

The council conducts research projects and provides loans, information, and technical assistance on homelessness and low-income housing developments to rural housing agencies. It publishes the biweekly newsletter *HAC News*, the bimonthly newsletter *State Action Memorandum*, and fact sheets on rural homelessness.

HUD USER
PO Box 6091
Rockville, MD 20850
(800) 245-2691
(301) 251-5154
fax: (301) 251-5747

HUD USER is an information service that provides research information through its on-line database of documents and reference materials. Its newsletter *Recent Research Results* contains short summaries of recent reports from the U.S. Department of Housing and Urban Development's (HUD) Office of Policy Development and Research, which sponsors HUD USER.

Interagency Council on the Homeless
451 Seventh St. SW, Rm. 7274
Washington, DC 20410
(202) 708-1480
fax: (202) 708-3672

Established under the Stewart B. McKinney Homeless Assistance Act, the council reviews, monitors, evaluates, and recommends improvements in federal homeless assistance programs. It publishes the newsletter *Council Communiqué* and information concerning McKinney programs.

Legal Services Homelessness Task Force
National Housing Law Project
122 C St. NW, Suite 740
Washington, DC 20001
(202) 783-5140

The task force uses legal means at the local, state, and federal levels to advocate for the homeless. It offers service providers assistance in litigation, administrative and legislative advocacy, and community education in health, public assistance, child welfare, and housing. Its publications include the bimonthly *Housing Law Bulletin* and numerous manuals on federal housing programs.

National Alliance to End Homelessness, Inc.
1518 K St. NW, Suite 206
Washington, DC 20005
(202) 638-1526
fax: (202) 638-4664

The alliance is composed of state and local nonprofit agencies, corporations, and individuals who provide housing and services to homeless people. Its goal is to end homelessness by changing federal policy and by helping its local members serve more homeless people. It publishes the newsletters *Alliance* and *Network Newssheets*, the report *Web of Failure: The Relationship Between Foster Care and Homelessness*, and the book *What You Can Do to Help the Homeless*.

National Anti-Poverty Organization (NAPO)
316-256 King Edward Ave.
Ottawa, Ontario K1N 7M1
CANADA
(613) 789-0096
fax: (613) 789-0141

The organization works on behalf of low-income Canadians on the issues of poverty, welfare, unemployment, job training and education programs, housing, tax and economic policies, health services, and child care. NAPO researches these issues and submits briefs to federal committees, task forces, and commissions. It publishes the quarterly newsletter *NAPO News* and other reports.

National Clearinghouse for Alcohol and Drug Information
PO Box 2345
Rockville, MD 20852
(800) 487-4889
(301) 468-2600
fax: (301) 468-6433

The clearinghouse distributes information on the relationship between homelessness and drug abuse and alcoholism. Its publications include the reports *Homeless Families with Children: Research Perspectives* and *Affordable Housing for Homeless Persons in Recovery from Alcohol and Other Drug Problems: A Case Study*.

National Coalition for the Homeless
1612 K St. NW
Washington, DC 20006
(202) 775-1322
fax: (202) 775-1316

The coalition consists of organizations concerned with homelessness. It lobbies for more government programs to help the homeless, conducts research, and works as a clearinghouse on information about the homeless. It publishes the monthly newsletter *Safety Network* and many pamphlets and reports, including *Shredding the Safety Network: The Contract with America's Impact on Poor and Homeless People*.

National Law Center on Homelessness and Poverty
918 F St. NW, #412
Washington, DC 20004
(202) 638-2535
fax: (202) 628-2737

The center provides technical assistance and legal advocacy to homeless people and to organizations that need access to or enforcement of federal programs for the poor and homeless. It publishes the monthly newsletter *In Just Times*.

National Resource Center on Homelessness and Mental Health
Policy Research Associates, Inc.
262 Delaware Ave.
Delmar, NY 12054
(800) 444-7415
fax: (518) 439-7612
e-mail: nrc3 pra@aol.com

The center provides comprehensive information about the treatment, social services, and housing needs of homeless persons with severe mental illness. It maintains an extensive database of published and unpublished materials. Its publications include the quarterly *Access* and the resource guide *National Organizations Concerned with Mental Health, Housing, and Homelessness*.

National Student Campaign Against Hunger and Homelessness
29 Temple Pl., 4th Fl.
Boston, MA 02111
(617) 292-4823
fax: (617) 292-8057

The campaign trains students to improve or create service programs to meet the needs of the hungry and homeless in their communities. It also holds workshops and conferences to educate people about the antipoverty movement. Its publications include the fact sheets *Veterans and Homelessness* and *Homelessness and the Mentally Ill*, the newsletter *Students Making a Difference*, and catalogs of academic courses, internships, and volunteer opportunities across the nation.

National Union of the Homeless
3434 Old York Rd.
Philadelphia, PA 19140
(215) 228-0795 or 923-5960

The union, founded in 1989, is made up of and led by homeless and formerly homeless people who have organized themselves to fight homelessness. It works to eliminate homelessness and related problems affecting poor people. More than twenty-five cities have homeless unions working on the political, economic, and social conditions that contribute to homelessness. It publishes the monthly newsletter *Union of the Homeless National News*.

U.S. Department of Housing and Urban Development (HUD)
Office of Homelessness
451 Seventh St. SW, Rm. 9206
Washington, DC 20410
(202) 708-4432

Office of Special Needs Assistance Programs
451 Seventh St. SW, Rm. 7262
Washington, DC 20410
(202) 708-4300

HUD is the federal agency responsible for housing programs and the development and preservation of neighborhoods. For the past several years, it has worked to encourage the private housing market to provide affordable housing for all. The Office of Special Needs Assistance Programs, under the aegis of the Stewart B. McKinney Act, funds a variety of homeless assistance programs. HUD publishes the report *Priority Home! The Federal Plan to Break the Cycle of Homelessness*.

Bibliography of Books

Gregg Barak   *Gimme Shelter*. New York: Praeger, 1991.

Alice S. Baum and   *A Nation in Denial: The Truth About Homelessness.*
Donald W. Burnes   Boulder, CO: Westview Press, 1993.

Sheila Baxter   *Under the Viaduct: Homeless in Beautiful B.C.*
                               Vancouver, BC: New Star Books, 1991.

Judith Berck   *No Place to Be: Voices of Homeless Children.*
                               Boston: Houghton Mifflin, 1992.

Joel Blau   *The Visible Poor: Homelessness in the United
                               States*. New York: Oxford University Press,
                               1992.

Nancy A. Boxill, ed.   *Homeless Children: The Watchers and the Waiters.*
                               New York: Haworth Press, 1990.

Philip W. Brickner   *Under the Safety Net: The Health and Social Wel-
et al., eds.   fare of the Homeless in the United States*. New
                               York: Norton, 1990.

Philip Michael Bulman   *Caught in the Mix: An Oral Portrait of Homeless-
                               ness*. Westport, CT: Auburn House, 1990.

Martha R. Burt   *Over the Edge: The Growth of Homelessness in the
                               1980s.* Washington, DC: Urban Institute Press,
                               1992.

Catholic Institute for   *Disposable People: Forced Evictions in South Korea.*
International Relations   London: Russell Press, 1988.

Carol L.M. Caton, ed.   *Homeless in America.* New York: Oxford Univer-
                               sity Press, 1990.

Robert C. Coates   *A Street Is Not a Home: Solving America's Home-
                               less Dilemma.* Buffalo: Prometheus Books, 1990.

Lars Eighner   *Travels with Lizbeth.* New York: St. Martin's
                               Press, 1993.

Lisa Ferrill   *A Far Cry from Home: Life in a Shelter for Home-
                               less Women.* Chicago: Noble Press, 1991.

Theresa Funiciello   *Tyranny of Kindness.* New York: Atlantic
                               Monthly Press, 1993.

Benedict Giamo and   *Beyond Homelessness: Frames of Reference.* Iowa
Jeffrey Grunberg   City: University of Iowa Press, 1992.

Irene Glasser   *Homelessness in Global Perspective.* New York:
                               G.K. Hall, 1994.

Stephanie Golden   *The Women Outside: Meanings and Myths of
                               Homelessness.* Berkeley and Los Angeles: Uni-
                               versity of California Press, 1992.

Paul Groth	*Living Downtown: The History of Residential Hotels in the United States.* Berkeley and Los Angeles: University of California Press, 1994.
Maxine Harris	*Sisters of the Shadow.* Norman: University of Oklahoma Press, 1991.
Charles Hoch and Robert A. Slayton	*New Homeless and Old: Community and the Skid Row Hotel.* Philadelphia: Temple University Press, 1989.
Mary Ellen Hombs	*American Homelessness: A Reference Handbook.* Santa Barbara, CA: ABC-CLIO, 1990.
Mary Ellen Hombs and Mitch Snyder	*Homelessness in America: One Year Later.* Washington, DC: Community for Creative Non-Violence, 1983.
Interagency Council on the Homeless	*Outcasts on Main Street: Report of the Federal Task Force on Homelessness and Severe Mental Illness,* 1992. Available from National Resource Center on Homelessness and Mental Illness, Policy Research Associates, 262 Delaware Ave., Delmar, NY 12054.
Rael Jean Isaac and Virginia C. Armat	*Madness in the Streets: How Psychiatry and the Law Abandoned the Mentally Ill.* New York: Free Press, 1990.
Rene I. Jahiel, ed.	*Homelessness: A Prevention-Oriented Approach.* Baltimore: Johns Hopkins University Press, 1992.
Christopher Jencks	*The Homeless.* Cambridge, MA: Harvard University Press, 1994.
Ann Braden Johnson	*Out of Bedlam: The Truth About Deinstitutionalization.* New York: Basic Books, 1990.
Joan J. Johnson	*Kids Without Homes.* New York: Franklin Watts, 1991.
Thomas L. Kenyon and Justine Blau	*What You Can Do to Help the Homeless.* New York: Simon and Schuster, 1991.
Jonathan Kozol	*Rachel and Her Children.* New York: Crown Publishers, 1988.
Julee H. Kryder-Coe, Lester M. Salamon, and Janice M. Molnar, eds.	*Homeless Children and Youth: A New American Dilemma.* New Brunswick, NJ: Transaction Publishers, 1991.
Elliot Liebow	*Tell Them Who I Am: The Lives of Homeless Women.* New York: Free Press, 1993.
Dale Maharidge	*The Last Great American Hobo.* Rocklin, CA: Prima Publishing, 1993.

233

Lawrence M. Mead   *The New Politics of Poverty: The Nonworking Poor in America.* New York: Basic Books, 1992.

Robert M. Moroney   *Social Policy and Social Work: Critical Essays on the Welfare States.* New York: Aldine de Gruyter, 1991.

National Coalition for the Homeless   *Heroes Today, Homeless Tomorrow? Homelessness Among Veterans in the United States,* November 1991. Available from 1612 K St. NW, #1004, Washington, DC 20006.

National Coalition for the Homeless   *Shredding the Safety Net: The Contract with America's Impact on Poor and Homeless People,* December 1994.

National Housing Institute and The American Affordable Housing Institute   *Preventing Homelessness: A Study of State and Local Homelessness Prevention Programs,* October 1991. Available from AAHI, PO Box 118, New Brunswick, NJ 08903.

Margery G. Nichelason   *Homeless or Hopeless?* Minneapolis: Lerner Publications, 1994.

Ann Nietzke   *Natalie on the Street.* Corvallis, OR: Calyx Books, 1994.

Marvin Olasky   *The Tragedy of American Compassion.* Washington, DC: Regnery Gateway, 1992.

Kevin Phillips   *The Politics of Rich and Poor: Wealth and the American Electorate in the Reagan Aftermath.* New York: Random House, 1990.

Mark Robert Rank   *Living on the Edge: The Realities of Welfare in America.* New York: Columbia University Press, 1994.

Marjorie J. Robertson and Milton Greenblatt   *Homelessness: A National Perspective.* New York: Plenum Press, 1992.

Rob Rosenthal   *Homeless in Paradise: A Map of the Terrain.* Philadelphia: Temple University Press, 1994.

Peter H. Rossi   *Down and Out in America: The Origins of Homelessness.* Chicago: University of Chicago Press, 1989.

Betty G. Russell   *Silent Sisters: A Study of Homeless Women.* New York: Hemisphere Publishing, 1991.

John E. Schwarz and Thomas J. Volgy   *The Forgotten Americans.* New York: Norton, 1992.

Barry Jay Seltser and Donald E. Miller   *Homeless Families: The Struggle for Dignity.* Urbana and Chicago: University of Illinois Press, 1993.

David A. Snow and Leon Anderson   *Down on Their Luck: A Study of Homeless Street People.* Berkeley and Los Angeles: University of California Press, 1993.

Alice W. Solenberger — *One Thousand Homeless Men: A Study of Original Records.* Philadelphia: Press of William F. Fell, 1911.

Lois Stavsky and I.E. Mozeson — *The Place I Call Home: Voices and Faces of Homeless Teens.* New York: Shapolsky Publishers, 1990.

Thomas Szasz — *Cruel Compassion: Psychiatric Control of Society's Unwanted.* New York: Wiley, 1994.

Doug A. Timmer, D. Stanley Eitzen, and Kathryn D. Talley — *Paths to Homelessness: Extreme Poverty and the Urban Housing Crisis.* Boulder, CO: Westview Press, 1994.

E. Fuller Torrey — *Nowhere to Go: The Tragic Odyssey of the Homeless Mentally Ill.* New York: Harper and Row, 1988.

Walter I. Trattner — *From Poor Law to Welfare State: A History of Social Welfare in America.* New York: Free Press, 1994.

William Tucker — *The Excluded Americans: Homelessness and Housing Policies.* Washington, DC: Regnery Gateway, 1990.

William Tucker — *Zoning, Rent Control, and Affordable Housing.* Washington, DC: Cato Institute, 1991.

Jackson Underwood — *The Bridge People: Daily Life in a Camp of the Homeless.* Lanham, MD: University Press of America, 1993.

U.S. Conference of Mayors — *Mentally Ill and Homeless: A Twenty-two-City Survey,* November 1991. Available from 1620 I St. NW, Washington, DC 20006.

U.S. Conference of Mayors — *A Status Report on Hunger and Homelessness in America's Cities: 1994,* December 1994.

Steven VanderStaay — *Street Lives: An Oral History of Homeless Americans.* Philadelphia: New Society Publishers, 1992.

David Wagner — *Checkerboard Square: Culture and Resistance in a Homeless Community.* Boulder, CO: Westview Press, 1993.

Richard W. White Jr. — *Rude Awakenings: What the Homeless Crisis Tells Us.* San Francisco: ICS Press, 1992.

Jennifer Wolch and Michael Dear — *Malign Neglect: Homelessness in an American City.* San Francisco: Jossey-Bass, 1993.

James D. Wright — *Address Unknown: The Homeless in America.* New York: Aldine de Gruyter, 1989.

Susan Yeich — *The Politics of Ending Homelessness.* Lanham, MD: University Press of America, 1994.

Index